PRAISE FOR *BIPOLAR FAITH*

"A stunning, unforgettable read, *Bipolar Faith* grabs you with the first exquisitely composed paragraphs and won't let you go until the final page is turned. Even then, its impact lingers. To say this is a book about mental health severely limits its scope, which includes arresting reflections on race, womanhood, death, love, sex, community, and joy. A master storyteller, Coleman seamlessly knits together the personal and universal, the particular and the communal. Hers is one of the clearest and most compelling voices in Christian literature today. Let those with ears hear."

—Rachel Held Evans
Author of *Searching for Sunday*
and *A Year of Biblical Womanhood*

"Monica A. Coleman is a courageous and brilliant theologian whose wisdom and rigor helps sustain many of us. This unique and pioneering book opens a new spiritual zone for our serious attention!"

—Cornel West

"In *Bipolar Faith*, Dr. Coleman offers a brilliantly written narrative which provides a bird's-eye view of her early years marked by family strife, tragedy and loss juxtaposed with the joys of childhood summers spent immersed in a segregated black community in Washington, DC. She ushers us gently into her world in which, over time, through Ivy League baccalaureate study and pursuit of ministerial professionalism and spiritual scholarship, she comes to terms with a family history of mental health challenges and substance use disorder, her own traumatic experiences and a diagnosis of mental illness which finally explains her episodic changes in mood, outlook and activity level. The reader will admire Dr. Coleman's strong faith through it all, her existential questioning and the fact that she has emerged whole from introspective exploration, loving herself as is."

—Annelle Primm
Senior Psychiatrist Advisor for Urban
Behavioral Associates
and Former Deputy Medical Director of the American
Psychiatric Association

"I'm very excited about Rev. Dr. Monica A. Coleman's new book, *Bipolar Faith*. The church—and broader society—must do a much better job engaging issues of mental health, and Dr. Coleman's powerful story sets us on the right path. This will be a helpful resource for pastors and congregants across the country."

—Joshua DuBois
Author of *The President's Devotional: The Readings that Inspired President Obama*

"In her memoir, *Bipolar Faith*, Reverend Dr. Monica A. Coleman courageously shares the story of her own personal and private life struggles with God, death, loneliness, love, rape and a family history of mental illness. Once a taboo topic, Dr. Coleman's revelation of the need for a 'middle place' to balance the public demands of life and the private pain and isolation of depression helps the church begin the conversation about relevant ministries to meet the needs of our congregants who often find themselves in the dark place of mental illness. Our spiritual journey takes us through light and darkness. This book may help an individual or a congregation to honestly pull back the cover of secrecy to develop resources for hurting people and families. *Bipolar Faith* shines a light in those seemingly empty periods of darkness."

—Bishop Vashti Murphy McKenzie
117th Elected Bishop, African Methodist Episcopal Church
Author of *Not Without a Struggle*, *Journey to the Well*,
Strength in the Struggle, and *Swapping Housewives*

"In America, in Black America, we do not like to talk about pain, about trauma, about grief, about sadness, about depression. We work hard, we live, we survive, we pass the scars of emotional wars from one generation to another like a birthright, like a family heirloom. Monica A. Coleman's story is our story, her family is your family, and mine too. *Bipolar Faith* is one Black woman's journey through depression and faith, yes. But it is also the saga of an individual, a family, and a community that needs to confront itself, once and for all, so there is actual healing and redemption in a way that truly liberates. Brilliant and fearless with her writing and with her voice, Monica Coleman's freedom train is one we all need to board."

—Kevin Powell
Author of *The Education of Kevin Powell: A Boy's Journey into Manhood*

"Monica A. Coleman writes with the artistry of a poetic storyteller, the intimacy of someone who has studied depression from the inside, and the courageous transparency of someone who knows the cost of silence. Weaving cultural truths with the reality of hope and despair, Coleman's latest book is a testimony that unmasks psychological struggles, family discord, and the quest for wholeness. As a scholar and minister, Coleman has crafted a book that creates a safe space for people of faith to reflect on their journey toward truth, balance, and self-acceptance."

—Thema Bryant-Davis
Past President, Society for the Psychology of Women
Co-Editor of *Womanist and Mujerista Psychologies: Voices of Fire, Acts of Courage*

"*Bipolar Faith* is an insightful work on an important and neglected topic. The writing is terrific, it pulls you along like a runaway train and is full of poetic lines that speak to the ineffable human experience of suffering and hope."

—Jennifer Michael Hecht
Author of *Doubt: A History*

"*Bipolar Faith* is a beautifully written, brutally honest memoir of survival. With grit and courage, Dr. Monica A. Coleman shares her story of mental illness and abuse and her journey to wholeness. Guided by faith, Coleman never sidesteps the pain and hurt as she confronts her private demons head on, ending in triumph, recovery and healing."

—Linda Villarosa,
Author of *Body & Soul: The Black Women's Guide to Physical Health and Emotional Well-being*

BIPOLAR FAITH

BIPOLAR FAITH

A Black Woman's Journey in Depression
and Faith

Monica A. Coleman

Fortress Press

Minneapolis

BIPOLAR FAITH

A Black Woman's Journey in Depression and Faith

Cover image:© Anne Simone Photography
Cover design: Brad Norr

Library of Congress Cataloging-in-Publication Data
Print ISBN: 978-1-5064-0859-0
eBook ISBN: 978-1-5064-0860-6

The paper used in this publication meets the minimum requirements of American National Standard for Information Sciences — Permanence of Paper for Printed Library Materials, ANSI Z329.48-1984.

Manufactured in the U.S.A.

This book was produced using Pressbooks.com, and PDF rendering was done by PrinceXML.

To everyone who is looking for the words to describe
what defies language,
my brothers and sisters who know these experiences
all too well,
this book is for you

To my family – by birth and by choice

To God be the glory

CONTENTS

PROLOGUE: STEAL AWAY TO JESUS: DIED OF GRIEF

Fountain Inn, South Carolina: Mid-1920s

Fountain Inn, South Carolina: Mid-1920s

You can die of grief. You can literally get so sad that your heart shrivels up and dies. You can invest so much of what you need in others that you don't know how to live without them. You can't live without what they give you. I know this because my great-grandfather died of grief. That's what Mama told me and what Grandma told her.

Grandma's voice explained tersely: "My mother died of pneumonia. The youngest girl, LePearl, was only three years old. Six months later, my father died of grief."

I understand the story to go something like this:

My great-uncle Robert was a child. I try to picture the old man I know now—small, dark brown, with thick glasses and graying hair—as a little boy with a big grin. In my mind, boy-Robert is wiry and has the same spark in his eyes that Great-uncle Robert has when he banters with Grandma. The boy-Robert pulled the chair.

"Now hold the chair still," said his father. "You got it?" he asked, stepping onto the chair. I imagine my great-grandfather reaching up and fingering the rope. Checking to make sure he tied the knot right.

"Yes, Daddy." I imagine the twinkle of meeting a parent's approval in boy-Robert's eyes.

"Now when I say, pull the chair. Pull it all the way out, okay?"

"Okay," young Robert chirped.

"One, two, three, now!"

Was my great-grandfather calm and relieved as the rope closed in on his neck? Were his eyes bulging? Did his face contort into someone barely recognizable to his sons? Or was the immediate loss of consciousness his first taste of peace in ages?

Did boy-Robert think it was a trick? Look at how Daddy's arms and legs thrash! And then stop! Is this a game? Or did he immediately know something was wrong? Did he run to show his brothers and sisters? Did he tell "Uncle Sam," a former slave and family friend? Or did he go outside and play, expecting to see his father later? Did he know he was helping his father commit suicide?

The questions raced to my mind. Why did my great-grandfather kill himself? Was he that overwhelmed with the idea of parenting eight children on his own? Did his wife's death leave a hole in his heart that escaped words? Did he wrestle with mood swings? Did he fear what he might have done to his children if left to his own devices? Did he think he could push through no more pain, poverty, and farmland? Why did he involve his son? Couldn't he do it alone? Did he think of what this would do to my uncle

Robert? The other children? His grandchildren and great-grandchildren? Could he think of anything but escape?

No one is alive who can tell me these things.

But I know Uncle Sam raised the eight orphan children; some stayed down south, and some moved north. I was in my late twenties before anyone told the story. One Christmas season, LePearl's daughter Grace fussed in her kitchen, grabbing serving spoons and paper plates to dole out to my awaiting hands and those of my cousins. My cousin Theresa asked what Grace remembered about the South.

Grace wiped her hand on her apron and recalled, "When I was fifteen, we went back to the old house. The rope was still in the shed. They never took it down, you know."

Grace lifted her glasses from the beaded chain around her neck and situated them on her nose. She started opening cupboards in search of paper napkins. "People will be here soon. Get the table ready."

With spoons and plates in our hands, my cousin Theresa and I walked slowly toward the dining room. We started adding in our heads. Our great-aunt LePearl wasn't even eighteen when she had Grace. We looked at each other with the same realization.

The noose was in the shed for thirty years.

When I think of growing up in that setting, I begin to understand. Every time they played in the shed, they saw the rope. At least once a week. Ten times a day. They got used to it; it became normal—part of their days. And a heaviness hung over each life, and the sadness remained. Like a heavy fog.

The fog was so thick the children had to leave. They couldn't see themselves or each other for the ghostlike presence of their father. Maybe the oldest stayed because only he remembered "Daddy" before the rope. As for the others, "Daddy" and the rope were synonymous. I understand. They had to leave. Some went as far as the next county; others left the state, moving north to Washington, D.C., Baltimore, New York. As adults, my grandmother's generation refused to speak of it. When forced to, they called it as they felt it, and Grandma said it from her heart: "He died of grief."

Depression is like grief. It's a sadness that creeps in on you and slowly overwhelms you. Sometimes, I feed it like a repast after a funeral; other times, I sing and shout my way through it. But after the relatives leave, and the food is eaten, and the lights go off, it's still there; and it feels so bad that you try to escape it by any means necessary.

No one diagnosed my great-grandfather with depression. No one diagnosed Grandma. Who's to know or care about the mental and emotional state of poor sharecroppers from South Carolina? And who can stop to think of a clinical illness when the children need to be fed? What's the difference between depression, war, being black in the Jim Crow South, and plain old hard living? Who would know to alert children or grandchildren to the slippery slope of despair?

Without the story of Great-uncle Robert and his father,

I only knew that grief kills. There was no judgment or blame. Just a fact. Two breaths out of slavery, and my great-grandfather still wasn't free. He was oppressed by the memories of his wife, his fears, the burdens of what lay ahead. Sadness can own you. You can die of grief. It took me years to learn what generations of African Americans have long understood: there are things worse than death.

PART I

WILL THE CIRCLE
BE UNBROKEN?

Teenager: Michigan, 1988–1991

1

GRANDMA

Washington, D.C.: February 1988

The South Carolina cousins placed buckets of fried chicken on the piano bench, and my faith decreased and my depression increased with each wing that was eaten. We treated Grandma's funeral like a family reunion. "Have you got yourself some chicken, baby?" "Who's your mama?" "Are LePearl and them here yet?" "She always adored you grandchildren." Brown wrinkled fingers picked up a napkin and wiped a bit of grease from the side of a mouth. As the relatives stood up, the plastic covering on the pale blue sofa made a creaking sound.

I was thirteen and too young, my parents said, to wear a black dress. So I donned a navy dress with a Peter Pan collar with soft yellow-and-blue lace trim on the sleeves that my great-aunt sewed just for the day. I slid into the back of the limousine with my two first cousins. It was the first time I saw a dead body. I stood in front of the casket and looked for a long time. I stared so long that I swore I saw

Grandma's chest move up and down. Not much, just a little. I wanted to yell and grab Mama and tell her to call the doctors and morticians and say that a mistake had been made and Grandma was not really dead. Just very sick. I blinked again, and everything was still.

During the final viewing, I walked up to the casket with Mama's hand in mine. "But Mama, it doesn't look like her? What's wrong? It doesn't look like her."

Pulling me to an angle, Mama said, "Look from this way. She was lying on this side when she died. Look from this way."

I moved to the right and tilted my head, trying to see what Mama saw. I looked another thirty seconds, and she still didn't look like Grandma to me. The woman in front of me had darker skin and was thin enough to be called skinny. Her wig wasn't centered, and she didn't have on her glasses. This woman's eyes were closed and looked as though she had never baked, fussed, insisted, laughed, or doted. The body in the casket didn't look anything like my grandma. I squinted my eyes.

From the sides of my eyes, I saw the deacons in the front row. Black suits, black ties, old and slim, their backs seem hunched as they rocked back and forth.

When Israel was in Egypt's land
Let my people go
Oppressed so hard, they could not stand
Let my people go

Go down, Moses, way down in Egypt's land
Tell ole Pharaoh to let my people go.

The funeral was getting ready to start and it was time to sit down. I squinted my eyes again. I turned to Mama. "Now I see. It looks like Grandma from this angle."

My mother smiled, and I walked away mumbling to myself: "Imposter." The woman in that casket was not my grandma. That's not how I remembered her.

When I thought of Grandma, I thought of D.C. and D Street. As far as I could tell, black people lived in D.C.; white people lived in Washington. It took years for me to realize that the place with the White House, Georgetown, the Supreme Court, and Congress is the same city to which I traveled every summer of my preadolescent life. Every summer after age five, my parents boarded me on a plane with shiny patent-leather shoes, a friendly flight attendant, and the promise of a good time with my grandparents and cousins. There was often another child traveling alone—like the girl with blond Shirley Temple curls and a red-and-white-checkered jumper. We chatted and ate peanuts all the way from Detroit Metropolitan Airport to Washington National Airport. We became friends in the air, but we parted on the ground. I ran from the attendant's hand to my grandmother, grandfather, aunt, or uncle; Shirley Temple, too, ran to her responsible relative. At that point, we separated. She went to Washington, and I ventured into D.C.

D.C. was a place filled with corner stores, alleys, and

row houses. D.C. had broken bottles, screaming ambulance sirens, sidewalks for hopscotch, scratched-out stickball fields, and wire fences high enough to make climbing a challenge. When I went to D.C., I stayed in the same section of the city, and that section was filled with black people. In fact, most of the black people that I knew in D.C. were either related to me or knew my relatives. As far as I was concerned, D.C. was one block long and two alleys deep on either side of the center of the world: Fifteenth and D Streets NW.

Grandma made it seem like the world revolved around us grandchildren. We were all special—for different reasons. Wesley was the oldest, and the only boy. Theresa was the baby. And me, I was the oldest girl, and I came from far away—only on vacations. The summers belonged to my cousins, Grandma, and me. We could always expect our favorite foods—upside-down pineapple cake, barbecued beef, and the apple turnovers Grandma called "apple jacks."

Grandma was a woman too old, in my mind, to wear the short dresses I saw in older pictures. She took five minutes to read the menu at the McDonald's drive-through, and I often played her affection off my parents' restrictions: "But Grandma said she'll get it for me," I'd say, whatever it was I wanted that had been vetoed by my parents. Grandma was a woman who believed that little girls should wear frilly underwear, even though it itched. And she believed in braiding hair every morning, even if it looked fine from the day before.

While most of my time was spent playing with my cousins, Grandma always made sure that we had time alone.

"Grandma, why do we go to church every Sunday? And why do we have to stay there all day? How come I can't sleep during the sermon anymore? What's a revelation?"

"Just keep quiet and watch after me" was the usual response to my weekly questions.

As a deaconess at Shiloh Baptist Church, Grandma had a lot of church business to attend. We made the Communion. On the Saturday before the first Sunday of every month, we broke the crackers into little bits so that everyone could eat them. Actually, I didn't do anything. I was supposed to sit in the corner and read my book, but I watched so intensely I could have been serving the Communion myself: First, open the large orange-and-green boxes of flat crackers. Eat a couple to be sure they are fresh. Give some to the children to keep them quiet. Then lay them out on the long shiny table and begin to break them. Keep your gloves on! Then get the Welch's from the refrigerator and don't let the children have any of this. Pour it very carefully into the little cups. If you spill it, you have to clean up the whole mess and put on new gloves. Then put all the little cups into the little holes in the shiny gold container. Wash your hands and done! And the most important thing is to tell the children that they can't have any until the Sunday that they walk down the aisle for themselves and are baptized in the name of the Father, the Son, and the Holy Spirit.

Grandma grasped my hand and led me down the spiral

staircase back to the car talking about bedtimes and young minds. She told me how God had blessed us, and that tonight she'd answer some of the questions as best as she could. My mind tried to think of the most important question, in case there wasn't time for all of them. Meanwhile, Grandma pressed a five-dollar bill into the mitten of a homeless man next to the car. Before I asked, she said, "He needs it more than we do. You give a dollar to the Lord, and He will reward you tenfold, hundredfold, thousandfold." Grandma saw God in a homeless man.

Then the cancer returned. When I heard the word, I didn't know what it meant. I didn't know that people died of cancer. I didn't know that it could sweep in like a windstorm and knock the breath out of a person, a family. I didn't know that it could leave as quietly as it seemed to come and could lie dormant for years. I didn't know that it required children to act like parents. I didn't know how hard it was to ask your granddaughter to give you a bedpan because you couldn't lift yourself up. I didn't know how terrible the large spoonfuls of Kaopectate tasted when there used be a time when you could chew a steak. I didn't know anything about death or unfulfilled dreams because Grandma refused to let anyone know she thought about it.

Grandma was diagnosed with breast cancer in 1963, but by 1983 she had been in remission despite lymphoma, leukemia, and the double mastectomy. Quickly, we grandchildren were informed of her condition, and we came to know all the actions that made up daily living with and fighting cancer. That summer we lifted, fed, and held Grandma. We combed her hair, straightened her wigs, brought back bulletins from church services, and ran water for her baths. We were scared, but silently followed the orders of our mothers: "Do what Grandma asks, and be good."

One day in August, Grandma got up, walked into the kitchen, said the peaches were rotting and needed to be canned, and told us, "You better pick those apples for some apple jacks if you want them by dinner." Grandma was back, and we never really thought a time would come when she wouldn't eventually get up from the bed to can food and cook our favorites. We continued to dream and talk of our future careers, discuss where we would go to college, and ask, "Grandma, will you come to the embassy when I'm a famous interpreter for all the big events?"

"Of course, I'll be there. I'll buy a new hat for the occasion."

Remission came and went with Grandma. Although I had wiped saliva from her mouth, run baths, given medication, and accompanied her on numerous trips to the doctor, I never believed Grandma would die. She had been sick before. Sick enough that everyone thought she was dying—for good this time. Most of her adult nieces and nephews huddled around her bed that Christmas.

But she only pursed her lips together as if to spit, gathered all her available energy, and said, "You all need to go home. I ain't dead yet." Turning to the other side, she called out, "Maxine-Pauline," the names that sent her twins running to her bedside, and we knew, as always, that this was not the end. Grandma was invincible.

But remissions end, and Grandma moved from the dilapidated but love-filled row house in D.C. into Theresa's room in a cozy Baltimore neighborhood nestled between Reisterstown Road Plaza and the Jewish community of Pikesville. It was then that cancer became real. This time, Grandma's hair did not grow back when Theresa and I plaited it, telling her it was beautiful. This time, Grandma did not get up to cook, but winced away when we held the spoon of liquid medication. This time, it took forty-five minutes to move Grandma into the living room to watch us open gifts on Christmas.

I watched my grandmother transform from the Grandma on whose knee I sat into a woman who needed my help to turn to her side. In three short years, I saw her skin darken permanently and her cheeks sink into the cavity of her skull. I heard her voice grow weaker as I watched the pain remove all pride and embarrassment. By the time she died, she could no longer mother; she could no longer grandmother. Her strength and esteem seemed to slip away every time I wiped the crust from her eyes. At age eleven, I knew that "chemotherapy" meant to pick out a new wig. I knew that "morphine" meant the end was near. I knew cancer. And I hated it.

Despite all of this, my memories of Grandma don't focus on stuffed bras and vials of blood. I remember the row house packed with the D.C. relatives, mothballs, Grandma's church clothes, and plastic-covered furniture. I like thinking about the twenty-five-cent candy bars at the corner store and Grandma's threatening voice about climbing the fence. I think about giving money to the homeless and finding holiness in grape juice.

I planned to move to D.C. one day. I told people in Michigan that I wanted to live in a city with subways, train stations, and dirty streets. I told my friends that I would live rent-free with an aunt or uncle. I even said that I longed to live in a city with more black people. What I did not say is that I wanted to go to Arlington National Cemetery. I wanted to be able to wind around the curves circling the nearly identical white markers until I stopped the car at the nearest pathway. I wanted to ignore the numbered placards that distinguish the Vietnam veterans from the WWII heroes from the children of Korean War fighters. I wanted to walk until I saw the tree with the low bending branch and the stone with two engraved sides: Grandpa's name on one side and Grandma's name on the other. I knew that I would need immediate access to this particular hill of dirt in order to survive.

I imagined living in D.C. I would sit down and hug the stone. I would talk to Grandma as if she were still here. I would ask her if she could believe all the foolishness that cousin so-and-so had gotten into. I would ask her if she liked the way I did my hair. I would tell her about my school papers and grades. I would tell her that I still needed her to believe in me.

My thirteen-year-old faith was buried with Grandma that rainy day at Arlington. Grandma did not just believe in my dreams, my future, and my potential. Grandma believed me. Although I don't remember ever telling her with words, I believed that she knew. She knew all the reasons that I was there every summer. She knew about the life I lived in Michigan: a life that I lacked a vocabulary to voice.

I hated being an only child. I always wanted a sister. I wanted an older sister. I conjured her up in my mind. She would be sophisticated and savvy. She would know the words to all the latest songs and know all the moves from the corresponding videos. Her hair would be cut in the most modern styles, and she would smell like Estee Lauder's "Beautiful." She would be very popular and have her choice of boyfriends. She would have a tight circle of girlfriends who were so cool that they let me hang out with them too. Because she was so pretty and charming, she would walk the mall and heads would turn to see her and her friends walking four abreast. She would be . . . in essence . . . everything I was not. And she would teach me how to be all those things I desired.

But there would be no more children. I am the only child my mother could have. There would not be the four children she and Daddy planned. No "rusty butt boys, maybe two." And no sisters. I am, she said, "the miracle baby." I am, Mama always said, "the one God wanted her to have."

There's another reason I wanted a sister. I wanted someone else who had the same parents and knew what it was like inside our house.

It was like walking on a balance beam with my arms

out, trying not to fall to the left or the right. Creeping on the corners of conversations, tiptoeing out of bed after I was supposed to have been tucked in, walking on the edge of the carpeted hallway to avoid the section in the middle that creaked when you stepped on it. I caught pieces of sentences through the door. I was less interested in their content than their tone. How high was the inflection? How much anger was there? Were the harsh whispers exchanged at a distance, or were there whimpers of a twisted arm, the thud of a back against a wall?

I was not spying. I was monitoring—checking to see how things were. I was making sure they weren't . . . whatever the worst could possibly be. I devised a plan when I was six years old. I would stop things somehow. I would knock on the door: "I can't sleep," "I'm scared of the dark," "I had a bad dream," "Can I get a glass of water?" Some kind of middle-of-the-night plea a child would make that wouldn't seem too obvious. Something that wouldn't seem like I was listening in. I thought of it as intercepting a bad moment so that my presence, my request, the time it would take to tend to me would be just enough time to diffuse the worst of the argument. And, I imagined in my head, if that didn't work, if I knocked on the door too late, I would run to the bathroom and lock the door. Or I would run outside to my best friend's house next door. I would knock on Mark's bedroom window until he heard me and let me in the back door. No stuffed animals or Star Wars action figures in my fists. Mark would know that this must be serious. I would call 911 and then Grandma. And after "everything" happened, I would go live with Grandma and play with Wesley and Theresa after school everyday.

I was six years old, and I had a plan for what I would do the night my father killed my mother.

I never told this to Grandma. But I believed that she knew. I believed that she was just as scared as I was. And my summer trips were more than "time to get to know your relatives." They were the respites my mother gave me from the tense air of our household. They were two months of the year when I didn't have to be afraid.

There was a constant fear of my father. In part, because I could see that fear in my mother. Mama told me that Daddy did not physically hurt her. She told me that I should not have been afraid. It took twenty years for me to tell Mama that I had an escape plan when I was six years old.

She sighed, "I had one." She paused. "I didn't think you would too."

"Of course I did." I replied. "I lived there too."

There was an unspoken understanding between the two of us that there was nothing that we should put past Daddy. He might have done anything when provoked. The goal, my mother and I learned, was not to provoke him.

"Don't run up and jump on your father when he first gets home." These were Mama's words of admonition when I was seven years old. "Stay up here with me, then I'll let you know when you can talk to him."

Daddy went down the stairs of the bi-level house where we lived then. Unbeknownst to me, he was pouring a drink. Or two. He took off his tie, settled down in his reclining chair, and watched half an hour of the news. Then he came upstairs, into the kitchen, and I could sit in his lap and recount what I learned in school that day. This was the pattern of my school days—waiting for Daddy to be okay to talk to. As I grew older, I realized that he needed a drink to be civil. I awoke each morning thinking little of the small glasses with traces of orange juice in the sink. As a teenager, I counted the number of drinks Daddy had. At the restaurant: one before the meal, one with the meal, one or two after the meal during conversation. Stop by the store on the way home. Come out with green bottle in paper bag. Drive home. Next morning, small glasses in the sink and empty bottle in the trash. I didn't know if Daddy's rages had anything to do with alcohol. I reasoned that Daddy was just plain mean.

Mama called it the stress of the job. I now imagine that it was the stress of life. Daddy was the oldest of eight children who grew up high yellow and dirt-poor in various sections of D.C. He was named for his father's brother and took pride both in carrying the legacy of his favorite uncle and in not being named for his father.

His father, my Granddaddy, lived in a small room in the basement of a house not far from Nana's apartment. I never knew Nana and Granddaddy as living together. Everyone said that Granddaddy had more bad habits than good. I often heard Daddy talking about what an irresponsible man Granddaddy was. When I overheard angry phone calls, I learned that, to his children, Granddaddy was a "no-good, irresponsible, womanizing drunk." He could barely keep a steady job, and he wasn't good to his wife. "He was a mean drunk," my aunt told me. But that was not the Granddaddy I knew.

Granddaddy was a tall nut-brown man with smooth skin and salt-and-pepper hair who took me on the subway, introduced me to his friends, sent velour sweaters in the mail for Christmas, and let me sit on his lap until I fell asleep. I loved Granddaddy.

Granddaddy was from poor, uneducated folk in western North Carolina. He and his siblings moved north to D.C. looking for jobs and a better life. He drew the short straw. Literally. Drafted into the Second World War, his company was in battle but left something back at the campsite. They drew straws on who would return to get it. Granddaddy drew the short straw and returned to camp. When he got back to the battle site, everyone had been killed. Mama told the story over dinner one night. "He was never the same after that," she laments as if she knew him as a youth. "He said," she continues, "that everything changed. That's when he began drinking, I think."

Granddaddy married up when he married Nana. She, also from western North Carolina, was the child of a child of a blacksmith. She traced her genealogy back a couple generations. She had pictures of her parents and grandparents, and she pointed out the relatives.

"But they're white," I said.

"Yes," she said, telling me who married whom and how long Great-great-great-aunt Sally, a former slave, lived. She showed me the newspaper article about her. Granddaddy and Nana met in D.C. when "I was young and sassy," Nana said with a light laugh. She presented black-and-white pictures with her two sisters and her brother as young people. They all moved to D.C., looking for their fortunes "up north."

Life up north was still hard. Daddy was poor in a way that I cannot imagine. Mama remembers seeing him go through the trash when they were ten years old. Looking for soda bottles, change, food. He went to work, looking for errands or chores that would keep his family until the next month. They were so hungry that families from the church left them food. Daddy had to take on the role of provider long before he should have.

Daddy was determined to do better than what he had. He was the first in his family to go to college and finish—paying for it through the Army's ROTC program. He sent Nana money every month. He was determined to be different from Granddaddy. Daddy never put himself in the same category with his father. The only thing Daddy was willing to admit sharing with Granddaddy was premature gray hair.

Mama, on the other hand, was a chosen one of the chosen one. Grandma was the one her siblings chose to finish high school. Her seven sisters and brothers stayed home while Grandma traveled to a neighboring town to finish high school because there was no twelfth grade in Fountain Inn, South Carolina. Grandma was the one they sent to Benedict College. They could only afford one, and she was the one. Grandma married up, from a gaggle of orphaned sharecroppers raised by an ex-slave into a family of teachers, one of whom went to Spelman College. My grandfather was a military man my grandmother adored. He was working on a graduate degree when he died suddenly, leaving Grandma a widow with twin baby girls.

Grandma protected and guarded her twins. Grandma told them that they were special and that they always had each other. She hung her hopes, dreams, and high standards on them. Grandma insisted that they finish master's degrees before marrying. She wanted them to have careers of their own before birthing children. Compared to Daddy's family, Mama, Aunt Maxine, and Grandma were solidly middle class. Mama and Aunt Maxine went to a private (white) women's liberal arts college. Yet Grandma thought of herself as the teacher who was locked out of the world of other black female teachers—because her family was too poor, too dark, too unconnected, and too single-parented to receive the privileges of D.C.'s black middle class.

So my life was as split as Washington and D.C. In one part of my life, I felt happy and buoyant, smart and supported. I ran and played with my cousins. I relished in Grandma's home cooking and church excursions. I held tightly to Granddaddy's firm hand in the subway. I felt the support of my family. I knew that they worked hard to do better than their parents, just as their parents had done as well.

Daddy picked me up on the last day of school and bought me whatever I wanted when I made the honor roll—like the red Sony Walkman I got when I was in fourth grade. He set up a summer reading program for me where he taught me black history from books by Benjamin Quarles, and read aloud from Dostoyevsky hoping I would love *Crime and Punishment* as much as he did. He scrambled eggs for me and put them on grape-jellied toast, dubbing the result "the Coleman breakfast sandwich." Mama's hugs were generous, allowing me to sit in her lap as I recounted the previous night's dream or lie at her feet with my blanket and pillow while she typed out her doctoral dissertation late into the night. When we lived in the bi-level house, Mama took me up and down our street on Sundays, picking a combination of Queen Anne's lace, brown-eyed Susans, marshy cattails, wild lilac, and tiny daisies for our dinner of pot roast with potatoes and carrots. We always lived in a safe neighborhood, in a house that, Mama said, "You can run around without running around your neighbors' houses too." We had a vegetable garden bound by marigolds and wooden slats rather than weeds, a chain-link fence, and an alley. Although not divided by the seasons, these moments, hours, and days were the color of sunshine.

The other side of life was gray. I huddled by closed doors and worried about saying the wrong thing. That life was filled with curse words hurled like the neighbor boy's BB gun, stinging whatever soft flesh got in its way. I felt smaller and smaller the more Daddy yelled. I grew increasingly resentful at Mama for sitting silently by while he yelled at me, and while he snapped at her. I spent hours of days figuring out ways not to be home: Chinese language lessons after school, Girl Scout meetings, creative writing club, manager of the volleyball team, track and field, summer programs in the sciences, elaborate plans for financial independence after college, summers in D.C.

I sought friendships, surrogate families, and boyfriends like lifelines. I needed more than family for support. I needed other people who could hear me—and the words I didn't say—without expecting me to be grateful that I had more than they did. When I was five and six years old, I nestled in the high branches of our street's strongest trees with my best friend Mark. Knocking our Zips tennis shoes together as our dirty shoelaces dangled below, we whispered about secret hatreds: his mean older brother, my parents. As a teenager, I confided about "how bad it is" to a teenage boy I liked. He would whisper, "I believe you," and I felt less alone. More often, my voluntary relationships were tenuous threads to the bright yellow light where people knew me as funny, smart, hard-working, and nerdy. Sometimes I felt that happy. Other times, I lied to keep the darkness at bay.

My two lives were intertwined, but I saw the seams and felt the frays where they joined. I knew how to live in duality. I knew how to perform and smile while being sad. I lived with both great lows and great highs, and I learned how to hide it.

I suspect that Grandma did the same thing.

Mama inherited photo albums of old pictures from Grandma's collection. As I spent hours flipping through photo albums of Mama's youth, I noticed two things: how truly identical the twins were and how sad Grandma was. My cousins and I spent Sunday afternoons guessing which girl in the picture was my mother and which one was theirs. We took our surmising to one of our mothers: This one is you! No, this one!

There were pictures of Grandma in the same album. In every picture of my mother and aunt's growing-up years, Grandma looked as if she were on the verge of tears. Her eyes looked sad.

"She missed my father," Mama said. "It's the grief."

The sad eyes were my other connection to Grandma. I believed Grandma knew what I lived. Every vacation, she embraced me with open arms and hugs that made me think that we shared a secret understanding. I think she knew about Mama and Daddy, their fights and the alcohol. I think she knew a debilitating sadness that had to be suppressed so the work could get done. But I don't think she judged those who couldn't. She seemed to know that some people could work through it and that others self-medicate with alcohol. Some do both. Who knows what happens to you when your family hangs all its dreams on your life? Who's to say what happens to the developing brain chemistry of children who grow up in fear of their lives? These are not questions for my parents, their parents, or their parents.

Grandma's response to these unspoken quandaries was a sanctuary of hugs, food, and church. I needed her and her home at Fifteenth and D Street. Once Grandma was gone, I was done with God. What kind of God would take away the only person who knew the truth of my life? Grandma's God betrayed me and left me alone with my parents. Alone in the gray parts of my life. No more of that God for me.

2

MIDDLE PLACE

*Jackson, Michigan: Six Months
after Grandma's Death*

Six months after Grandma's funeral and I still felt like I was floating in nothingness. I spent a lot of time crying. I wanted to die too. No, I didn't want to die. I didn't have a plan. I just . . . didn't want to have to live anymore. I needed a middle place between the activities of my life and killing myself. I wanted to go there and stay awhile. Until I had to come back.

I missed Grandma. I knew Mama did too. In fact, I was so concerned about Mama's sadness that I didn't share mine with her. I lied to Mama:

"Yes, it looks like Grandma in that casket."

"No, I don't mind if you sell Grandma's house."

"It's fine, as long as we're together; we don't have to have Christmas in D.C."

I saw the droop in Mama's eyes, and I didn't want to be one more thing for her to worry about. She had to deal with money, hospice bills, and estate taxes. Grandma was a Depression-era woman—she had money everywhere except under the mattress: in five different banks, two credit unions, and on and on. Settling Grandma's estate was more like a treasure hunt than a financial arrangement. So I didn't tell Mama how sad I was. I wanted to be strong for Mama.

I went to my bedroom when it hurt the most. I hugged my knees to my chest and bit my lip to hold back the tears. When that didn't work, I pushed my face into my pillow. I wanted Grandma back.

Nana convinced me that God was punishing Grandma.

"You know," Nana said without looking up from her game of solitaire at the kitchen table. "God promises the righteous seventy years in age. Three score and ten, the Bible says. I'll be seventy in two days."

Nana was referring to Psalm 90:10, a scripture that suggests that God fulfills life-span promises to age seventy. I imagined that Nana was feeling proud. Pious. She birthed eight children, survived a battering husband, two heart attacks, and a stroke. She earned her pride. She had a right to celebrate. But Nana also knew that Grandma died when she was sixty-nine. Her remark felt cruel and malicious. Was she implying that Grandma was not righteous?

I was sure Grandma heard the same thing. They went to the same church. Did Grandma die feeling guilty that she had somehow failed God?

Grandma was the best person I knew. If she ever made a mistake or did anything wrong, it didn't matter. I believed Nana's words, I believed the scripture, and I believed

Grandma was perfect. Nothing was wrong with Grandma. It was God. God was unjust to punish her, to keep her from her seventy years.

I had to live without Grandma. I didn't have to live with God. Grandma's God did not answer my night prayers of tears. I didn't need a God who punished Grandma and then took her from me. I had no words for such a God.

I started praying to Grandma. I asked Grandma what she thought about my new dress, my haircut, or the guy I liked. I thought about what Grandma would say about my friends. I asked Grandma if it . . . if the sadness . . . would get any better. I asked her to watch over me and talk to me. I implored: "And if, if, there is a God, can you tell Him to just make it better?"

I felt guilty about my faithlessness, and I kept that a secret as well. In my family, going to church is like brushing teeth. It's just something you do. Good spiritual hygiene. Once Grandma was gone, Christmas was never the same. My great-aunt LePearl's family adopted us into their customs. Like we did the Christmases before Grandma died, we went to Baltimore and stayed with Aunt Maxine. I shared a bed with Theresa. She complained about me pushing her off the bed, and I complained about her toenails. Just like before. But that year, we went to Cousin Grace's house, ate the food she cooked, and gathered all the chairs in a circle around the living room. Although she sat in a corner, "Aunt Pearl" was the focus. Aunt Pearl was the only living member of Grandma's generation in the D.C. area. Grace and her three younger sisters swarmed around

Aunt Pearl: "Mama, do you need this? Mama, are you comfortable?"

Grace began the ritual of going around the room while we each shared what we had to thank God for. At the end, Grace passed out song sheets and we sang carols while her sister, 'Cille, played the piano. 'Cille was a church pianist and played for choirs. She, her sisters, and her children all sang beautifully, giving solos and ensembles of hymns and popular gospel songs.

Theresa and I sang and hummed along. The songs were familiar. But singing them was a lie. I didn't need God. I could still be a good person, understand why other people believed, and be okay. I had to sing the songs. I had to fake it. If Mama found out I didn't believe, she would be sad, and it seemed that she was so often sad. If Grandma knew, she'd be disappointed. She would say that she raised me better than this. But I refused to believe in a God that betrayed Grandma, and, by taking her away from me, betrayed me as well. I would not believe in a God that could let me be so sad. I could not believe like I did when Grandma was alive.

Finally, 'Cille stopped playing the piano, and one of the grandchildren begged Aunt Pearl to sing.

Aunt Pearl stood up and sang in her creaky yet solid voice, "Myyy God is so high." Her grandchildren, knowing a tradition that my first cousins and I did not, chimed in, "You can't get over him." We figured out where and how to sing the chorus.

Aunt Pearl continued, "So wiiiiiide." She stretched out her arms to go with the verses.

We sang together, "You can't get around him."

Aunt Pearl dropped to a surprising bass tone, "So looooow."

"You can't get under him."

I didn't know the next line that Aunt Pearl's children and grandchildren knew: "You must come in at the door."

As Aunt Pearl finished, she flashed the toothy grin that all Smith women have. I turned to Theresa sitting just inches from me.

"She looks so much like Grandma." I lowered my eyes so no one could see how glossy they were becoming.

"Yeah. Just like her," Theresa whispered.

We both sniffed back our tears.

Death stalked me. Turning up in corners where it shouldn't have been. Less than a month after Christmas and Grandma showing up in Aunt Pearl's smile, the English teacher assigned *Beloved*. I didn't understand all of it, but I knew why Sethe killed Beloved. She didn't want her daughter to experience what she had. Sethe didn't want her daughter to live in the terrible world of slavery that she knew. I understood that. I wrote in my journal:

The whole world is terrible! I have been a wreck all week. I've been searching for some kind of escape. I tell myself I can't escape. I can't disappear. I need to stay here. But trying to stay here is making me sick. I'm pale and have dizzy spells at school. I can't pay attention in class. I try really hard not to cry. I don't understand why no one sees me or how much I'm hurting. I say it in my head, "Help! Someone help me!" But no one is here. No one can see me, and all I see are ghosts. I see the ghost of Grandma in Aunt Pearl. I ask Grandma for help. I don't get any answer. And now there's some ghost in my book who wants back into this world. Doesn't Beloved get it?! She has the better end of the deal. It's Sethe who is sad without the one she loves. Like me.

I looked for other people who would understand me. People who didn't know my family or the girl I was supposed to be in the yellow parts of my life. Like Maurice. I met Maurice during an educational program at Michigan State University. I was there to learn advanced trigonometry and computer languages. There were several summer programs for minority youth housed in our dorm. My program was six weeks long. Some programs were shorter, with a new set of teens swarming in every week or two. Maurice was in one of those programs.

We met in the cafeteria. My roommate saw him staring at me and pulled my arm, "Don't look now, but I think someone likes you."

We talked later on that evening in the lobby. Maurice, who had recently moved to Michigan to live with his mother, was the first Californian I had ever met. "There's nothing better than the ocean, dude." His West Coast slang made him different from the Detroit, Flint, and Saginaw boys, and he'd rather use his lean basketball-player body to hold a skateboard. Maurice was dark brown by the sun but naturally a medium brown, the color of a wooden picture frame. He had short, curly hair that beaded when wet but felt silky between my fingers when I held his head. He was so tall that to kiss him I stood while he sat, and I still had to reach on my tiptoes. He was my first boyfriend, and my best friend.

For one week that summer, we spent every lunch, dinner, and free evening time together. We sat on the couches in the lounge or in the dorm stairwell sharing stories about our lives. He told me how much he missed the sun and the sand of the Bay Area. He talked about how rough Detroit was. His high school had to be, he concluded, the most dangerous place he'd ever been. He had to act much tougher than he felt inside. He talked about his mother's remarriage to a tall white man who thought he could tell Maurice what to do, and about how disconnected he felt from his mother's new life and his baby sister. I listened attentively, rubbing his hands while he talked. I kissed his cheeks as if that could make it better.

I told Maurice my secrets too. I told him how much I missed Grandma and how sad it made me. I told him about how scared I was. I didn't know what I was afraid of, but I was scared and the fear was always with me, even when I looked happy. It was, I said, like a river that runs beneath the earth—if you dig deep enough, it's there and it's just sad.

He said he wished there was something he could say or do to make me feel better. He put his arm around me and held me close to him. I didn't tell him that just being there right then was enough. I didn't think I could talk about

Grandma or my fear to anyone without crying. I never talked about it. Telling Maurice somehow made things better, and he made me happy.

Maurice left four weeks before my program was over, but we wrote each other every week. He even had a friend drive him up from Detroit on my birthday. He meant to surprise me, but I was away from the dorm and I missed him. He left a note on my door and told me to go to security. There he left me a silver necklace that I wore everyday. For his birthday, months later, I sent him an engraved silver ID bracelet from Things Remembered. We matched together.

Once school started, we were ninety miles apart, and it seemed like an entire continent since we were both too young to drive. We were determined to keep our love alive, and our long letters talked about school and family and how much we missed each other. I told Maurice things I never told friends at school and church. He knew how empty I felt and how much I cried. He supported me with declarations of love and acceptance. He didn't care about my grades, my church activities, the designer labels that weren't on my clothing, or how fast I did or did not run track. It was like my childhood friendship with my next-door neighbor Mark. Another boy I trusted, someone who seemed to get me.

One night there was a letter from Maurice waiting when I got home. I served myself dinner on a plate and rushed upstairs to my room. I planned to sit on my bed and read it over and over again. I lifted the pages to my nose, knowing it smelled like his cologne. Dry, sweet. These letters were my lifeline. They kept me from holding everything inside.

Just as I was opening the envelope, Daddy yelled up the stairs. "What's wrong with you? Come down here and eat dinner like a family!"

I wanted to read my letter, but I laid it on my bed, picked up my plate, and ambled down the stairs to sit at the table. In the mornings, the breakfast nook was as picturesque as it was designed to be. The paneled windows formed the top half of a hexagon looking out into the backyard shrubbery. During the spring bloom, you couldn't even see the neighbor's backyard down the hill. Just greenery and the squirrels and robins that made it their playground. At night, however, it was an expanse of blackness that seemed to go on forever.

As if there were something to see, I stared out the window while eating my food. I had one concrete thought: if I just eat this quickly and quietly, I can go back upstairs and read Maurice's letter. If I don't say anything, Daddy'll just leave me alone.

Mama sat across from me while Daddy stood in the kitchen. Having arrived home earlier that day, he had eaten already and was moving the pots into the dishwasher.

He began: "What the hell is wrong with you? Why can't you be a part of this family?!"

I had learned that these were rhetorical questions. I kept my face turned toward the window.

"Look at me when I'm talking to you! You walk around here like some kind of stuck-up snob. You think you are some kind of social butterfly because you have all these friends. But you're not. You treat me like shit. You don't talk to me, but you want to talk on the phone all night long."

I said nothing. I knew better than to respond. That only led to punishment and grounding. There was nothing I could say that would have calmed him.

"Well, no more. You think you have a boyfriend?! You're not allowed to have a boyfriend. You need more female friends. No more phone privileges." He turned toward my mother. "Take the phone out of her room. And no more letters. I don't want to see any more letters coming from Detroit. You are not allowed to have any friends who aren't black girls, you understand."

I tried to remain stoic, but I began to imagine my life without Maurice. I tried to imagine having no one but my journal. Who would I talk to? Who would hear—and actually believe—everything I had to say about how I felt? Maurice didn't know the public Monica from school and track and church. He didn't know the "Goody Two-shoes" everyone believed I was. I had to look perfect on the outside even though I knew that inside I was not. It was a two-ness that fed into itself.

When I presented myself as sad or depressed, I only looked spoiled. Because, as Daddy kept asking, what did I want that I didn't have?

I knew the answer to that. I wanted someone who knew the real deal about me. Grandma was gone, but Maurice knew and still loved me. And there, Daddy was trying to take that away from me. He didn't understand! He had seven younger siblings. Mama had Aunt Maxine. They didn't know what it was like to come home and be alone. No one else knew what it was like to be their kid. No one else lived in this house of whispered-sometimes-yelling arguments at night when they thought I was asleep. I began to cry.

"Why are you crying?"

I said nothing.

"Why? Answer me!" Not a rhetorical question.

"I don't know," I sobbed. I couldn't explain what I was thinking. That wouldn't go well.

"You're lying!" he yelled back. "You know why you're crying, and if you don't, you're just crazy! Only crazy people don't know why they do something."

"Don't call her crazy." Mama's voice came from the other side of the table. Up until now, Mama had been sitting there, watching the scene unfold before her. I couldn't count the number of times that Daddy yelled and cursed while she stood there or sat silently.

So I was surprised when Mama spoke up.

"Don't call her crazy!" Mama said this in a tone lower than normal. Almost like a loud whisper.

Something about the word "crazy" bothered Mama. She sat through all types of name-calling from Daddy. Maybe they had one of those parental agreements about not arguing about the child in front of the child. If so, it was silly. I heard them fighting about me. Voices from the bedroom: "Monica doesn't see reality." "Let her grow, Allen." "Stop protecting her. What kind of mother are you?" "You try to control her." "I'm supposed to." "No you're not, let her . . ." Mama defended me behind closed doors, and I knew it. But in her moments of silence when he yelled, the backdoor defense was no consolation.

Apparently, "crazy" was a breaking point for her.

I didn't think of myself as crazy. I knew I was sad, but not crazy.

I barely understood the flatness of my depressions. It took an incredible amount of energy to smile when I wasn't happy, and it was nearly impossible to see, let alone feel, joy even when it was right in front of me. I must have seemed like an ungrateful kid. I wasn't hungry; I had more clothes than I needed; I went to a good school; I had two parents at home. These were things Mama and Daddy lacked growing up. They believed that having these things would create a happy life for them and for me. Why wasn't this enough for me? I had no answer to that question. I wanted to be happy. I wanted to be thankful for all the material things that I had. But they meant nothing to me. I felt nothing.

"Don't call her crazy!" Mama interjected this time.

Daddy looked at Mama, then continued back with me.

"He's my friend, Daddy. I'm lonely and he's my friend." I continued crying.

"You can't be lonely!"

Ask me how I feel and get mad when I finally tell you! "I don't have siblings like you all. My friends are far away."

"We're your parents. We're supposed to be your best friends!" Daddy followed with a list of things I was no longer allowed to do: talk on the phone, write letters to boys, have any visitors, the list continued. "Understand?"

"Mm hmm."

"What?!"

I lifted my eyes long enough to glower at Mama who returned to her normal silence. "Yes," I said to Daddy. "May I be excused?"

"Yes."

I walked as slowly as I could, but I wanted to run. When I got to the bottom of the stairs, out of view from the kitchen, I rushed up to Maurice's open letter on my bed. I pushed it to the floor, threw myself headlong across the bed, and cried: What did the letter even mean now? I can't drive or date. Daddy won't even let me get mail. I may as well forget Maurice. As for Daddy, I vow never to answer another question honestly. Daddy asks how I feel and then gets mad when he doesn't like the answer. He tries to tell me I'm not feeling something I am feeling. And when he finds out what matters to me, he takes it away. I know how I feel, and I know what I care about. I also know what to do. Keep it to myself, I reason. He will never, ever again know how I really feel.

So I turned to my piano. When I was four years old, Daddy bought me a piano. At that time, both my parents were in graduate school, and most days I ran around in Brand X clothing from Sears. I don't know how they afforded the piano. But I recall standing at the top of the stairs, holding onto my mother's pants and watching the movers turn and twist to get a mahogany baby grand Steinway through the front door.

Daddy's piano skills consisted of a two-finger half of "Chopsticks" and a short song he played by rolling his knuckles across four black keys. Nevertheless, he loved the sound of a piano well played. Mama was classically trained from childhood, and I spent much of my fourth year sitting on the right side of the piano bench, legs dangling while Mama played Bela Bartok's "Bear Dance."

I started taking lessons when I was five, and ten years later I still was not a talented or gifted musician. I couldn't keep time, theory always eluded me, and I couldn't sight read well or play by ear. But I was a disciplined pianist. I learned Daddy's favorite songs and played them for him and all visiting company. Did that for years. He loved Canada's national anthem. In my early high school years, I practiced two hours a day. I was better than decent. Two hours a day of scales, arpeggios, and chords before honing and memorizing Bach's inventions and Beethoven's and Mozart's sonatas. For that skill, my parents enrolled me in the local Bach and sonata competitions one year. It was terrible. With others watching, my fingers forgot where to go, and I lost all sense of timing. After each failed performance, Daddy cursed at me all the way home. He believed I could do better. I came home feeling smaller than I did on stage.

Playing the piano was for me. The notes on the page spun into a force field around me, and I got lost in the sounds, the forward and sideways sway of my torso to the crescendos and decrescendos. When I practiced, Mama and Daddy left me alone. Their arguing became mute, and the music turned into the soundtrack of my life. When I dreamed, I heard certain runs in the background, and I fingered out songs on my leg or on my desk at school when I felt frightened or lonely. That night, I wiped my damp face and tiptoed down the stairs and into the living room. I pulled out the piano bench as quietly as possible and dove right into a sonata. The music was my cocoon from the world. Music was somewhere between the tears in my bedroom and the activities of my public life. Music was my middle place.

It took years for me to realize that I will always search for a middle place. Left to myself, I live in extremes. I need a neutral space for equilibrium, for escape. I need a place where I can forget both the sadness and intermittent happiness. I don't naturally live in that place. Bipolar cares nothing for balance. I need exercise, creativity, and the arts. I don't want to perform or compete. My teenage lexicon had no words for how much I needed to find a grounding to bring me back to center. I didn't know such a grounding was a lifetime need. I didn't know I'd need this center to survive.

3

THE MASK

Brighton, Michigan: Two Years after Grandma Died

Depression was my secret. It was the thing I said in whispers to very few people. People I could trust. Otherwise, no one needed to know. They would not understand. They wouldn't care. I managed it by myself. I mean, I wanted help, and I had friends. But it came down to me. When I cried at night, I was the only one there.

Sometimes I felt okay. Like when I was out with my girls. My circle of friends consisted of three other black girls who were also only children. We were all younger than our peers because we all skipped a grade along the way to high school. We walked the mall like we owned it—scoping for boys, trying on clothes at Merry-Go-Round, and checking out the latest releases at Recordtown. There was only one thing missing: letter jackets. Our look would be complete with letter jackets. Letter jackets were the key to cool. It was bad enough that we didn't go to public school where all the cute boys were. Kids our age assumed we were snobs or smarty-pants because went to Greenhills.

Greenhills was a small college prep school that I never wanted to go to. When I was in sixth grade, Mama and Daddy insisted that I needed to be academically challenged. I took the required entrance tests and found myself among sixty-five other kids my age that were just as overachieving as I was. The unassuming flat-roofed building of white brick squares fostered an environment that was both relaxed and competitive. Just one story high, there were no locks on the lockers, but we considered any SAT score under 1400 as "failing." The architecture and honor code masked our internal drives.

People often asked me, "Are there any black people there?"

There were only thirty black students at Greenhills, and that's in grades six through twelve. Only fifteen blacks in the high school, and eight of those fifteen were in my grade.

"Yes!" I sighed in response to the inquisitors. "We are there."

After Grandma's death, my world seemed whiter and whiter. With Mama and Daddy's job promotions came more money and bigger houses and more suburban subdivisions. The suburban life was balanced by the naïveté of childhood and long summers in D.C. I mean, it was a bigger deal that my childhood friend was a boy than that he was white. I just liked Star Wars action figures more than dolls and dress up. But once I was in high school, the largely white environment of home and school bothered me more. The good part was that it made me more of an activist.

My girls and I decided that we needed a black students' organization. One guidance counselor was discouraging black students from applying to Ivy League schools. We were all having trouble with one English teacher when reporting on books by black authors. We were all tired of having to speak for the entire race when a question came up in a class. We were motivated to organize.

So we invited the black students from other private schools in southeast Michigan and northern Ohio to an all-day conference, with dinner and a party to follow. We wanted to assert that it bothered us when our classmates said, "I don't think about your blackness. I mean, you could be purple or polka-dot for all I care." We wanted our blackness known, represented, and appreciated. We found the most radical speakers we could.

We invited a local scholar of Afrocentric thought who gave two lectures. One lecture taught the principles of Afrocentricity, and the second lecture talked about the influence of Africa on Western art. We invited the president of a local high school's black student association. He was a student of the Nation of Islam and spoke about Black Nationalism and the need for a separate black nation within the United States. Although my friends and I were hardly nationalist or separatist, we derived great joy from watching our fellow classmates cringe at his speech. This young man, only a year or two older than us, spoke eloquently and fiercely of hating every drop of white blood in his body. He talked about white supremacy and revolution. Best of all, he brought a friend who stood silently by his side wearing a dark suit. Our white classmates asked, "Is that his bodyguard? Is he Fruit of Islam?" We didn't know and we didn't care. For the first time, we saw on the faces of our classmates the feelings of estrangement, alienation, and exclusion to which we were accustomed. We were revolutionaries with spiteful edges.

But most times, we just wanted to be regular teenagers. With letter jackets, the question people asked us in the mall would be different: "So what do you play?"

I chose track, thinking that running didn't require a special skill. My friend Kelli and I decided to join the team together. (Kafi and Robin chose softball.) Kelli and I giggled together, taking turns singing the verses to The Jet's latest song, coming together on the chorus with our hands in fists of imaginary microphones: "How did you know? 'Cause I never told. You found out, I've got a crush on you!"

Kelli took running seriously enough to pull her hair back and put in another thirty minutes passing the baton after track practice was over. Still, she refused to run in the rain the weekend before a big dance because, as she told the coach, "If you don't understand that I have black girl's hair, then I just can't explain anymore to you." I, on the other hand, was never in a relay because I didn't run very fast.

One time, I ran the 400-meter race. Before the race, when I had asked the coach how to pace myself, she said to sprint the whole way. I was running my hardest, and I saw the girl next to me gaining as I was going around the first curve. I clearly thought, "I guess she's just faster than me. That's good for her." She passed me, and I huffed and puffed my way to the finish line.

I lacked the competitive spirit that sports require. I didn't care enough about winning. I came to practice, tried every event the coaches suggested, even the 300 hurdles that scraped my leg when I jumped too soon and came down on top of the hurdle. Greenhills was a class D school, and so every runner was needed just for points. I lettered after my second year, and I sported that jacket every day the weather was cool enough.

Late track practices on Fridays often led to a girls' night out. "I got the Galant!" Kelli held up the keys before school started. Eight hours later, we tumbled into Kelli's dad's new gold Mitsubishi, rolled down the windows, and turned up En Vogue.

"Ooh! My first mistake was . . . ," we crooned as we pulled out of the school driveway to Showcase Movie Theaters. The chore of running aside, these days with friends, music, and malls were the color of sunshine.

So I knew I could wait it out. When I got down, like when I missed Grandma, I could let myself be a little down. Even cry. But I could make it through. It might come back. There might be other things that hurt me, but I would be here. I was ready to challenge them. I could fight it. I would never think about taking my own life again. Life was too much fun. I would never give up again. This is what I told myself.

Some quiet part of me suspected: it's coming back. The

lows will come back again. I'm not really strong. I am not so convinced that life is good. I am lying. I am keeping secrets. I am wearing a mask.

The mask was designed to keep people from knowing how I felt inside. I was like the poem by Paul Laurence Dunbar:

We wear the mask that grins and lies,
It holds our cheeks and shades our eyes,—
This debt we pay to human guile
With torn and bleeding hearts we smile
And mouth with myriad subtleties.
Why should the world be overwise,
In counting all our tears and sighs?
Nay, let them only see us, while
We wear the mask

Mama and Daddy introduced me to this poem in elementary school—supplementing my Catholic school's curriculum with their knowledge of black literature and history. Dunbar, they said, is referring to the ways that African Americans learn to operate around white people. African Americans protect themselves from a cruel racist world by giving white folk what they expect: a minstrel show and "yes, massas." All the while, they are teaching themselves to read at night or hiding their attempts to escape in song lyrics. Mama and Daddy taught me about the ingenuity of black folk. They taught me how to live in the world. I would be like that, I decided.

I took my natural personality to an extreme. If you wanted me to be happy, I would be ecstatic. You wanted me to smile, I would grin. You wanted me to be grateful, I would thank you until you were sick of hearing it. It might have looked as phony as it felt, but I didn't care. I couldn't take the risk of sharing myself with others. I gave my parents, my girlfriends, and the world what I knew they wanted: a smart, religious, well-behaved young woman. It wasn't all pretending. There was a part of me that was everything the mask was. I have a naturally effervescent personality. I wasn't faking my laughter with friends, my energy for learning, or the joy I found with my church class. I just had to be that "me" all the time, even when the private me was sad.

I told one adult. I had a relationship with the mother of a classmate. I once called to talk with her son, but he wasn't home and we began to chat. I always enjoyed talking with adults, and she told me that her daughter was away at college, leaving her with her husband and two youngest sons—a house full of men. We talked about girl stuff, and I called just to talk with her.

Mama knew about my conversations with Mrs. Myers and encouraged them. Mama long believed in what black female scholars call "the community of other-mothers." When I read about them in Patricia Hill Collins's *Black Feminist Thought*, I knew exactly what she meant. Since I was old enough to learn my own phone number, Mama made sure I knew Grandma's and Aunt Maxine's as well. "You don't have to tell me everything," she said, "but always talk to someone." Other-mothers filled the gap in Mama's parenting. Mama was simultaneously subscribing to the African American traditions she inherited in her own relationships with her aunts and acknowledging her limitations as a parent.

I was not thinking about other-mothers when I thrust the phone into Mama's hands. In my junior year, and at nearly sixteen, I had figured out a way to survive. I increased my extracurricular activities and decreased time at home. I joined a homework club and stayed at school or church as late as possible. I drew charts in my journal minimizing time at home: wake up, eat breakfast, and head out the door—one and a half hours. School, then Girl Scouts, or youth choir rehearsal, or SAT prep until six in the evening. Home at six thirty. Dinner at the table until seven. Take shower and go to sleep. Sleep until six thirty or seven the next morning.

I slept ten to eleven hours a night, a classic sign of depression. I preferred to think of it as avoidance. Sleep allowed me to avoid Daddy and Mama, their arguments, and my own sadness. I might dream, but I couldn't feel if I was asleep.

I told these things to Mrs. Myers. How much I slept, and how much I hated Mama and Daddy. I imagine she thought I was just being a teenager—trying to find my own identity amid my parents' rules and regulations. I can imagine how easy it is to miss depression in teenagers. Where is the line between normal angst and frustration, and a desperation that can kill?

But I wanted her to know. I read my poetry to Mrs. Myers. One poem was about a girl who set herself on fire. I wrote it in iambic pentameter for an assignment in the Shakespeare unit of English class. I sent a copy home with her son. She asked me outright. She asked if I ever thought about suicide. I told her I didn't want to be alive. *Is that the same thing?* I knew that she worked in a mental health program, and I knew that she would take me seriously. This was the only way I knew to ask for help.

She thought that I should tell Mama. "I would want to know if it were my daughter," she said. I tried to tell Mama, but I didn't know what to say. We rode home in the dark together, the sun setting early during Michigan winters. I opened my mouth to say something, anything, but nothing came out. Where would I begin?

"I hate him," I muttered under my breath. Daddy is the problem. "I hate him."

"Don't say that." Mama chided.

I yelled back, "Why? Because that's how I feel and you don't want to know how I really feel, do you? You can't handle it anyway!"

We pulled into the garage; I leaped out of the car with my book bag in tow. I ran to the phone, dialed Mrs. Myers, and wailed, "It's Monica. You tell her! You tell her!"

Mama walked in the door, I handed her the phone and said, "Here!" I ran up the stairs to my room.

I'm not sure what I expected to happen. I wanted Mrs. Myers to tell Mama that I wasn't okay, that I needed someone to notice what was wrong with me. I didn't know how to tell her myself, but Mrs. Myers was right, Mama needed to know. I needed help.

Mama told Daddy. Exactly what I didn't want. He was the enemy. Mama was supposed to be my ally against him. I thought Mama would keep my secret and find a way to make it better. But she didn't. She told him. Daddy said he cared, but I didn't believe him. He seemed less upset that I was suicidal and more upset that I didn't tell him about it.

"Why didn't you talk to your mother or me about this if you were feeling so bad?" His deep voice boomed.

It was as if I had aired the family's "dirty laundry" by talking to Mrs. Myers about my feelings. I had one conclusion: he didn't care about me. He only cared about the image of the family I presented.

Mrs. Myers's revelation created incessant parental questioning: "What's wrong? Why are you in your room?" Every ten minutes, I swear.

I wanted Mama's compassion and sensitivity. I wanted Mama to be attentive to my needs. After all that, I just wanted them to leave me alone.

Mama decided I needed to see a psychologist. Maria was a child psychologist who handed me paper and asked me to draw a picture of my family. I looked at her like she was out of her mind.

"I'm fifteen," I snapped. "I'm not drawing pictures with crayons. If there's something you want to know, just ask me."

"So what's the problem?" Maria used a tone meant to

calm me. It only irritated me. I wasn't feeling peaceful, and I didn't think she should sound nice and even right now.

"I hate my father."

"Your mother says that you were suicidal."

"Yeah, a couple of years ago." I said flatly.

"Are you still suicidal?"

"No, I just hate my father."

I was supposed to open up to her, but I didn't think she could help. Mama went through a lot of trouble to get me to Maria. Mama suggested family counseling shortly after talking with Mrs. Myers, but Daddy refused.

"We don't need therapy," he said. "The child needs to stop being so ungrateful."

So Mama lied and told Daddy that we had a late-night meeting while she tried to figure out how to pay for it without it showing up on the joint checking account or insurance forms.

It didn't last long. Daddy found out and confronted us when we came home one evening.

"What's this?!" he asked Mama while holding up a sheet of paper. We had barely made it out of the garage.

Mama went into the kitchen and looked at it. I made moves toward to my room.

"You sit right there!" he snapped.

I went to the table and sat down.

"Monica's therapy," she said. Mama looked at me. I looked back at her. We both inhaled.

"What's this for? I thought we talked about this." Daddy bellowed at Mama.

"She needs someone to talk to." Mama replied.

"She can talk to us. Can't you?" Daddy turned toward me.

The kitchen counter and barstools separated us. I arched my feet so my toes touched the floor. I bounced my legs up and down and gripped the sides of the table. I looked down.

"What's wrong with you?"

"Nothing." Hell if I was telling the truth.

"Something must be wrong. What's wrong?" he prodded.

"Tell him," Mama urged in a quiet voice.

"Was I talking to you?!" Daddy turned around swiftly and grabbed Mama's arm and twisted it. He pushed her against the cabinet. "I wasn't talking to you."

Mama winced.

My silence immediately escalated to anger. For months, I was silent, evasive, sleeping. I tried to avoid conflict. Tried to avoid that moment. But it wasn't Mama's fault. I stood up. "You're what's wrong! I hate you. I have to see a therapist because I hate *you*!"

Hatred was my primary emotion. I was convinced that most of my problems were Daddy's fault. He yelled at me. He cursed at me. He kept me from my friends by making us live so far from school. Getting out of the house, growing up, and going away to college was my salvation. A couple months prior, I decided I would leave home the day after my seventeenth birthday. I began a countdown to liberation. I put hatch marks on the inside covers of my notebooks. I started at 865 days. Now I had only 489 more days. I felt guilty for hating Daddy. I knew that I wasn't supposed to hate anyone. But I thought long and hard about it and, yes, it was hatred.

I hated Daddy for making me wear a mask. For making me pretend like I was happy all the time when I wasn't. I saw myself as waging a battle for my soul, and I didn't have enough armor. I recognized a vulnerable part of myself—a part that was scared and didn't have enough faith and didn't have any answers—but I didn't know how to protect it from criticism and harsh words. I didn't know how to protect myself from the depression.

When I wasn't depressed, another part of me thrived. The part of me with a letter jacket and friends and choreography to MC Hammer's "Turn this Mutha Out." I knew that if I could get through the depression, I could be that person again. I could be "me" again. But I was too far into that episode to know it. I moved deeper and deeper into my second experience with depression. School kept me busy with the SAT, ACT, achievement tests, and Advanced Placement exams. I slept my way through as much of the sadness as I could. But wearing the mask made me tired, and I felt the sadness as rage. I felt it as hatred, and I said so out loud.

That night in the kitchen, I held my breath to see what would happen next. It felt good telling the truth, but I wasn't sure what the truth would unleash.

Daddy let go of Mama and walked toward me. I slid down into the kitchen chair as if I could disappear in front of them. Daddy must have seen my anger morph into fear because he stopped a couple feet in front of me.

"You don't hate me," he said. His tenor was lower. The harsh edges fell off his tone.

"Yes, I do," I spat back at him, squinting my eyes with determination. Meanwhile, I scooted the chair backward a couple of inches.

"No, you don't. You just think you do because you don't like the rules. But you know I love you, right? Right?!" he insisted.

"Yes, Daddy," I cowered.

"Tell me you love me."

I looked past his shoulder at Mama, who was still standing in the kitchen by the refrigerator. Her face said to keep the peace and get this conversation to end. At least that's how I read it.

"I love you, Daddy," I muttered.

"What?"

"I love you Daddy."

"Now give me a hug." I hugged Daddy's rotund body, and my stomach muscles tightened. My appetite dissipated, and I wanted to get out of his embrace. "You can go now."

I left my school bag in the kitchen and rushed into the living room to play the piano.

A middle place. Between truth and lies. Lying had become part of my life. I lied about loving my father. I lied about being happy. I lied about the harmony of my household. I lied with silences and masks. It was a cultural, psychological, and domestic habit. It was how I stayed alive.

But I always wanted to tell the truth. I wanted people to know. I wanted to be free to say it. But depression plays tricks with your mind. So does fear. It would take years for me to know that my happiness was as honest as my despair, and that the mask was as honest as my soul.

4

FAITH IN GOD

Ann Arbor, Michigan: Two Years and Four Months
after Grandma Died

I started to believe in God the day Mama told me that she was leaving Daddy. I was drinking raspberry juice through a straw, a delicacy I was allowed only on special days. It was the last day of exams for my junior year in high school, and Mama took me to my favorite café in downtown Ann Arbor. The place had omelets all day, crisp buttery pastries, and an item on the menu that left a salty spinach taste in my mouth. The lunch crowd was dwindling when we arrived, and we were virtually alone when Mama made her announcement and I realized that there was indeed a God.

I'd been content with my conversations with Grandma. I knew that Grandma wasn't God. I turned to Grandma because I believed that she was watching everything unfold and that she understood. Although she never said anything negative about Daddy, I sensed that she thought the marriage was a mistake. Maybe it was the way she embraced

Mama when Mama and I arrived in D.C. for Christmas three days before Daddy, who was still at work. Grandma held Mama like an eagle welcoming a fledgling back into the safety of the nest. Grandma looked up and down at Mama, shook her head, sucked her teeth, and insisted Mama come on in and get some greens and have a cup of tea. Food couldn't fix what was wrong, but it might give her strength. And Lord knows Mama needed strength for another six months of our life. Six long months before the summer visit.

Grandma was my strength. I took all my memories of her, pulled them into me, and turned them into something like an imaginary friend. I imagined her telling me to be patient—like the jazz vocalist Dianne Reeves sings in her song, "Better Days." I played it over and over again on my boom box. I liked the part where she shared her grandmother's wisdom:

> She said, "All the things you ask you will know some day, but you have got to live in a patient way. God put us here by fate and by fate that means better days." She said, "Child, we all are moons in the dark of night; ain't no morning going to come till the time is right. Can't get to better days unless you make it through the night. You gotta make it through the night. Yes you do."

These words helped me make it through my nights. Not unlike my parents and their parents, I too suspected that there was a better life out there. My vision had nothing to do with food, houses, school, or land. I had those things.

I harbored fantasies of living like the "me" I knew I was. If I was myself, who I really was, I would go to Africa. I would dance in the grass with a long skirt on. I would live in the city with Kelli as my roommate, and we would leave our high-powered jobs that allowed us to have amazing wardrobes. We would order Chinese takeout that we knew how to eat with chopsticks, then hit the club. I knew it wasn't the real world. It was the world I hoped for.

I felt there was no hope in the real world. My life was always going to be as it was: jubilant at school, and returning home at night to hatred, anger, fear, and that damn mask of pretending I was okay. After the fight in the kitchen, Daddy forbade me from seeing Maria, and while I had no deep affinity for her, I took it as a sign that there was nothing I could do to improve my life. I let my parents know that I was suicidal, but in less than three months, life was the same as before: I scowled at Daddy, refused to talk to Mama, and counted down the days until I got out of the house.

It never occurred to me that Mama would ever leave Daddy. She usually tried to mediate in our relationship, explaining to me, "Your father doesn't understand." "You know Daddy loves you." "He didn't mean it that way." Over and over again, I looked at Mama, and turned my head without speaking. Her loyalty amazed, and then bored, me.

During one of those times when Mama tried to convince me that Daddy wasn't as bad as he was, I muttered, "You're a punk."

"What?" Mama asked genuinely. She couldn't hear my

mumblings over the sound of the car driving back to Brighton.

"You're a wimp. I mean, you let him do all these things, and you don't do anything about it." I didn't even raise my voice. My frustration and bitterness became resolute acceptance.

Mama ignored my disrespect even though she must have thought that Grandma would've knocked her into next week had she talked that way. Mama kept her eyes on the road and softly said, "I try, Moni. I do."

"Yeah." I looked out the passenger window. There's nothing Mama could say to convince me that she could do anything to make things better.

That's what I thought until the café. As Mama told me she was leaving, she asked if I had any questions.

"You *are* taking me with you, aren't you?" My voice was soft and high like a scared child's. I didn't ask Mama if she was serious, or sure in her decision. I just wanted to be sure I got to leave as well.

"Of course I am."

Mama told me that things would be different if we left: "We won't have as much money, okay? I can't take you shopping every weekend."

"That's okay. I don't need any more stuff. We can live in one room, as long as . . ." I didn't finish my sentence.

Mama smiled, sighed, and said, "Okay. That's good."

Mama was afraid that I would be unhappy without all the material possessions that my parents' combined salaries allowed. Telling her that I didn't care took a visible burden off her. I wanted to say more. I wanted to say that money didn't matter at all. I wanted to tell her that the peace we would soon have carried no price tag. I wanted to tell her that she just found a way to let my insides match my outsides, and that was worth a million dollars to me.

We sat there in the café for over an hour talking about apartments, neighborhoods, and what to pack. Mama pulled her purse to her side and pushed her chair back as we got ready to leave the café. Being slightly facetious, I asked Mama the same thing she asked me: "Do *you* have any questions?"

Mama pulled her chair back to the table. "Why didn't you run away?" Her voice dripped with shame. I heard her feelings clearly saying: I wasn't there for you. I didn't protect you. I let everything happen to you. Why did you stay when I let you down?

I didn't think or pause before I said, "I wasn't going to leave you there. I mean . . ." I closed my eyes so I wouldn't cry.

In some ways I was lying. I was fully prepared to leave Mama there when I went away to college. I counted the days until I left for college, and I was determined that I would never return. Of course, Mama could visit me in my dorm, but I would never, I swore, put my foot back in that house. That house and the house before it were dark places where kitchen-table curses and late-night arguments dominated my memories. I would fly away like Toni Morrison's flying Africans in *The Song of Solomon*. Maybe it's a myth or a fictive tale, but I found records of blacks in the Georgia Sea Islands who believed it, so I did too. Like them, I was going to fly back to Africa where I could be free. I knew I wasn't going to Africa, but I was going to college. And I was prepared to leave Mama there in Michigan if she couldn't save herself.

My words betrayed me, though. I thought that I could save Mama. Like the little girl with an escape plan, I thought that my vigilance could prevent something unthinkable from happening. I took the yelling, the cursing, and the anger if it deflected some away from Mama.

I started to hide my feelings. I began to joke and said, "Where would I have gone anyway? To Kelli's house? You would have found me and brought me home. And then I really would have been in trouble." This is what I started to say, but Mama stood up, moved to my side of the table, and pulled me into her side.

"You don't have to do that anymore," she said. "You don't have to protect me anymore. I'm going to take care of myself, and you too, okay?"

"Okay, Mommy."

It was a miracle. Mama's decision was a miracle. Instantly, I knew there was a God. Grandma had looked at Mama with concern on her face, but Mama stayed with Daddy. But more than two years after Grandma's death, Mama decided to leave. Only God could do this. Instantly, I transferred all my energy for Grandma to God.

I wrote my journal entries to God. I told God about the activities of my day, asking if the boys I liked were interested in me too. God was my new savior. God saved me from the angst of my household and, by proxy, my sadness. I was so grateful that I barely knew what to do. How many ways, I asked God, can I show you how much I appreciate that?

With my belief and trust in God came an overwhelming sense of guilt. I hated Daddy for all the ways he hurt Mama and me. I knew I was supposed to forgive people who trespassed against me, but I didn't know how.

I wanted to be as faithful to God as I was to Grandma. But I was torn. I wrote my prayers in my journal:

Oh how You have changed my life. I want to be a messenger for You. Let me praise You to others. Let me sing your praise. Let me serve. Teach me how to serve Thee. There is an unresolved issue though. Daddy. Help me, Lord. What to do, what to say, what to believe, what to ignore. . . . It's so hard to forgive and not to let the tears and pain and hurt become anger and hatred. God let me forget, forgive—don't let me hate him.

I was honest with God. When I felt sad, angry, or frustrated, I told God all about it. By the fall of my senior year, I was ready to openly declare my belief in church.

Throughout high school, going to church was mainly another opportunity to see black people. We became members at Bethel African Methodist Episcopal (AME) Church when I was ten years old. My parents chose Bethel because the pastor was active in the community and because it had an eight o'clock service. The service there was shorter than at Grandma's church, but as far as I could tell the only other difference was the music. When the Baptists sang

"Sweet, Sweet Spirit" at the end of the service, the AMEs sang "I Surrender All."

I loved being in the high school Sunday school class. Reverend Blake and Mrs. Jordan taught a room full of teenagers who circled the table, some of us in chairs against the walls. With envy, the younger students peered through the glass partitions that separated the classrooms in the church basement. As high schoolers, we didn't use lesson books; we had our own topics of discussion. One week, Reverend Blake and Mrs. Jordan began class by asking what we thought of the recent high school shooting. Other times, they began by asking about the new programming on BET. Or if we thought the Pistons were playing dirty. We always talked on top of one another giving our opinions, sharing what we heard from others. Reverend Blake and Mrs. Jordan somehow wove in a bit of scripture and what a Christian response might be. I loved that they knew what was happening in our world and that they cared enough to ask what we thought about it before giving us an adult lecture.

The high school church class was more than Sunday mornings. Every other Thursday evening, we gathered at Reverend Blake's house to watch *The Cosby Show* and *A Different World*. Early arrivals were caught up in discussions of the football game between high school rivals. We quieted promptly at eight o'clock. During the commercials, Reverend Blake initiated conversations about the sitcoms' topics: Are you ever tempted to cheat like Denise? What are your friends saying about sex?

We felt comfortable talking with Reverend Blake about

these issues, and he didn't give us moral platitudes we were going to ignore. He talked frankly about which other teens were pregnant, asked if we knew who the father was, whether or not they were staying together, and if we knew how to avoid situations like that ourselves.

One night, Mrs. Blake left a chocolate cake that we devoured while playing Bible trivia. I stood out as a private school kid because I didn't see any of them in school the next day, but my letter jacket was my passport into the verbal world of sports, competition, and laughter. Sitting at the kitchen table with chocolate on my fingers and my partner's trivia card in view, I felt cool and popular. Here, I acquired the fashion trends and slang that rolled off my tongue the next day at school. I joined the youth choir and drama ministry, and happily spent every Saturday at a rehearsal of some sort. It wasn't about faith; church was social.

But Mama leaving Daddy changed that, so I walked down the aisle. It was time to tell the truth about what I believed. I was already baptized. Six years earlier, when I was ten years old, Daddy decided it was time for the family to join Bethel. My parents came on "Christian experience," but I hadn't yet been baptized. I was christened as a baby in the Baptist tradition. Mama and Daddy took me back to Shiloh in D.C. for the event. I loved looking at the pictures of me with the curly Afro and long white baby dress. Rev. Henry C. Gregory held me up to the sky as Mama and Daddy stood nearby with my godparents, Aunt Maxine and Uncle Ernest, standing to the side. Grandma, Nana, and

Granddaddy stood in the front row. I was only four months old when my family dedicated my life to God through christening and promised to raise me as a Christian.

Baptism was withheld until I made a decision for myself. In Baptist practice, at the age of reasoning I would declare my belief in Jesus Christ as my Lord and Savior, and get put under the water. As a Methodist church, Bethel had no baptismal pool, but that wasn't a problem. Bethel had a relationship with the local Baptist church. I stood at the back of a long line at New Hope Baptist Church. I wore a magenta swimsuit under the white cotton shorts and frock the church provided. Children my age and a couple years older and younger stood in front on me. They were members of New Hope.

I peered out from backstage, watching Reverend Lightfoot talk about the Father, Son, and Holy Spirit before he pushed a kid under the water. Everything stopped when it was my turn. The church sang a full chorus and three verses of "Wade in the Water" so that my pastor, Reverend Woods, could take Reverend Lightfoot's place. I stepped into the water. Reverend Woods talked to the congregation and whispered to me, "Hold your breath."

I inhaled, and before I knew it, I was steered to my right into the awaiting towels of the stewardesses. Within moments, Mama bustled her way to the space behind the pulpit and pool. She had a wide smile on her face like she knew I would be going to heaven now. I had done nothing special, and no one ever asked me if I believed in God and Jesus. If they had, I probably would have said yes. I didn't know that there was anything else to believe. Mama hugged me, and I said, "The water's cold."

"It always is." Mama knew the tradition of which so many gospels and spirituals sing: "The water chilled my body but it warmed my soul."

"You didn't tell me that. It was really cold."

My journey into and out of the cold water made me feel privileged. At ten years old, I was a full member of the church and allowed to take Communion—something I previously had to watch from the sidelines when my Catholic school classmates went through their First Communion in second grade.

At sixteen, I walked down the aisle for myself. After the sermon, the pastor issued the invitation to discipleship. I stood up. I didn't look at Mama or my friends from the high school class. I looked straight ahead and I walked. Mama cried as she smiled this time. That time, someone asked me. The pastor asked the whole church, but I heard it as if he were talking specifically to me: "If you believe that Jesus Christ is your Lord and Savior, come make your confession of faith." I do. I believe. I believe in God.

With some faith, my newly acquired driver's license, and pleas to borrow Mama's car, senior year was perfect. Indeed, my last year of high school was everything I had hoped. Having completed all of my standardized tests during my junior year, I took one Advanced Placement math course and cruised through the rest of my classes. I gave myself pleasures I denied for years. I didn't run track because I didn't want to run in the snow and rain during my senior year. I didn't participate in any piano competitions so I could grow my fingernails longer, get a manicure, and begin my dating life. I spent hours at Kelli's house, curling my hair, applying lipstick, talking about boys, and perfecting our Kid 'n Play dance moves for the teen nights at local dance clubs.

Senior year also gave Mama and I something we hadn't felt in years: peace.

I didn't really understand that Mama was also afraid. We didn't talk about it. We didn't have to. I imagine how Daddy must have felt. He had to know that there were problems with the family, but he must have been just as surprised as I was when Mama left. He was doing better than every model of fatherhood he had witnessed. What more did he know to do? Maybe he thought that I would outgrow my sullenness and that as suddenly as I had changed into a belligerent teenager, I would change back into a mature version of the little girl he knew and loved on Daddy-daughter days. He had loved Mama for nearly twenty years of marriage and four or five years of dating before that. The house that was too big for three people had to feel like a cold palace with just Daddy and half a house of furniture. Truth be told, getting away from Daddy did not usher me into heaven on earth. I was still depressed.

My new therapist saw Mama and me together.

"You're still depressed, Monica." She turned to my mother. "Do you hear me?"

"No, I'm not." I protested. "Don't listen to her, Mama. I'm not depressed anymore. I'm okay."

With the fear of living with Daddy gone, my life was so much better that I assumed the depression was gone. For brief moments, I was completely honest with myself. I had trouble sleeping. I begged for rest. I asked God to watch over me when I sat in my room in the dark, radio on, shaking and crying. I didn't understand why I wasn't happy. I was supposed to be happy, but I wasn't. I assumed that no matter how happy I was, there would always be sadness too. That was just how life was. But with the fear gone, it should have been bearable. I should have been able to handle it.

My therapist understood that I wrestled with something that couldn't be fixed with one life change. She knew that depression was bigger than something a teenager could handle with grit and resolve. If I had known that, I would not have blamed myself as much. I would not have believed that something was wrong with me.

PART II

EVERY TIME I
FEEL THE SPIRIT

COLLEGE: MASSACHUSETTS, 1991–1995

5

INVISIBLE

Cambridge, Massachusetts: Freshman Year, 1991

Depression followed me to college. I ended up at Harvard as an afterthought. I applied to Harvard just to see if I could get in. When I was accepted, I didn't know what to do. I didn't know anything about Harvard. I didn't even know where Cambridge, Massachusetts, was. My college guidance counselor was convinced I couldn't make a fair decision without adequate information, and helped arrange my campus visit. I arrived in Cambridge during the special weekend for minority students who were accepted but had yet to make a decision. Within twenty-four hours I knew that Harvard was the school for me. It only took one party.

The weekend began a ritual that my black female classmates and I invoked most of my first year. I traded clothes and shoes with another girl in my dorm until we perfected our look. We bound out of the dorm an hour before we hoped to arrive at the party. We were off to Matthews Hall to pick up three more people. We waited in the common area watching another classmate in the bathroom apply a quick layer of mascara while bumping her hips to the new jack swing rhythms of "Nice and Smooth and Funky."

"Hurry up," we yelled from the living room. "We still need to go by Canaday."

We went dorm to dorm, waiting for someone to finish curling her hair or to pick out earrings, acquiring another couple of women until ten or twelve of us bustled onto the Number 1 bus to the frat party at MIT. We sashayed the short distance from the bus stop to the student center. We later ran down this walkway in the winter months when we concluded that it was impossible to be cute and warm at the same time, and, having chosen the former, we made a mad dash in our short skirts and tank tops. We were a cohesive group and made sure we had the original twelve before we hailed cabs or hoofed it back to Harvard Square four hours later, after the buses stopped running.

The morning after my first party on visit weekend, I called Mama and said that Harvard was my choice.

"You sure? It's only been one day."

"Yeah! This is it."

"What about it?" Mama knew there wasn't any time to visit classes or meet with faculty. That was set up for the third day.

"I like the people. These are the people I want to go to school with." A sketchy way to make a college decision, but I chose from another Ivy League school and a private university in the Midwest. I knew that all these schools could educate me well. Where, I wanted to know, would I be happiest? Happiness ranked high in my criteria.

"Well, anywhere you want to go baby, we'll find a way to get you there."

Once I got to Harvard, I picked up where I left off, falling easily into a circle of women who lip-glossed and danced our way into a relationship that shuttled back and forth between Harvard Yard and MIT. The best parties were at Chocolate City. Chocolate City was an MIT dorm turned party center every couple of months. The residents were known by the brown satin jackets they proudly wore, "C-C" embroidered in mustard yellow across the back. The all-male dorm threw parties that drew students from all the Boston area schools and a couple in Rhode Island. We crammed our way inside as the men at the door gave instructions: "No one allowed in the dorm rooms unless you live in CC. No exceptions." "Reggae on the third floor." "No coat room, so watch your stuff." We immediately fell into the groove, making room for the sorority sisters to do their steps. The whole crowd crouched down to the floor as the DJ spun "Engine, engine, number nine on the New York transit line. If my train goes off the track, pick it up, pick it, pick it up!" We raised our arms and jumped up and down in unison with the rest of the partiers. I don't know if CC was a black-male-only dorm as it appeared those evenings, but it was a piece of heaven. These pearly gates opened under a banner with the George Clinton–inspired quotation, "In a world of vanilla, we all need a chocolate city."

Harvard had no analogue to MIT's Chocolate City, but

we had a significant black community. At Harvard, I met other black teenagers like me. With few exceptions, my classmates were also from predominantly white schools where our identities were formed by the often competing interests of family, academic pursuits, Afrocentricity, hip-hop culture, and fitting in at school. For me and everyone else I knew, the pressure to succeed came from our family or ourselves. We pushed ourselves hard. We set the goal of being "group I," a grade point average of A- or above. It was our own choice to participate in countless extracurricular activities and to party and study at the same time. Harvard never demanded it.

My personality fit in well at Harvard. Harvard saw itself as gathering the so-called best and brightest minds. That also meant that they congregated many young, type A, overachieving, perfectionist minds. And among that group, many of us probably came to Harvard with our own sets of neuroses and mental illnesses. But no one was looking for depression. In fact, I quickly learned that at Harvard, you had to be an independent person. No one took care of you. No one offered anything. If you didn't ask, you wouldn't know what was going on. But if you were that kind of person, and you asked lots of people lots of questions, the resources were endless. After the first couple of weeks, proctors and tutors stopped holding our hands and passing out pamphlets. "If you need something, just knock on my door." If you didn't knock or ask or join or talk, you easily faded into the background. No one watched the students closely enough to notice if someone began to get too close to the edge.

I liked the idea of anonymity. In many ways, I wanted to disappear. Well, I oscillated back and forth between wanting to hide and wanting to be noticed. The depression returned after a terrible romantic breakup. I think. It's hard to draw lines of causality. Was it the breakup? Unresolved feelings about my parents' divorce? Was it the months of cold and gray weather that killed any spirit sensitive to sadness and in need of bright light? Was it the combination of hormones and biology? Was I still weak from the anemia I learned about just months before starting college? Or some savvy cocktail of it all? I only know that I had an extraordinary reaction to a tumultuous breakup. What should have resulted in the calling of close friends and two to three weeks of cursing and crying instead sent me into months of emotional trauma and physical illness. I stopped sleeping. I vomited everything I ate. My skin became pale and dry. My blood count dropped, and the student health center gave me iron rather than a cure for a broken heart, damaged self-esteem, or major depression.

My connection to community was the Christian organization to which I belonged. I became active with Harvard's branch of Campus Crusade for Christ my first month of school. My first-year roommate and I signed up the first week when all the campus organizations were presented to new students. It began with a phone call from Lanh. Lanh spoke in a soft, secure voice when she said that she had both of our names on her list of first-year students interested in Christian Impact's activities. She was contacting all the women in our dorm who signed the sheet. There were four or five others who wanted to have Bible study, and if we thought our room was big enough, did we mind hosting? After all, it would be convenient.

Bible study with Christian Impact was more than reading scripture. It was the core unit of a larger network of friendship and faith. We began our Bible studies with check-ins on the past week. We quickly learned each other's favorite classes, first loves, and what hometown traditions we missed. As we read through the book of Philippians, we shared notes from study guides. We talked about the historical context of Paul's letter and what the words meant to the church at Philippi. We also talked about how those words spoke to us and how they might encourage or challenge us in our individual relationships with God.

That was the first time I thought of myself as having a personal relationship with God. At Bethel AME, I learned Bible stories, memorized hymns and litanies, and heard countless sermons on the social and political issues that affected the black community. Personally, I fostered a rapport with God not unlike Celie's in Alice Walker's *The Color Purple*. Celie writes to God in her journals because she has no one else to tell her deepest secrets. There is no one else she can trust. God was my confidant and my rescuer. I responded out of gratitude, asking what I could do to repay God, how I could best praise God. But Christian Impact suggested that there was something more personal involved.

"How is your walk with God?" Lanh asked me this every week when we met one-on-one over lunch.

I loved walking to North House to meet her. I waited for her outside the main doors—freshmen needed resident escorts to enter the upperclass dining halls. Lanh greeted the dining hall worker with words of recognition while I displayed my student card. After moving through the assembly line of students and cafeteria-style food, we hovered over a small table away from the majority of diners.

"It's okay, I guess." No one had ever asked me that question before.

Lanh opened the side of her mouth to blow her bangs out of her face. Lanh's round face was framed by dark straight hair that was wispy on the ends. She used her hand to push them aside after her first gesture failed.

"I mean, is there anything God is challenging you to do? Or have you learned anything new about God this week?"

She expected me to talk about relating to God the way I talked about a friend. I had no language for that. I followed Lanh's lead.

"Um, when I was reading chapter two, I came across something I never thought of before."

"Tell me more."

Although I looked up to Lanh as someone who could teach me more about Christianity, our weekly meetings also gave me a chance to learn more about her. Lanh slowly shared stories about being Chinese from Vietnam. A church in Chicago helped to bring her entire family to the States. "We were the boat people you hear about," she recalled. Her family settled in the Midwest, and Lanh was raised with a combination of evangelical heartland Christianity and traditional Chinese values about hard work and women's purity. I enjoyed hearing her stories, but Lanh always returned the discussion to me. She understood herself to be my discipler, and in the model of Jesus and the twelve, she wanted our friendship to focus on how she could help me to be the best Christian I could be.

Over time, her questions became a casual exchange in an easy-flowing conversation: "How are you and God?" Or "I become easily frustrated when I have a conflict with my family. God is teaching me patience right now. How about you? Do you ever feel that way?" We tracked the answers in our spiritual notebooks. Lanh showed me her notebook. There were several pages of grids with her daily schedule. She blocked out hours for class, study, extracurricular activities, and prayer time. She showed me how to make a similar chart for my own schedule, planning an hour every day for prayer and Bible reading. With Lanh and Christian Impact, I learned to integrate my faith into my everyday life. I was a disciplined student with all of my classes, and Lanh showed me how to apply that same discipline to my relationship with God.

"God's like anyone else," Lanh said. "You get to know God because you spend time with Him. You get used to the sound of His voice."

"Makes sense."

"Try this for a week and we can talk about how it went." Nearly every week, Lanh offered new tools for developing my relationship with God. She gave me forms about different ways to pray and how to break down my study of a biblical passage with nothing more than a Bible, a notebook, and a thick Bible dictionary. Lanh showed me that being faithful was more than a declaration of belief. She showed me *how* to be a Christian. At the end of every lunch, Lanh hugged me as she said, "I appreciate you, Monica."

These were four simple words, but I repeated them to myself when I felt lonely and worthless.

"I appreciate you, Monica."

Lanh understood that I, like so many other students at Harvard, was rewarded for my accomplishments. In some ways, just attending Harvard was a reward for a high school academic career gone well. Did Lanh know that I needed to know that I was valued for more than the papers I wrote and organizations I joined? That I needed to know that I was valuable just because I was me? She didn't say, "I appreciate what you did." She said that she cared about me just because I was me. I heard her acceptance as an outgrowth of God's acceptance of me. So maybe, I thought, there was nothing I had to do to make God love me, or to make my family and friends love me.

Christian Impact created an overall environment of love and acceptance. I felt welcome when I went to Friday Night Live. The auditorium of Boylston Hall turned into a cross between a nightclub and a camp meeting. We crowded in, nearly two hundred strong, as if we had to arrive before they started charging. A small band of my classmates performed on stage with two men on one mic and two women on another. Some students filed into the theater-style seats while others stood in the aisles. Reading from the words projected onto a screen behind the band, we sang in rounds, the women's voices following the men's:

> More love (more love), more power (more power), more of You
>   in my life
> And I will worship You with all of my heart
> And I will worship You with all of my mind
> And I will worship You with all of my strength
> For You are my God

We closed our eyes, lifted our hands, or swayed back and forth as our music became prayer and celebration. Friday Night Live gathered other people my age who were as excited about God as I was. We believed that God heard our prayers and spoke to each one of us individually. We believed that God was giving us the tools to fulfill our purpose in life. All we had to give was our time and devotion.

After a while, we heard a short sermon from one of the young adults employed by the national organization to provide guidance to our campus. I don't remember the sermons. I remember the music and the way I felt like a part of something bigger and better while I stood next to a white male student I didn't see in any of my African American studies classes or black student organizations. For years, I referred to the music as "Christian Impact songs," as if they were written specifically for our organization. Only when I stumbled onto a Christian radio station did I hear Michael W. Smith or Twila Paris singing the lyrics that formed my early Christian spirit.

So I turned to Christian Impact when I lost the ability to sleep. I started going to evening prayer, midnight prayer, early morning prayer. If I wasn't going to sleep, I thought, I might as well talk to God, right? I couldn't stand to be alone with all my hurried thoughts. I focused on the recent catastrophe—the cheating boyfriend. How could I have misjudged him? How many people knew? Why didn't anyone tell me? What was wrong with me? Wasn't I pretty enough? Supportive enough? What could I change to be the woman he wanted? I replayed the thoughts like a tape recorder until my body believed them too. I couldn't take vomiting yet another bowl of cereal or slice of pizza. I needed to be around people. I was lucky enough to find people who embraced me just because God made me.

I slithered through the end of the semester without damaging my grade point average too badly, and I returned home for the summer where I caused a worried look on Mama's face. It was as if Lanh passed the baton to Mama. Mama watched me with furrows in her eyebrows, concerned, trying to feed me, encouraging me to get some sun. There were many mornings I woke up with her face just inches from mine. I screamed from the surprise.

"I'm just looking at you," she replied. "Checking to make sure you are breathing. Got into the habit when you were a baby."

I rolled over, mumbling, "I'm alive. Now stop doing that."

She didn't. When I ate, walked around the house, or watched TV, Mama watched me. Checking to see if I gained weight. Or if there was more color to my face. Or if I just looked sad. She never pushed or pried or tried to make me talk about the relationship or exactly what happened. She gently suggested a therapist.

I sat outside his office with a list of symptoms. Trouble sleeping. Disturbance in eating patterns. Crying for no apparent reason. Check, check, check. Within thirty minutes, the short white man told me that I was depressed. It had no effect on me. My preferred medication was two hours of working out in the gym with my coworker from my summer job: run three miles a day, light weight lifting, and a daily dose of endorphins. When I returned to Harvard for my sophomore year, I was thinner, but fit, and the furrows from Mama's forehead were gone.

I maintained my rigorous schedule running in weather conditions I complained about during high school track practices. I pulled on the sports bra, tank top, turtleneck shirt, double sweatshirts, and thermal running pants that are staples of cold-weather athletics and headed for the door. I pulled the hood of a University of Michigan sweatshirt over my head, tightened the drawstrings, and blinked the rain and snow off my eyelashes. Every morning at seven, I ran two to three miles through the neighborhoods to Porter Square and back. No Walkman; no praying or singing in my head. Just the sound of my running shoes against the cobblestones, and the wind chafing my nose and cheeks. Competition and letter jackets aside, I relished the moments alone with my body pounding over the concrete and asphalt. It was my sacred time of empty-mindedness. Unbeknownst to me, the endorphins were doing wonders for my mood, giving me a cheery disposition until two or three o'clock in the afternoon.

I was alone when I ran. In fact, I was alone more than I should have been. I began to disappear. At first, it was an accident. I decided to circumvent the Harvard housing lottery. I didn't like the idea of some computer deciding my roommate or residence for three years. I applied the universal rule of getting over: for every law, there is a loophole, and for every rule, there is an exception. There must be a way to get out of the lottery system.

Jordan W Co-op was "alternative campus housing." Directly behind the Radcliffe Quad, Jordan W Co-op drew little attention. It looked like high-rise projects, only with three floors. From the outside, it was cement and brick with different colored doors for the different entrances. The Co-op lacked the ornate wood, brick, and ivy that characterize all the other houses. The steps were concrete, the doors were heavy metal, and the carpeting in the front hall was flat and matted. Unlike the other houses, there were no grand pianos, darkrooms, or recreation rooms. Rather than the lettered or named entryways leading to the numerous residence halls within a house, Jordan W Co-op had two entrances—the front door and the kitchen door. I quickly made it home.

The Co-op was more like an apartment complex or a real house than the other houses. Inside was a large kitchen with two ovens, two stoves, a large pantry, and a small table. There was a dining room, which contained a larger table, and a living room stocked with donated and misplaced books, an out-of-tune upright piano, couches, a television, and a VCR. The basement housed a washer, dryer, and storage space. Above the ground floor were two floors of bedrooms with a bathroom on each floor. Most of the residents of the Co-op were older students who left Harvard for one reason or another and were now returning to finish their degree programs. They were, the housing office told me, students who lived on their own, and they wanted to maintain an independent lifestyle.

Although the cost of rooming was the same, the board price was half the cost of the house system. The Co-op was also completely vegetarian, and the residents took turns cooking and cleaning for each other. All the rooms were singles—even those that were intended as doubles. I wanted a single bedroom and assumed that I could learn to cook for fifteen to twenty people. I signed up for the Co-op, was given an official affiliation with Cabot House, and moved my books and hand-me-down student couch into my new room.

At the Co-op, I met residents who were completely unlike me. It was not the black social world I inhabited the previous year. It was a swing in the opposite direction. My coresidents were older, laid-back, vegetarian, cost-effective, and 100 percent white. My initial impulse was to live a single life in my bedroom and a community life on the first floor, emerging only to cook, clean, or eat. In the Co-op I learned that those three activities are enough to bind even the most unlikely friendships.

I made one friend while performing my Co-op duties. An exchange student from the University of Michigan Co-op system taught me how to bake bread: "If you are going to make one loaf, you may as well make six or seven." We finished our homework, and at midnight we ran water over our wrists to test it for the right temperature for the yeast. We mixed and kneaded until early morning hours and awakened other residents at three o'clock in the morning with the aroma. My bread lessons always brought the sight of slippered feet and half-opened eyes peering around the kitchen door: "You making bread? When's it gonna be ready?"

Although the residents of the Co-op weren't all friends, we shared the same space and worked out a grand peace. Diverse sexual orientations were respected. Every meal avoided the food allergies of all residents. The significant others of residents were accepted like family and often given their own keys. If I was reading about slavery all day for classes, my coresidents allowed me to gripe and mutter, "White people!" under my breath without taking any personal offense. We were all kind to each other and respected each other's cooking, and I found myself in conversation with people I never thought I would have liked.

There was the girl from Greece who stood on a chair

when she kneaded bread, swearing that it was the best way to get the right angle on the bread. It made no sense, but whatever she made on Easter morning was phenomenal enough to shut me up. There was the long-haired white male student with an uncanny resemblance to Christopher Reeves who taught me to cut butter into flour with two knives to make a flaky piecrust that later won awards at church cookouts. There was the red-haired guy who always cooked the same Spanish rice for dinner when it was his turn. Just when all the residents were set to mutiny and complain, we remembered that he also made the best chocolate chip cookies we ever tasted.

It's safe to say that many Harvard students had never heard of the Co-op. It felt like we were one of the best-kept secrets on campus. We were outside of the formal bounds of the undergraduate campus and outside of the mainstream. We were a part of Harvard that was kept quiet. We were not in the brochures, the website, or the housing manual. We were almost invisible.

Invisibility had its privileges. The Co-op was basically self-governing. Although a graduate student was assigned as a residential tutor for assistance, we made up and adhered to our own rules. Rather than a majority-rules democracy, we used a consensus method for all decisions. Our meetings were long, but every detail mattered. Sara Lee or Lender's bagels? To buy bread or to make bread? Should recycling be one individual's responsibility for the semester, or should all residents be held accountable for their personal recyclables? We also made decisions that were contrary to other university regulations. We thought it was ridiculous to make one gender walk up or down stairs to use the bathroom, so we declared the bathroom facilities coed. When we wanted a deck, we bought the wood and built it.

Invisibility also had its disadvantages. It facilitated disappearing. I began to disappear just four or five months into my sophomore year. No matter how much I ran or how healthily I ate, the depression was back. It started with the nightmare. My sleep was disturbed and troubled. When I awoke, I barely caught my breath. I barely remembered the dream.

Someone is chasing me. I can't see his face, but it is definitely a "him." He is there in my dorm room, coming toward me. So I bolt out the door and run. I run down the stairs of the Co-op. He follows me. I run around the kitchen, into the dining room, and around the circle to the basement door. I fake like I'm heading toward the basement. I hide behind the door as I hear him stumble in the dark down the stairs. Quietly, I creep into the closet and stoop down between the vacuum cleaner and mop. He'll never find me here, I think. He'll just go away mad. I hear him run by. He stops in front of the closet, opens the door, and reaches out . . .

I jumped up. I panted. Thank God it was only a dream. It was only a bad dream, I told myself. Go on back to sleep. When I slept, I dreamed the same dream. Nearly every night, I dreamed that he found me in the closet. Again I awoke right before he opened the closet door. I was afraid for what he would do to me. I turned on the ceiling lights, the halogen lamp, the desk lamp, and the night-light. All the creaks in the building sounded especially loud. I turned on the television and watched four hours of late-night mystery movies. I didn't know if my insomnia was real or voluntary. Maybe I was refusing to sleep. I would do anything to avoid the man when the janitorial door opened.

I called my friends. They trudged through the snow, one by one, to the little building behind Cabot House. Over the weeks, Keith came, Doug came, Kevin came, Ray came. Within ten minutes, I fell asleep. But if they left while I slept, I woke up and couldn't get back to sleep. I begged them to stay the night on the couch. They never asked me anything. They just sat there. That was all I needed: a bodyguard from the dreams.

I wanted to tell them what I remembered. I wanted to tell someone about the dream. But the dream was all that I had. I couldn't remember anything else. And I couldn't explain why an otherwise normal, happy, and healthy life was filled with such inexplicable terror. Somehow I knew that I couldn't be alone and that I needed someone to watch me. I needed someone to know that something was wrong with me, someone to keep me on this side of the fears.

But I also thought I was a burden to my friends, and I stopped calling them to come by. They thought the nightmares ended. They believed I could sleep. They asked me. I lied and said yes. Then I began to wonder if there was another way out. I didn't think about Lanh or my Bible study or Friday Night Live. I just had one question. If I disappeared, if I just fell off the face of the earth, how long would it take anyone to notice?

If I disappeared on a Thursday, the professors wouldn't

have a chance to notice my absence until the next Tuesday, and then it would take two weeks before they either realized I was gone or wrote it off as more than sickness. If I disappeared on a Tuesday, my housemates might assume I was hanging out and eating with a friend because I would have fulfilled my duties on Monday. If I disappeared on a Sunday, no one would notice I hadn't gone to any parties until the next week. My friends didn't call that often. They weren't paying much attention to me. What if I just disappeared?

6

ANOINTING

Cambridge, Massachusetts: Junior Year

My journey with God is paved with the tar of African American literature. That's why I decided to major, or "concentrate" as we said at Harvard, in Afro-American studies. I know when I fell in love with my chosen field: ninth grade, James Baldwin's *Go Tell It on the Mountain.* I was transported to the storefront church where spiritual voices circled the threshing floor. I imagined the old women with cotton doilies pinned to their heads singing songs they've known since before they could remember. The men in plain black suits and black ties, humming the verses and chiming in on the chorus. The voices drop out, the pianist pounds the keys, and hands clap a rhythm four times the normal two-four gospel beat. A middle-aged woman holds her skirt in one hand while the congregants sing, "When I think of His goodness and what He's done for me, when I think of His goodness and how He set me free, I can dance, dance, dance, dance, dance, dance, dance, all night."

That's probably not what Baldwin's narrator saw around him as he negotiated his parents' expectations for his leadership in the church and his own spirituality. But it's what I saw through the blurry memory of deacons on Shiloh's front row, singing "Ay-ay-ay-men, ay-ay-ay-men, ay-ay-men, aaay-men, aaay-men"—the last sounds I heard before falling asleep in Grandma's lap. When I awoke, I saw a woman's hat flying through the air as she arched her back, raised her arms into a large V, and shouted "Glory!"

"What's wrong with her, Grandma?" I asked.

"Nothing, baby. She's just . . . getting happy." Grandma hugged me close to her, her right arm around my body.

"What's she happy about?" I inquired.

"God, sweetie. God."

In those early months after Grandma's death, I was drawn to the way Baldwin wrote about a life that was both new and familiar, and the English assignment became my passionate hobby. I read the latest African American literature in the library: Toni Morrison, Alice Walker, Gloria Naylor. I knew that I was reading fiction, but I believed every word. *The Bluest Eye* and *Song of Solomon* portrayed Midwestern landscapes I'd seen many times, and I believed that somewhere people really *did* drive down the neighborhood streets of Linden Hills. These books vividly recounted truths I picked up from family time in D.C.: collect your hair from the comb after getting your hair done; don't eat everyone's cooking; "Go outside and bring me some leaves from the third plant from the gate—I'll make a tea that will help you feel better." Nature, story, religion, culture, and dance wove together a tapestry that felt like Great-aunt Ozie's quilts—sent to Michigan from down south because, as Aunt Ozie said, "You need to stay warm up there."

Cambridge was much colder than Michigan, and the blanket of African American literature warmed my soul. I took a class on Harlem Renaissance literature as an elective my first semester, and I was hooked. I was supposed to major in mathematics and economics. I planned it during my last two years of high school. I had a natural aptitude for numbers and an interest in corporate business. But in the fall of freshman year, I found out that I could major in my hobby. The black students were all talking about Harvard's newly revived Afro-American studies department, led by Henry Louis Gates Jr. I'd heard of Dr. Gates before Harvard. Mama fed my high school interest in black literature with a gift book of African American literary criticism edited by Dr. Gates. I ignored most of the postings about the freshman roundtables with senior faculty until one advertised dinner with Dr. Gates. The Henry Louis Gates! Of *Our Nig* and *Signifying Monkey*!

That night in the small room off of the Freshman Union Dining Hall, Dr. Gates was jovial, telling jokes and laughing at them himself. He talked about hip-hop, politics, and the move to Boston. He was more relaxed than I imagined he would be. He turned toward me, asked me what I was studying, and invited me to his office hours.

I called home talking about "Afro-American studies." Mama and Daddy's reception was not as warm as Dr.

Gates's. They asked the question I heard all the time: "And what are you going to do with that?"

Their question was followed by declarations about how I would never get a job, and they didn't have to send me to Harvard to do that, and "Can't you minor in that?" and "Economics is a better plan," and "No, you are not."

I worked hard to convince my parents that I was not throwing away an expensive education on slave narratives and Black Arts poetry. Each year, I found a new research fellowship and spent my summers in Radcliffe's Schlesinger Library, Harvard's Widener Library, or the Library of Congress working on an independent project or copying pages for a postdoctoral fellow. That version of a summer job was a far cry from the summer job at General Motors after freshman year where I trained the medical division on new diagnostic software. I didn't know when I would again make that kind of money for three months of work. But I felt like I shriveled under the fluorescent lights of an eight-hour-a-day job at a desk. I lived for my daily runs. As I traded my dreams of a corporate career for an academic one, it probably seemed like I was choosing Mama over Daddy.

I didn't choose black studies and academia to alienate Daddy, but I was no longer in a field where he could open doors or give sage words of advice. Daddy loved black history, having studied it during his days at Howard University, and he exposed me to it during my elementary school years. But he knew little about literature and my plan to be in school "how many more years?" I no longer shadowed him professionally, and we lost the last secret code of the Daddy-daughter bond. The truth is that Daddy probably started it all when he put black historians on my summer reading list and insisted I learn James Weldon Johnson's "Creation" for the elementary school forensics contest. In my heart, I don't think it was Dr. Gates or Harvard or Daddy. It was James Baldwin, 125th St., and the storefront church.

While Baldwin's lyrical description drew me to the study of literature, it also invoked an affinity for the black church that was drenched in memories of Grandma, Shiloh, music, and the faith of southern folk moved north. Boston's black churches reflect New England's historic black community. Boston blacks have centuries of freedom under their belt and generations of college education. They solidify their faith amid Massachusetts's secular humanism and offer it to all the city's immigrants and transplants. I looked for Grandma's Shiloh Baptist Church as soon as I first arrived at Harvard. I visited three different churches with other self-described black Baptists from my class. While my classmates quickly found a home at Union, Massachusetts Avenue, or Concord, I still felt like something was missing.

St. Paul AME Church had the recognizable liturgy of AME churches around the world: "I was glad when they said unto me, let us go into the house of the Lord." The air filled with whoo-hoos, yeahs, and alleluias after the first three words. Everyone was glad to be at church, and that alone made going fun. St. Paul is the oldest black church in Cambridge and the place where every young adult wanted to be. St. Paul is two blocks over, one block back, and a little way down the street from the Central Square T subway stop. My friends and I walked past Dunkin' Donuts, two Indian restaurants, and a Popeye's Chicken on the way there with thoughts of where we would stop after church. And we would be hungry. The six different choirs that kept us rocking for two or three hours were enough to entice many who had not previously been to an AME church to join St. Paul.

I went to St. Paul's eight o'clock morning services after partying on Saturday nights. I wasn't the only one. The church auxiliaries welcomed us with weekly meals on Monday nights to kick off the College Fellowship meeting. College Fellowship lured twenty to thirty college and graduate school students to the Christian Life Center every week with the prospect of home-cooked food and relevant conversation. After eating, we held devotionals with songs I learned in Vacation Bible School: "What a Mighty God We Serve," "This Is the Day," and "I Will Magnify the Lord." Like children, we bowed down and jumped up, doing the different body movements to each song, but our burgeoning adulthood was obvious through heated discussions of how Christians should party, dance, date, and buy music. One of the nearly fifteen ministerial assistants guided our conversation by highlighting biblical passages and keeping it as real as we felt it. We came to know each other well through both our perspectives on these issues and the time we took to pray for our success on the LSAT, midterm exams, or final papers.

St. Paul was a fourth family to my existing communities of Harvard's blacks, Christian Impact, and Jordan Co-op. I still talked with and visited Mama and Daddy and my cousins, but I didn't get home very often. I created families of my own. Everything seemed better amid the warm hugs of the parishioners at St. Paul, so I faithfully went to church each Sunday morning I could. Actually, Cynthia and I went together.

I met Cynthia during my sophomore year, and, just as Lanh did with me, I called her freshman dorm room to see if she was interested in a Bible study with Christian Impact. Christian Impact sent me on retreats and leadership training with other college groups, and I acquired all the tools to lead four to five women through a study of Philippians. I lacked Lanh's quiet piety and affirming personality, and the Bible study I led was not nearly as cohesive as the one I had attended. I rarely had all four students at one meeting, and my relationship with Cynthia never fit the discipler-disciple model that I had with Lanh. Cynthia and I made better friends.

A native of Nashville, Tennessee, Cynthia was loyal to the southern press-and-curl and wore her hair straight down her back on most days. She had a model's body without the prissiness, easily challenging her male classmates to a game of one-on-one. She had a demanding fashion sense so acute that the whole Bible study understood when she told us that she just couldn't schedule a second date when she opened the door and homeboy stood there in a teal suit. "A teal suit!" she said incredulously. We nearly fell off the couch from laughing so hard.

I called Cynthia to the Co-op so we could go to church together.

"How much money do you have?" I asked.

"About a dollar in change," Cynthia replied while fishing through her purse.

"I think I have seventy cents, but some of it's probably in the couch. Come over and help me find it." I crawled on my hands and knees, lifting up cushions.

"Does the T take pennies?"

"I don't know."

Cynthia and I pieced our change together to get on the subway, knowing that if we made it to church, someone would give us a ride home.

We climbed snow banks with change in our mittens to make it to church. We sat on the right side of the church facing the pulpit, taking notes on the pastor's sermon. He preached a series on the first chapter of Joshua. I leaned to my left and whispered to Cynthia: "Have you ever thought maybe this is for you?"

I referred to the first verse: "Moses, thy servant is dead."

I knew that Cynthia was destined to be a minister. She came from three generations of well-known Christian Methodist Episcopal (CME) ministers. Her grandfather was a bishop and one of the first black graduates of Vanderbilt University. Her father died in climactic fashion while preaching the words, "And one of those days they are going to roll me down that aisle." He had a massive heart attack and left Cynthia with no guide when, four years later, she began to wonder if she was called to preach as well. God gives Joshua leadership over the wandering Hebrew clans, and it seemed a natural corollary to Cynthia's place in her family.

"You ever think maybe this scripture is for you?" I whispered during church.

Cynthia looked at me from the sides of her eyes. "Yeah, I was thinking that."

The pastor finished the sermon and opened the doors of the church. Several members walked down the aisle to pray at the altar. Although the pastor asked for people who had never accepted Jesus Christ and those looking for a church home, St. Paul's invitations always allowed for open prayer at the altar rail. I often took my tears to the altar and walked away relieved. There was nothing magical about the wood, and I knew that. A minister whispered a prayer into my ears, and he touched my hand, and I knew that I had a church family that could uphold me with their belief. That was the altar's magic.

That time I stayed at my seat, but accustomed to the mystery of what happened on my knees, I knelt on the floor in the narrow space between my pew and the pew in front of me.

I thought my prayer in my head and began to whisper it out loud. When I opened my mouth, something different came out. They were not the words I tried to say. I closed my mouth. I continued to praise God in my mind.

"Thank you for being there for me. You are my God.

You are so wonderful. You are holy and magnificent and mighty."

I tried to say the words aloud, but it happened again. I knew instantly—I was speaking in tongues.

I had heard about speaking in tongues before. We had an entire College Fellowship session on prayer, and one member asked about prayer language. Is it okay, she asked, if you are praying by yourself and you speak in tongues even though Paul says in First Corinthians that there must be an interpreter? The minister said that there should be an interpreter when people speak in tongues in public. Like one Sunday at St. Paul when a man spoke in tongues loudly after the choir sang. The organist played softly. I followed the congregation, who seemed to know what to do. The minister did not proceed to the next event in the order of worship. Everyone seemed to be waiting. A woman in the corner stood up. She turned toward the pulpit and spoke loudly of who would be blessed and what our church was called to do. There it was in real life—something I had only read about in scripture. Someone spoke in tongues, and someone else interpreted. It was a holy word for our church community. It was a word directly from God.

"It's not to show off how holy you are," the minister told College Fellowship. "And, yes, there are people who speak in tongues when they are by themselves, praying alone. In those cases, it's a prayer language."

My colleague seemed satisfied, and the minister added one more note: "But not everyone speaks in tongue, and it doesn't mean you aren't saved if you don't. Some people do. Some people don't." I assumed that I was one of those people who didn't. Not raised among Pentecostals or in any environment where I saw it regularly, I didn't even envy it. It was just another spiritual gift, and one I didn't have.

But when my English-thought words moved my lips another direction, I knew I was speaking in tongues. Cynthia asked me if I wanted to go to the altar. I shook my head. I was staying right there until it stopped. I would have time to figure it out later. But it didn't stop, and Cynthia took my hand and led me to the altar to pray with one of the church ministers. I don't remember anything after this point, but Cynthia later told me what happened. She and I stood before the altar, not standing out much among the other people who were moving to the front of the church. We moved to the right and began to speak to each other in tongues. A minister that we knew from a Harvard doctoral program stood in front of us, and we had a three-way conversation in tongues. The music continued to play, and the congregation sang along with the choir welcoming people to join our church. Our three-, five-, or maybe ten-minute process barely distracted from the sounds and activity that typified the end of a worship service at St. Paul. But it still felt like everyone was staring at me when I collapsed into the front pew with church mothers fanning my face with programs and cardboard funeral-home fans.

Cynthia sat next to me on the front pew, and she turned to me and said, "Well, we have to be friends now. God anointed it."

"Yeah, He did." I smiled, and we sat there for the two or

three minutes until the service ended. We returned to our original seats for our purses and coats.

"Hungry?" I asked.

"Famished!"

"Indian?"

"Yeah!"

We took our ecstatic experience in stride. We believed in the Holy Spirit, and we constantly prayed for God's anointing. When I prayed for God's anointing, I hoped God would show me my purpose in life. What was I supposed to do with my career? What was I supposed to do for God? Would it be the same thing, or would I serve the church in my volunteer time? I didn't want to make a decision based solely on my skills or what other people wanted me to do. I wanted to do what God wanted me to do, what God anointed me to do. That's what I meant when I prayed for God's anointing. I spoke in tongues. I was anointed by the Holy Spirit, and in front of my entire church. My conclusion: God had something special for me.

7

CALLING

Cambridge, Massachusetts: Four Months
after the Anointing

My academic interests in African American studies inadvertently brought me to ministry. It was the third day of the Race Matters conference at Princeton University. I was trying to beat the morning rush when I was ushered through a chatter-filled room of conference attendees at PJ's Pancake House. There was no privacy at PJ's. The tables were lined up in rows, positioned approximately six inches from one another. There was just enough room between rows for a server to move in and out with plates of pancakes, sausages, or eggs raised high above shoulder level. It was always crowded, and you quickly became collegial with those at tables near you since you were going to overhear their conversations anyway.

As soon as I ordered my pancakes, Angela Davis was seated next to me. *The* Angela Davis! I had read her work on race, women, and class. I had seen old posters and buttons from the Black Power movement days with the famous words, "Free Angela." I recalled old pictures with her large light brown Afro and her fist raised high in the air. At this time, she wore long dreadlocks and wrote about the growing number of women in prisons. She was right there, six inches away from me.

We began to chat. We talked about natural hair and having mentors. She asked what I was studying and I mentioned my senior thesis. I wanted to read slave narratives written by women and see how they talked about God. I didn't talk ministry. Preachers say that they can "see the call" on others long before people see it for themselves. I think Angela Davis saw it on me because I didn't say anything about preaching.

Angela Davis asked me if I had ever met Renita Weems.

I had never heard of Renita Weems, but I chose my words carefully so I would sound like a well-researched and world-wise student, "I'm not familiar with her work."

"You must meet her! You must!" Angela Davis gave me her card, told me to call her, and said that she could arrange for my attendance at a conference the following month where both she and Weems would be speaking. As soon the conference ended and I returned to Cambridge, I looked up Weems, then purchased and read her books. I made some calls and got funding to travel to the conference so that I could meet Weems.

The tenth anniversary conference of the National Black Women's Health Project was in Atlanta, and I thought I had died and gone to black-woman heaven. I walked around gleefully overwhelmed at my surroundings: poets and activists, politicians and mothers, young women in suits and older women in kente cloth. I took a shuttle from the Westin Peachtree Plaza hotel to Spelman College and the Atlanta University Center where many events took place. I attended a lecture on journaling, and I learned the real names of authors who write with pseudonyms. I reveled at the natural hairstyles of the conference participants. Few of my classmates wore their hair without chemical straighteners. It was nice to be part of the crowd instead of fielding questions about how I "get my hair like that."

A Bible professor at Vanderbilt University, Renita Weems was also known for her bold preaching and writing on women's issues. She was scheduled to speak during the Sunday brunch. I sat at a round table near the back with seven women I didn't know. I had Weems's books with me so that she could sign them after the sermon. As soon as she began to speak, my mind wandered. I thought about preaching.

It scared me. I hated public speaking. I had a lisp long past what I deemed an acceptable age. Although I went to speech therapy classes as a teenager, the lisp still comes out when I am nervous and my speech quickens. If I had to preach, I would be nervous, and I would lean into a microphone and say, "Jee-thuth." But there was a recurring sermon in my mind.

There is a section of Luke 19 that Bibles subtitle "The Triumphal Entry." Jesus is getting ready to enter Jerusalem. He asks his disciples to go inside the city first and borrow a young donkey so that Jesus can ride it. Jesus rides into the city and the crowds surround him. "Hosanna! Blessed is he who comes in the name of the Lord." They celebrate Jesus and wave palm branches as they cheer. I've heard the story every Palm Sunday that I can remember. With the church members around me, I have held my single strip of palm leaf and waved it back and forth in commemoration. But I didn't want to preach that sermon. I read and reread the passage, and I was stuck on the following verse: "Jesus saw the city and wept." Why is Jesus crying? What does he see?

I sat in the pew at St. Paul AME tuning out the pastor's words. I flipped to Luke 19 in my Bible. I imagined myself constructing the sentences that could answer these questions. In one version of the sermon, Jesus sees the need the people of Jerusalem have for salvation, and it makes him sad. In a second version, I imagined Jesus crying over his knowledge that he will soon be crucified in Jerusalem. In yet a third version, I was preaching about the social conditions of the city, and Jesus' heart for the poor and disenfranchised.

I couldn't get those verses out of my head. I knew that I would have to preach it. It's ironic. Of all the passages in the Bible, I focused on this one. Jesus is surrounded by people who love him and celebrate him. It's a time when he should be happy and joyous. Maybe part of him is. But he's crying. Something is making him sad. I understood that. I thought—and still think—that there is something God wanted me to tell people about Jesus. But the cynic in me wondered if my own experiences with crowds, jubilance, and quiet tears didn't draw me toward this passage. Maybe there was something I needed to tell people about myself, and I was using my faith as a smokescreen. Maybe that was the case. I can't argue against it, but that's not how I felt it. I believed deeply that God wanted me to point out the combination of exuberant joy and quiet sadness.

Renita Weems preached on stage and I was preaching in my mind. For the first time, I thought about being a minister and I wasn't afraid. I tilted my head down and closed my eyes. I said a short prayer: "Okay, God. I'll do it."

When I looked up, the black women filling the room were clapping and standing up as Renita Weems finished her sermon. My epiphanic moment went completely unnoticed to my tablemates who listened attentively to Weems's inspirational message. I picked up my books and moved to the line already forming on the left side of the room. I took my place in line, repeating the lines over and over in my mind: "Okay, God. I'll do it. Okay, God. I'll do it." Weems sat behind a table with an ink pen between her fingers. Her manicured short natural curls faced the audience when she looked down and as she signed the books. As the women moved through the line, Weems chatted briefly with each one, listening to their stories of how a particular essay in the book helped them see something more clearly or gave voice to their secret thoughts and suspicions. Weems smiled mildly and asked the correct spelling of their first and last names. By the time I stood in front of Renita Weems, I was crying and stumbling over my words:

"I have a sermon on my heart. I have a sermon on my heart." I held the books tightly in my hands. "I have a sermon on my heart."

In caring and practical black-woman fashion, Weems said, "Well, good for you. Now sit here and collect yourself while I finish signing books. Then we can talk."

Through my teary vision, I saw women come and go as they told Weems how much they liked her writing and preaching. There were about ten women left in line when Angela appeared at my side. "This is the young woman I told you about." I'm sure I missed Renita Weems giving Angela Davis a questioning look: this heap of blubbering girlhood? That's what I thought as I calmed down enough to be embarrassed. But Weems didn't treat me like a child. She signed my books and gave me her card. She told me to call her if I came to Nashville.

Less than two months after I said yes to God and ministry, I was in Nashville where Cynthia preached her first sermon. I thought nothing of buying the plane ticket to Tennessee, and Cynthia's family quickly became mine as I started calling her relatives by their family nicknames: "Mama Cleo" and "Grandma Sapp." I read the scripture for her first sermon. She would read the scripture when I preached my first sermon. We were barely twenty years old, and we pledged to walk together in our journeys in ministry.

My first sermon came from Psalm 91. "He that dwelleth in the shelter of the most High shall abide under the shadow of the Almighty. I will say of the Lord, He is my refuge and my fortress: my God; in Him will I trust."

"*She* that dwelleth," Cynthia and I laughingly revised the King James Version.

Although I thought about Luke and Jesus' tears for a year and a half, I believed that God wanted me to preach about something else for my first sermon. "The safest place in the whole world is inside the will of God," I said. "We just have to go boldly into that which God calls us. We shouldn't run and we shouldn't be afraid." Cynthia helped me write the end where I gave examples of biblical characters that followed God. This was the first of many times that Cynthia and I planned to talk through sermon topics, read scripture, or introduce one another for preaching engagements. Over the miles, we wrote sermons together—even then I was better at introductions, so Cynthia helped me with my closings. We prayed together on the phone before we preached: "May God use my sister to reach someone in that church today."

They say that ministers preach to themselves and about themselves, especially in the first sermon. Under the guise of preaching about my run from ministry and my knowledge of freedom struggles, I tried to respond to my deepest insecurity—what does it mean to be safe and how do you get there? I thought that I would always be safe if I was doing God's will. That meant accepting the call to be a preacher. A small part of me suspects that that answer is too simple. Was I outside of God's will when I was a child afraid of my father? When I was afraid of going home? Had God abandoned my grandparents and their parents whose experience in the Jim Crow South and racist North made assurance of safety tenuous on most days? What does God have to say to people like me whose major death threats come from some untraceable place inside their brains? Part of me believes that I will find a safe place by being a good Christian. Part of me believes that other Christians have a calling to help the world be safer in the places where it is not. And part of me knows it is all a lie. I know that I can never live without the threat of death.

The audience clapped, and the receiving line was full of people I knew: former high school English teachers, gym instructors, elementary school teachers, leaders from Girl Scout camp, Sunday school teachers. There were also many new faces—Daddy's second wife, her family members, and their friends. And Peter, my boyfriend.

I first noticed Peter at a campus concert honoring World AIDS Day the previous December. He played the piano and sang "Everything Happens for a Reason." As he performed, tears and sniffles were heard throughout Memorial Church as family members and friends of those who had died from AIDS asked themselves whether everything happens for a reason. Or was the death or their friend, cousin, or brother as senseless as it appeared?

I liked Peter's voice and his ability to sing into people's hearts and minds. That's what I told him when I saw him in the divinity school library a couple of days later. We talked for hours that first day; we called each other over Christmas break and were an official couple by mid-January. Peter was also a minister, and told captivating stories about his life in the streets and experimenting with drugs before he got it together and heeded God's call. He was a preacher's kid with siblings, and eight years my senior. I was, well, a Goody Two-shoes whose experience with Christian Impact called me to live out the teachings on premarital celibacy. We appeared to have little in common. But every conversation lasted hours, and we guided each other as we forayed into a new world—ministry for me and Harvard University for him.

We planned on breaking up when I graduated, but we were too attached to each other to actually do it. He flew out for my first sermon. He stayed days after everyone else left, and I showed him all the places I had told him about. The trip takes up pages in my photo album: sitting on the swings in Gallup Park, feeding the geese on the banks of the Huron River, standing with high school friends on my twenty-first birthday (the waiter took that one), our improvisational merengue dance after my first three legal drinks, Peter sitting at my piano playing the song he wrote for me, our faces leaning in as we kiss (we set the camera up to do that). We held hands, acted as if the future held no questions, and promised to visit each other in Cambridge and Nashville after I started divinity school at Vanderbilt.

Nashville—located squarely in what news reporters call "the Mid-South"—was a shock to my decidedly northern system. I didn't realize I was moving to the South because I was so focused on going to Vanderbilt. I was excited about learning more about my faith, and by proxy what it meant to be a minister. I looked forward to classes on preaching, ethics, and Bible. I was drawn to the prospect of cross-registering in other departments across the university—English, or maybe anthropology. Vanderbilt is a place, I wrote in my application essay, where "I can be both a Christian intellectual and an intellectual Christian." When my friends asked where Vanderbilt was, I glibly replied, "I don't know. Somewhere south of Ohio."

The real shock of Nashville was environmental. When it snowed in Cambridge or Michigan, Nashville offered hours, nights, and days of rain. My disdain for rain returned with a vengeance. I had hated rain since I was nine years old. The rain was beating on the windowpane and flooding the remains of our garden the November morning I stormed into my parents' bedroom, tearful and indignant. Mama and Daddy had just told me that Granddaddy died of cancer. Four years later, Mama's first cousin held an umbrella over Theresa and me when we stood graveside at Grandma's interment. So I expected, with no disappointment, the summer shower that traveled through suburban D.C. a year prior when I sat at the breakfast table in my uncle's house with Daddy and three of his siblings. Nana died a month before my senior year at Harvard. I had seen her just a month earlier when we made plans for her trip to my graduation. Of course, I thought, it is raining. It is always raining when someone dies.

Ordinary rain recalls the veteran's twenty-one-gun salute and an adult life without grandparents. When it rains, I turn over, pull the covers over my head, and go back to sleep. I can barely think of reasons not to curl up into a ball and stay still until the storm passes over. Oddly enough, it's the rain that makes Nashville bearable. The rain washes away the pollen that makes every non-native-Nashvillian miserable each spring. When March and April came, I had headaches and sniffles I had never known before. I thought it was the flu. Student Health Services mentioned something about sinuses, but my colleagues told me that it was allergies. A classmate gave me a basic geography lesson one day: Nashville sits in a basin, surrounded by mountains. The pollen never blows out. It just sits over the city. People who grow up with it don't feel it so much, but the rest of us—she paused to wheeze into a tissue—just suffer. So I both dreaded and anticipated the rains that cleared the yellowish-green dust off my car and allowed me to breathe deeply again.

My enthusiasm for Vanderbilt's curriculum was also muddled by the cultural shock of leaving New England. Nashville had none of the things I assumed accompany university life: rare bookstores with the sweet-stale musk of old paper and binding, coffee shops with fresh, fat bagels you can't put your finger through, cobblestone walkways that made me quickly trade in my Wild Pair flats and pumps for rubber-soled brogans. Ann Arbor, Michigan, and Cambridge, Massachusetts, were like this, and I assumed Nashville would be as well. I quickly learned the difference between a college town and a city with colleges in it. As excited as I was about Vanderbilt, I didn't plan for the changes or the rain.

When I complained to Professor Weems about my loneliness, she almost laughed aloud and looked at her watch.

"Right on time." She reclined in her office chair and asked me if ever took Twenty-First Avenue past campus.

"No. Why?"

"Go all the way out and you'll see an independent bookstore on your right. Go past the grocery store, but not all the way into the neighborhoods. It'll still be a commercial area. There's a café in there, and I know it's not the same, but it will feel a little bit like Cambridge."

A graduate of Wellesley College, Professor Weems knew the collegiate atmosphere I missed. She, like me, might have spent weekends in Harvard Square or at Harvard Bookstore. Maybe she ate bagels, sat at a coffee shop with an assigned book, and watched the snow fall outside the window. Finding the bookstore she mentioned, I bought a book and ordered a pasta salad with sundried tomatoes and artichokes. A place where I could read and eat! I exhaled as I plunged the fork into the wide bowl and flipped through the first couple of pages with my left hand. I silently thanked Professor Weems for pointing me toward such a haven. I knew then that, although there would be a lot of adjusting, I wasn't completely alone in a new place. Perhaps, I found just the right place to sort out how to be the new me that ministry was creating.

Mrs. Wingo died during my first Easter as a minister.

Mrs. Wingo was the urban chic cool mom I often wished

I had during my teenage years. She was Kelli's mother, and the coolest mom of all my friends. Not surprising because Kelli was "the cool one." Kelli had her pulse on Detroit happenings, where the cute boys were, and what clothing was really in style. She was a model, and was the first among the four of my crew of black girls to wear makeup, shave her legs, rock the polka-dot style of rapper Kwame, and wear the fashionable asymmetrical hairstyle that Salt-N-Pepa had. Whenever there was anything we wanted to do that was outside the rules, we always had Kelli ask her mom first. Her mom always convinced the other moms. Then they convinced the dads. That's how we managed to go to our junior prom before we were all sixteen, the age when we were officially allowed to date.

Mrs. Wingo seemed to understand teenage girls and cared about our small joys in ways that the other moms didn't. She left us alone when we pushed back the couches and choreographed dance moves to MC Hammer or Kid 'n Play or The Jets playing on the forty-fives we bought. When Kelli and I crooned the opening lines of Keith Sweat's "Right and a Wrong Way," Mrs. Wingo yelled from the front seat: "Oh yes, you are young, and no, you are not ready!"

We burst into laughter offering up explanations: "We know, Mom!" "It's just a song, Mrs. Wingo."

I started calling her "Mom" after living with Kelli for four weeks when Mama had back surgery and couldn't take me to school. Every day, Mrs. Wingo fussed at how long we took to get ready for school, asked about homework, made arrangements for dinner, and tucked me in. I was enthralled by the peace and quiet of their home. The only people making noise were Kelli and me. No arguing. No shouting or cussing. Soft tones. Quiet movement on carpet. Gentle—not desperate—nights.

I saw Mrs. Wingo less than a year before—after college graduation, before my first sermon. She was in the hospital, her dark brown skin still shiny and more noticeable because of her bald head. I came in the room all smiles and hugs and pulled the chair up close to the bed.

"Hi, Mom."

"Hi, baby," she said, slowly turning her head, evidently weak and tired. She still smiled.

It was easy to call her "Mom."

I think I believed that Mrs. Wingo, like Grandma, would live a long time after diagnosis. I think I believed she would be fine. She knew better. That afternoon in the hospital room, Mrs. Wingo told me that she was scared. She held my hand tightly in a way she might not have held Kelli's and said: "It was a cold that wouldn't go away. And then pneumonia, they said. But when I looked up, they were wheeling me into oncology." Tears ran down her face. She didn't try to brush them away. She continued, "I've never smoked a day in my life, but. . . ." She swallowed and shared the facts, "but it began in my chest and now it's in my brain. I don't know when I'll get back to work."

We sat silently for a while. Mrs. Wingo closed her eyes and I held her hand. When she opened her eyes again, we talked as if I were in the living room on a trip home from college. What are you studying now? How's the preaching going? Have you seen Kelli? Because I wasn't her daughter, she didn't have to be strong or hopeful or pass on words of wisdom she wanted to make sure I had before she died. Because I wasn't her daughter, I didn't stop the activities of my life or sit bedside like Kelli did. But she was one of my "other-mothers."

I knew Mrs. Wingo would die. Sooner than later. But death never feels real until it is. The news of her death made some trapdoor beneath the pit of my stomach flip open.

As soon as I could, I went to church. Payne Chapel AME is tucked in a black neighborhood in northeast Nashville. If you aren't looking for it, you can easily miss it. The pastor told a story about being a young minister, serving in one of his first churches where the pastor was an alcoholic. Some days, my pastor explained, he arrived at church and his lead pastor couldn't stand up and so he would have to preach without notice. As a result, he trained the ministerial staff to always "have a sermon in our Bibles." He often gathered us in his office before the early worship service, turned to one of us, and said, "You're on." The members were used to supporting young ministers who were still trying to find their voices and their ways in ministry.

When Pastor invited people to come join the church or just come to the altar for prayer, I headed toward the altar. While I could just as easily have prayed at home, there was something different, something special about being on my knees, touching the wood, collapsing in the midst of other people who cared about God, with the sound of the choir filling the air. The tears erupted.

I flew out to Michigan the next day.

Mrs. Wingo's dead body was like Grandma's. It looked like her, and it didn't look like her at the same time. I walked up to the body, took my time, stared at her. She lost her hair, so they put a hat on her. It didn't look right. She didn't wear hats. But she had her glasses on. That looked right.

I hugged Kelli.

"You didn't have to come," she said. "But I'm so glad you did."

"Of course I'm here. I didn't think twice." I hugged Kelli even tighter and whispered. "I know we lead different lives now, but we'll always be friends. Always. No matter what. No matter what." We held hands and cried together.

Mr. Wingo put his arm around us and said, "She really loved you, Monica." I cried more.

As the family left the church, I stood in the back with my high school friends. We held hands and hugged Kelli one last time. We didn't have to say it aloud. Our collective had changed. We were no longer the four only-children black girls at the small private school. We were no longer the teenagers talking our mothers into letting us wear makeup, buy a new dress, or go on a date. There would be no pictures of the four moms at our respective weddings. We were four girls with three moms.

Not so deep down, we also knew that Mrs. Wingo's death was too random. This week it was Kelli's mom, but it could just as easily have been one of ours. Our mothers were around the same age too. It could have been Mama. And that didn't just make the three of us sad; it terrified us. For more moments than we dared to verbalize, we were Kelli, and Mrs. Wingo was our real mom. All of us imagined ourselves without a mom. We shuddered.

By the time I got back to Nashville, I looked about as bad as I felt. Between a student conference in New York and Mrs. Wingo's funeral, I missed two weeks of school with just a month left in the spring semester. Somewhere in the weather changes and plane rides, I caught a bout of the flu, and I was thrown into the pre-Easter Holy Week services at church and school. I tried to be a good minister, but I wanted to go home and crawl into bed.

There were still two more days until Easter when Peter called from the train station. Weeks earlier, he had asked if it was okay if he stopped through Nashville while he was in the South on another business trip. The sound of his voice and his warm embrace felt like a piece of heaven in the midst of my grief and illness. Although we had broken up six months prior, we were still friends.

The chance to be around someone I knew, someone who knew me, meant I could really exhale and fall apart. The sermons had been preached; I studied for a couple hours. Now, I thought, I can fall apart on the outside as much as I have fallen apart on the inside. I knew that, for just a day or so, there would be someone to take care of me. I didn't take time to clean up. The apartment was strewn with piles of books, photos from when other friends came to visit, luggage that was full of sweaters and corduroy pants. Peter stayed with me and plied me with cups of hot tea and my favorite Indian foods while I tried to sleep off how shitty I was feeling. We went to early service on Sunday morning. The worship was a short necessary break in the middle of what appeared to be the beginning of an upswing out of the reality of death.

And then we got in an argument.

PART III

WADE IN THE WATER

MINISTRY: TENNESSEE, 1995–2000

8

RAPE

Nashville, Tennessee: April 1996

Rape. The sound of the word hurts my ears. The sound of the long *a*. Like the *a* in "pain." It sounds less like a scream, and more like a slow scraping. Rape. It elicits silence whenever it is said. It's the kind of thing that happens in the news. To the nameless victims in Central Park. I've always shuddered at the thought of a woman on the ground, at the mercy of her predators. Eyes closed, limbs twisting, screaming aloud . . . or muffled. Like in the movies. And then I close my own eyes. Because of the horror of rape.

But it's something else to hear the words "rape" and "I've been raped" said to you. By a friend. Who hasn't been herself lately. I remember when Lanh said it. I ran through the cold December wind to get to her dorm room. I wanted to hug her. To cry for her. To express my mutual grief and anger. She was running . . . at night . . . through the park . . . not too far from campus. They saw her . . . they said horrible things . . . they pinned her to the ground . . . they had a gun . . . just like in the news. Just like in the movies.

I remember sitting around the hospital room. Lanh lay in bed, self-hospitalized to prevent hurting herself. I ran my fingers over the straps around her wrists that she requested. I sat around the bed with two other women from our Bible study group. We were trying to tell jokes to make Lanh laugh. We were trying not to cry. And Lanh spoke, "They say that one in four women will be raped." Silence. We sighed, and simultaneously bit our bottom lips. There was nothing to say.

But it's different to hear the words "I've been raped" from a classmate or friend than to hear it from your own voice, from your own mouth. At first, I thought it was not so much what Peter did but the words he used, the look on his face, his anger, his disrespect, the cursing. But the word "rape" makes it real, makes it tangible. He read my journals. Rape. He questioned me on their contents. Rape. He cursed my God. Rape. For six to eight hours, he cursed me. Rape. He touched my breasts begging the nipples to rise. Rape. Despite the pained look on my face. Rape. He lifted my shirt. Rape. He mistook my struggling for orgasm. Rape. He pressed his penis to the dryness of my vagina. Rape. I almost gave in. "You've taken my heart and soul," I thought. "What more do you want? If I give up, will you just go away?" Just go away. Rape.

The sound of the word screamed in echoes in my head. RAPE RAPE RAPE RAPE. I loved him and he raped me. I loved him and he raped me.

I was simultaneously aware and unaware of what was happening. As he cursed, begged, and touched, I tried to separate nightmare from reality. Slowly the scream of the word "rape" became the discreet whisper, "death."

And I screamed, "No." Just no. I ran to the bathroom. Water, water, water. If I touched my own body under the water, it would be just like before. It would belong to me. Under the water.

9

DAY BY DAY

Nashville, Tennessee: The Day after the Rape

DAY 1

I couldn't wait until noon. That was when I was supposed to meet Tanya. I called Tanya twice that morning. Once at two or three o'clock in the morning. To my surprise, she answered. It wasn't like me to be awake at that hour, let alone to call anyone. I didn't remember what I said or even why I called. Some part of me knew that someone else needed to know what was happening with me. Some part of me knew that I was afraid. By the time I called her back, hours later, Peter was gone. I showered. And I could barely put two words together.

That was when I asked Tanya if we could meet on campus.

Today.

It wasn't our usual day. We usually met on Thursdays, only varying the time and location of our meal: lunch at a restaurant or dinner at one of our apartments. That was one of the requirements of our relationship.

We were pretty formal in starting our friendship. When the professor of the elective class in spirituality told us to "Turn to your neighbor and discuss this topic," Tanya and I found that we were often turning toward each other. After each partner exercise, we wished we had more time to talk. One week we had an assigned book that had a chapter on spiritual friendships; we looked to each other and said, "Let's be spiritual partners!"

We first met in a local coffee shop, and I often joked that we should start our own business with the same name, only ours would really be a bean store. All kinds of beans: coffee beans, beanbag chairs, Mexican jumping beans, adzuki, lentil, and northern beans. Yes, Tanya agreed, and every day at lunch we would sell the bean of the day over brown rice for two dollars for paying customers and free for homeless people. This was our vision for ending hunger in the local community—one bowl of beans at a time.

More often that not, we met in each other's apartments and ate food we cooked for one another. Tanya made sparse meals she learned to cook when in the Peace Corps in Niger, West Africa: a stew that tasted like peanut butter, adapted, she said, for vegetarians, and the one good mango she found in the grocery store. The meals came with stories about the elderly woman who taught Tanya how to make the stew, or about the first child who brought a mango to her hut.

In most ways, it was an ordinary friendship between women. We talked about our long-distance relationships, our classes, and our lives before Nashville. But there were two rules: we had to meet regularly, and we had to ask each other this question: "How are you and God?" Many weeks, the answer was some version of "Hell if I know."

How does being a minister affect my prayer life? Am I supposed to pray more? Pray differently? How can my boyfriend and I worship together? How do we even share our faith with each other when we are so far apart? How do I know what I'm supposed to be doing? And how does what I am studying every day factor into that? I'm worried about love. I'm worried about whether or not God wants me to have the things I so desperately want. The things that once connected me to God don't work anymore. How do I even recognize God's voice?

Sharing these questions meant that we knew each other's deepest insecurities. But sharing these questions made it easier to live without the answers. In my friendship with Tanya I learned that sometimes the holiest thing in the world is two people sharing a piece of fruit.

Tanya had a class at eleven, so I had to wait until noon.

I told myself: it's just four hours, just four hours, just four hours. Read something. I have homework to do. Can't focus. Can't stop thinking about everything. Watch TV. There's nothing on. God, I hate talk shows. Well, let me just go to school. I can drive to school, right? Yeah, I can do that. I can hang out for an hour or so. I'll see people, chat about nothing. That will fill the time until I see Tanya.

As I walked in the door to the Div School, I saw Tanya walking toward me. I saw down the hallway. On my left was the elevator that goes to the second floor of classrooms, administrative offices, and the Refectory. The third floor had faculty offices. Directly opposite the elevator was the door to the classroom. The linoleum floor made the short hallway between the outside door and the corner toward the common room look more like an elementary school than a graduate school. Almost all first-year students were in that class, and I heard the din of about forty of my colleagues chattering and getting comfortable in the classroom. Tanya rounded the corner from the common room area, and the twenty feet between us evaporated. I flung myself at her and buried my nose into her light brown hair. I inhaled the strawberry scent of her shampoo and wailed into her shoulder. The elevator door beside me opened. I couldn't move; I couldn't see. I heard the professor's voice to Tanya. "Don't worry about class. You can use my office." She handed Tanya her keys. Tanya pulled me into the elevator, keeping her arm around me the entire time. I didn't look up. I don't remember walking down the corridors to the faculty offices. I don't know how long I cried before I said anything. It doesn't matter. If I had never spoken another word again it would be okay. I just wanted my best friend, and here she was. Here she was, knowing all the things I could not say.

DAY 2

I called three former boyfriends asking them the same question: "Am I just pussy to you?" An odd question given that I never had sex with any of them.

I imagine how odd the question sounded to men who hadn't so much as kissed me in years. Calling was not unusual because we maintained something between collegiality and close friendship. But it was unlike me to ask about sex before asking how their day was or how their family was doing.

"What?"

"Am I just pussy to you? I mean, is it all about sex with men? Do you care about anything besides getting it? Am I just pussy to you?"

That was how I felt. And I needed someone, I needed men who once held, loved, kissed, and caressed me, to reassure me that I was wrong. To tell me that the truth Peter just introduced into my life was really a lie.

They reminded me of our friendship that endured personal struggles. They told me that I was smart and beautiful and a good friend. They told me that sex was good, but we wouldn't have been friends over time and space if it was "just pussy" to them. They told me that they loved me, and for a few moments I believed them. But once the conversation ended and I was home alone, looking at the tussled burgundy sheets, the unmade bed, my half-full suitcase in the corner, I knew they were lying. They were lying to help me feel better. They didn't know what happened. I didn't tell them. I couldn't. I hadn't yet told myself. I only knew that Peter was right, and I was only as valuable as what lay between my legs.

DAY 3

I took a shower. I still didn't make my bed or really go back in there. I laid down on the couch. I felt so hurt. So naked. Peter knew more about me than any other person. And then he read my journal. That made me completely naked before him. The words, the actions. I just kept saying "fucking bastard" over and over again while he tried to kiss me, take off my clothes, touch me. I prayed he would go away. Just go away. That God would make him stop. The look on my face showed the pain. But he wanted me—it—so bad.

I had to get up. I had two theology papers due. I needed to clean the bathroom, the kitchen. I needed to make my bed. I wanted to burn the sheets. I needed to get up and go to class. I needed to pay my rent. How was I going to do all this? How was I going to do this? Okay, start with breakfast.

DAY 4

Cynthia came to my apartment. She was back in Nashville for Easter and then spring break. She said that there were evil spirits in my place. Evil spirits that Peter let in my home. She laid her olive-oil coated hands everywhere. On the walls and doors and hallways. Praying. I sat on the couch and watched her. I hoped whatever she was doing worked. I hoped it would help me sleep.

DAY 6

I went to church with my classmate. I sat in the common room with stacks of books around me. I needed to get some work done. Nothing was getting done at home. I didn't really want to go home anyway. Still hadn't made the bed. The sun was setting, the books were all around me, and I stared ahead not paying attention to anything. My classmate asked if I wanted to go to church with him. Yes, on a Saturday evening.

The church had no pulpit. There was no raised area designated for ministers and the choir. Everyone sat on the same level. The ministers in chairs on the left; the piano on the right. In the middle was a platform of plants with a bay window behind it, opening out onto a park while the sky slowly darkened during worship. It was like nature burst into the middle of the church. God's created world was center stage. Human beings were peripheral.

I didn't remember the service, and there was no wooden altar rail like in an AME church, but I was at church so I knew I could talk to God about it. As the service ended, I asked my classmate, a staff minister at the church, if I could kneel at the front and pray.

"Of course."

I knelt, but I didn't pray. I cried. I cried and I cried and I cried. I didn't hear the pianist leave. I didn't hear the other parishioners close the door. I didn't even hear the pastor tell my friend to keep the church open for me. The world around me disappeared while I lay crumpled up in front of the altar. By the time I looked up and wiped my face, an hour had passed. My minister classmate patiently sat in a chair in the hallway.

"You okay?"

Of course I wasn't. "Better." I said.

"I'll take you to your car. Come by and have dinner with us tonight, okay?"

"I'll be okay." I lied. "Really."

I liked this church. They waited while I cried to God. They changed their schedule, took their time, and waited while I cried. And still treated me like a human being when I was done. These were good people. This was a good church.

DAY 8

At five in the morning, I still needed to do laundry. I couldn't imagine going to work. I had already missed two days. No real excuse. I was going to lose my job. I wanted to stay in all day. I felt like that a lot at the time. Even when I slept, I woke up feeling like I hadn't slept. I had oodles of work to do. I wanted to stay home and hide under the sheets, watch TV. I was really tired. What I needed to do was get myself lost in the library and read until my eyes fell out. But I couldn't focus.

DAY 11

My therapist told me to try to think of ways this whole thing made me stronger. I didn't feel stronger. Empty, hollow, bitter, violated, stripped, scared. That's how I really felt.

I had been in therapy for months. It was actually one of the things that excited me most about attending Vanderbilt. I would be somewhere long enough to explore the issues I wanted to resolve. I never mentioned my earlier diagnosis of depression. I went to the Psychological and Counseling Center asking for someone to help me process the events of my adolescence.

"Help me to stop hating my father. Because Christians aren't supposed to hate."

Nancy couldn't get me to stop hating Daddy, but she was able to help me to start loving myself.

Early in our sessions, she asked me if I had any secrets. "Is there anything about yourself that you don't want anyone to know?"

"Not really. My life isn't that exciting."

"Nothing at all?"

"No . . . well, wait. There is one thing."

"What?"

"I'm not telling you. I just met you." That's why it's called a secret.

"Fair enough. But tell me why you don't want anyone to know about it."

That was easy to answer. I immediately ran on about how much I had screwed up. How I had done something that no one thought I would do. How I had done something I wasn't proud of. Something I didn't want to do. It was a mistake. I made conscious decisions, but I. . . .

I concluded, "I really screwed up. And I think that hurts God and I broke a promise to God. I broke promises to myself."

Nancy replied with a gentleness that I needed, "And that makes you . . . what? Human? Don't you think God knows that God made you human?"

Her simple question broke down years of type A overachiever development. I worked so hard to get things right and good. This mentality brought me far. It helped me work hard, study hard, get good grades, get into school, start a magazine, apply for fellowships, and accomplish the host of things noted on my résumé. But it didn't do anything for how harshly I judged myself for one thing.

Nancy continued, "If God made you human, and you did something that all human beings do—screw up sometimes—don't you think God still loves you?"

For the first time, I applied to myself the unconditional love of God that I preached about. If there was nothing I could do to make God stop loving me, then maybe I didn't have to do anything to love myself. I could really love myself for the imperfect but pretty darn interesting person I was. I laughed out loud when I said that to Nancy. She laughed with me. "Well, Monica, you are pretty darn interesting."

It would take years for me to address the issue that brought me to therapy—making peace with Daddy. I realize now how hard it must have been to help someone who didn't tell the whole truth about herself. I wasn't trying to hide things from my therapist. After all, I sought her out. I wanted to be a better and stronger person. I just couldn't tell her things I didn't tell myself. When I talked about a "bad fight with an ex-boyfriend," it made sense that she would try to help me move on. It made sense for her to ask me to look for the lessons.

DAY 13

I walked through the hallways at school, sat in classes . . . I couldn't say how empty I felt when people asked how I was. I couldn't say how violated. I hated it every time someone asked me how I was doing and I said "Fine" or "Okay." I wanted to look in their eyes and plead, "No I'm not okay." Tanya and I went out for bagels. She said she was concerned about me. She thought I was holding too much inside. "Internalizing," she said. She didn't want me to turn my anger and sadness in on myself. I didn't feel like I was. But where else was all this supposed to go? I was pretty bottled up about it. I didn't know what to tell my friends. I didn't want pity. I had too many friends who knew Peter. I couldn't tell them. What was I supposed to say?

DAY 14

I preached at church. I pulled out one of those sermons that was tucked in my Bible. Pastor says "Amen." Other ministers said they liked it. I felt like a fraud. How could I minister to anyone? I needed someone to minister to me.

DAY 15

I laughed. At a rerun of *Seinfeld*. I actually laughed.

I called Nancy and asked for another therapy session. I was still sleeping on the couch and counting laughs. I needed help from someone who really knew what to do. She used the word "abuse." She used the words "sexual violence." Was that, I asked myself over and over again, what happened to me?

DAY 21

I stopped praying. I had probably stopped praying three weeks prior. I was mad at God. I just didn't have anything to say. I didn't want to share anything with Peter—not even God. I found ways to be a student of theology and a minister without praying. All I had to do was talk about God. I didn't have to talk to God. I had three prewritten unpreached sermons in my Bible. If I needed to preach, I would pull one of those out and read it. I recited one of five prayers I memorized for all those occasions when people ask ministers to pray: grace, the invitation to join the church, an upcoming surgery or medical procedure. I went through the motions for months. Because hell if I was going to talk to the same God Peter talked to.

DAY 23

Nancy told me to do what was best for me. That just

sounded so selfish. Maybe it was white privilege that let her say that. Maybe it was a secular thing. I thought that ministers were supposed to give of themselves. We're not supposed to be selfish.

I took a long bath. A bubble bath. I stretched my legs upward and lathered. I thought of how flabby my legs had become in these weeks without working out. In any event, they were my legs. God made them. Crooked and all. And they worked. They were beautiful. A temple, a body, me acting-in-the-world. My own spirit incarnated. I looked at my arms. I put soap on my entire body. And just felt it. And held it. I dried off. I lotioned. I painted my toenails and put on satin pajamas. I drifted off to sleep.

I slept!

For a couple of hours anyway.

DAY 24

I was writing a paper for my class on the book of Psalms. We learned that the psalms were the hymns and prayers of the ancient Hebrew Israelites. We learned the devotional quality of psalms. When you can't find the words yourself, use the words of other faithful people. I found myself drawn to Psalm 55. I wrote the verses I liked in my journal:

Give ear to my prayer, O God; do not hide yourself from my
supplication. Attend to me, and answer me; I am troubled
in my complaint. I am distraught by the noise of the enemy,
because of the clamor of the wicked. For they bring trouble

upon me, and in anger they cherish enmity against me. My heart is in anguish within me, the terrors of death have fallen upon me. Fear and trembling come upon me, and horror overwhelms me . . . It is not enemies who taunt me—I could bear that; it is not adversaries who deal insolently with me—I could hide from them. But it is you, my equal, my companion, my familiar friend, with whom I kept pleasant company; we walked in the house of God with the throng. Let death come upon them; let them go down alive to Sheol; for evil is in their homes and in their hearts. But I call upon God, and the Lord will save me.

It was comforting to know that I was not the first person to be hurt by someone I once called friend, by someone I once loved. But I called upon God, and God did not save me. This psalm only went so far. I picked the verse I liked the best, "Let death come upon them; let them go down alive to Sheol." God, go get him!

DAY 25

God answered the prayers I could not pray—in the middle of the library. I was determined to finish out the semester without completely flattening my GPA. I took a stack of books and papers to the library and told myself I could not go home until I got something done. I tuned my Discman to a local college radio station and settled in with my research. I tuned the music and chatter to the back of my mind as I flipped through book after book looking for quotations to support my argument, and then I heard the radio announcer read from the eighth and fourteenth chapters of the biblical book of Jeremiah.

> *I would comfort myself in sorrow; my heart is faint in me. Listen! The voice, the cry of the daughter of my people from a far country: "Is not the Lord in Zion? Is not her King in her?" "Why have they provoked me to anger with their carved images—with foreign idols?" "The harvest is past, the summer is ended, and we are not saved!" For the hurt of the daughter of my people I am hurt. I am mourning; atonishment has taken hold of me. . . . You shall say to them this word: Let my eyes run down with tears night and day, and let them not cease, for the virgin daughter—my people—is struck down with a crushing blow, with a very grievous wound.*

I heard these words as if for the first time: "For the hurt of the daughter of my people I am hurt. I am mourning. Astonishment has taken hold of me. Let my eyes run down with tears night and day, and let them not cease, for my daughter is struck down with a crushing blow, with a very grievous wound."

For the first time, it occurred to me: God cried when I cried. I heard God saying to me, "Don't you know that I cry when you cry? When you lament, I lament. It hurts me when it hurts you. I'm hurt that this thing has happened to you. I'm hurt that Peter did that to you. I'm hurt by what he said in my name. I really am right here with you."

141

This wasn't the God I was mad at. It wasn't the God I was taught. This wasn't the God who parted the Red Sea but ignored my pleas. It wasn't the God I asked to make Peter stop. This was some new God. This was a God that said to me: "I'm not ignoring you. In fact, I hurt with you. I'm right here, and I'm pretty undone too."

The radio program seemed to end as quickly as it entered my consciousness, but it left an imprint on my needy soul. I burst into tears right in the middle of the library. I pushed my books and papers to the side, placed my hands in front of my face, and sobbed with no regard for how much noise I made or how much attention I drew to myself. Maybe, just maybe, God cared about me after all.

As far as most of my friends knew, I overreacted to a fight with an ex-boyfriend. They had no idea what was happening. They didn't know that I was faking my ministry. They didn't know I was losing my ability to really talk to the God that made me want to be a minister. That was my first glimpse of the only God I could believe in.

DAY 28

I had three terms papers to write and all I could think about was the trauma I could not name. Every time I read books or articles for my Human Sexuality in the Bible class with Professor Weems, I cried. I had proposed my paper topic over a month earlier. I submitted the outline for Professor Weems's approval. All I had to do was follow the outline, but I couldn't. Using a payphone in the law school, I called Professor Weems at her home.

"I can't do this. I can't do this. I need an extension. I can't write this paper." I nearly hyperventilated on the phone.

"Why can't you write the paper?"

"I can't. I just can't. I can't. I want to, but I can't. I just can't." I stammered repeatedly.

"Yes, you can. Calm down. Breathe. Are you breathing?"

"Uh huh."

"You can do this. You have the outline, right?" Professor Weems reassured.

"Yeah." I managed to get out.

"Follow the outline. Just follow the outline."

"Follow the outline?"

"Follow the outline."

I can only imagine how I sounded. I felt like a lost child who needed someone to hold my hand. There was no apparent reason why a term paper would cause me to fall apart at the seams. The truth is that the attack left me with invisible scars. I might have looked tired, but I didn't have cuts or bruises that anyone could see. I probably sounded like a stressed-out student at the end of the semester. In reality, I was a student who couldn't get a good night's sleep. I was a minister who was losing her faith.

DAY 29

I remembered my dream. I dreamed it. I dreamed the rape.

That would not be such a big deal if I weren't known for dreaming the future.

I come from people who dream. Sharing the previous night's dream is a ritual I remember from my childhood. Ambling sleepily out of my bedroom, down the hall, into the light of the kitchen and into Mama's lap where she sat at the table, back to the window, hands at typewriter. She pushed back from the table so I could settle into her legs, chest, and shoulder. It's hard now to believe I was ever so small that I had to exert energy to climb up and onto my five-foot-five-inch-tall mother.

"Morning, baby."

"Mm."

"How'd you sleep?"

"Mm mm mmm mm."

"Really?" I loved how Mama never made me talk before I was awake enough to, and always managed to decode my pitched grunts and humming so accurately.

"What did you dream about last night?"

The pattern was the same at Nana and Grandma's house—only they didn't tolerate my sleepy tonal utterances. They demanded words: "Speak up, child!" And they took whatever I said as information for the right digits to play when the numbers man came by.

There was always someone who cared about what I dreamed, and dreams meant something. I usually dreamed ordinary snippets of life. In the dream I knew who the people were and we were somewhere, talking or working. But when I awoke, I realized I didn't know any of those people at all. Years later, I would find myself in that situation and halt, thinking, "I've dreamt this."

"Like déjà vu?" friends ask if I say out loud, "I've dreamt this."

"No. I dreamt it. I remember dreaming it. I didn't know them then, but I dreamt this." I try to remember to say this only in my head or to Mama, who will understand.

There were difficult dreams, like when I dreamed of Grandma dying but no one told me. In the dream, I was at Grandma's house on Thanksgiving—which is weird because I was never there on Thanksgiving. Grandma and I were in the kitchen, and Grandma was getting ready to make dinner. It was early in the morning. I was the early riser in the family. Everyone else was asleep. Grandma told me to go to the basement and get the turkey. For some reason, I expected a live, wild turkey to be down there, and I had every intention of grasping it by the neck and bringing it to Grandma to kill for dinner. (As if that is the most normal thing to do.) So I went down the stairs to the basement and found myself down there in a pool of dead fish. On the carpet, about four inches deep, everywhere. Against the boxes and against the hinged door leading to the small room with the washing machine and washboard.

I started screaming. "Grandma, there's dead fish down here! Come down here! There's dead fish down here!"

She replied calmly, "No, there's not. Stop yelling. Get the turkey, baby."

"But there's no turkey! There are fish everywhere!"

Why was I still standing in the vast pool of dead fish?

Why didn't I run back to the stairs to get away from them? Why didn't I run back up the stairs?

Grandma repeated, "There are no fish down there. Just get the turkey."

The oddest dream I ever had. When I told Mama, she said she didn't know what it meant. She told me to tell Aunt Maxine, who said she didn't know what it meant. We would have to ask one of our cousins or great-aunts who had a dream book. They would know. Every couple of months I asked them if they knew what the dream meant. "No, baby. I don't know what fish means."

They lied. They knew. They knew what my dreams knew. Grandma was dying. Sooner than later. And she wouldn't want to admit it. No one would want to accept it. But she was dying. And they didn't tell me what my dream meant because that meant that they would have had to accept that Grandma was going to die. Soon. I just found out that Aunt Maxine and Mama knew what the dream meant. They could have given me any excuse—something about how I was only eleven or twelve years old, something about how they didn't want me to worry, something about not being able to reach a cousin who knew. But they didn't lie this time. They just said, "We weren't ready to deal with it yet. So we didn't tell you."

So I knew that I dreamed the future.

I had one of those chasing dreams—the dreams where I'm being chased by someone, by people I know, who want to get me for some reason I never understand during or after the dream. I'm not afraid of my typical chasing dream, always in the same building, a building my waking self has never been in, but one that I know well in the dream. I know I'll outrun them, outhide them, outmaneuver them by the time I wake up. That dream makes me tired, but it doesn't scare me.

This dream was different.

I knew him. I couldn't see him in the dream. I didn't know who he was, but I knew he wanted to rape me. I was running. I ran into my apartment. Yes, the apartment where I lived in Nashville. I closed and locked the door, but I still wasn't safe. He was taking the hinges off the door from the outside. I still wasn't safe.

I woke up, terrified. Breathing hard. I called a friend. I don't remember who. Tanya? Someone back in Cambridge? Male friend? Female friend? Told him or her about the dream. She or he said what I probably would have said to myself: "It's just a dream. It's just a dream. It's okay. Breathe. Turn the lights on. Get out of the bed. Go to the bathroom. Wash your face. It's just a bad dream."

But I knew differently. I knew that dreams were not just dreams. Not dreams like that. I couldn't forget this dream. But I didn't remember it that night. I remembered twenty-nine days later. And I was horrified.

I dreamed this, I said inside my head. I dreamed this. I knew this was going to happen and I couldn't stop it. Just like in the dream.

I only knew one way to get through nightmares like that. I did the same thing I did in college. I called my friends to come sit on the couch while I napped. I asked them to let me sleep on their couches. When night came, I begged Tanya, my minister classmate, a friend from the law school, whomever, to sit with me and protect me from the sleeping and waking nightmare I was living.

10

LOOKING FOR HOPE

Nashville, Tennessee: Six Weeks after the Rape

I was looking for hope as I drove north on Interstate 75. I didn't tell Lanh why I was coming. In our two-hour conversation, we talked about school, church, her Ohio State Buckeyes, and my Michigan Wolverines. She reminded me that I was always welcome to visit; I proposed a date for the day after my last paper was due. I didn't say anything about Peter or what happened. I didn't have the words. I knew that with Lanh, I wouldn't need them.

I watched Lanh quietly heal from her rape three years earlier. I sat with her in the hospital. I brought small snacks to her dorm room. She didn't talk about what happened that night. She talked about what happened to her life. What her parents were saying. How hard it was to study. Meetings with the police. Hopes that Malcolm still loved her.

"Of course he does," I reassured.

Lanh and Malcolm met through Christian Impact, and

from a distance they made an odd couple. Malcolm had the all-American, Midwestern-turned-Ivy-League prep look. Corduroys in the winter, khakis in the spring and fall; sweatshirt for weekends, blue blazer for business events. His dirty-blond hair arched over his forehead, staying out of his eyes even when he lifted his head from prayer. A year ahead of Lanh, Malcolm started medical school while Lanh finished up her senior year. They planned to marry the summer after Lanh's graduation.

She moved knitting needles in and out of thick yarn. She started with a scarf. Within a month she was making sweaters for Malcolm. "It gives me something to focus on," she said. "You know it's cold in Ohio." Lanh turned the garment over. It looked like something out of an elite ski shop.

"How did you learn that?" I asked.

"A nurse showed me the basics in the hospital. I bought a book. I taught myself the rest."

Lanh never said anything else about her rape, and I never asked. But I saw how, one threaded loop at a time, she stitched her world back together. Lanh wore a white wedding dress and the traditional Chinese red for the reception. They moved into a family student apartment in Columbus.

When I arrived, Lanh and Malcolm welcomed me with hugs, warm food, and fresh sheets on the futon. Lanh explained her schedule and incorporated me into it. I could stay inside or join her on her run. She shared the week's scripture reading so I could keep up in Bible study. She told me how wonderful it was to wake up next to the person you love. She showed me the rice cooker her parents gave them. "To make sure I don't lose my Chinese." We laughed together. As if that could be lost. Pasta with sundried tomatoes and black olives. Broccoli in a rich black-bean sauce. I sat at a table with other people and ate—a rarity for a single graduate student. I felt like I was with family again. For a couple of days, I felt sane.

I slept.

Perhaps Lanh recognized my trauma as similar to her own. Perhaps she identified thirty-seven sleepless nights in one glance. Perhaps she knew that healing from rape came in living through the ordinary moments of each day—the morning jog, a bowl of rice, evening Bible study, a cup of coffee with an old friend. Her routine inspired me to believe that there could be life, love, and normalcy after rape.

Without sharing the story I could not voice, I asked her the last question I allowed myself to pose about her rape.

"When did it get better?"

Lanh sucked her teeth and sighed. "It's bad. It's really bad. And then one day, you wake up, and it's not so bad. The next day, it's bad again. Then maybe in the next month, you have another good day. And then it's bad again. But then there's another good day. And you jump from good day to good day like lily pads. You count them up. You are grateful for them. And when you're not paying attention, you have another good day, and then another. And after a while, the good days outnumber the bad days. Then, you can count the bad days."

I couldn't even imagine it. A good day? But I saw it in Lanh—regular good days filled with regular good things.

Because of Lanh, I sensed that this was not the end of me. On the drive back to Nashville, I stopped at a jewelry store in an outlet mall. I pierced my left ear with a third hole to accompany the first and second ones obtained in elementary and high school female rites of fashion. This hole, I told myself, meant something. It symbolized the healing I would attain. I touched my ear and twisted the small stud whenever I doubted the recovery process. It was something I held onto when everything else felt like a vapor. For this reason alone, being raped thrust me into the best depression of my life. This time, I knew I would survive.

At that time, the bad days outnumbered the good days and I lost my job. I worked in the Christian Education Department of the AME Church—a job I inherited from an AME student who graduated months before I started my degree program. It was mainly office work: answering the phone, directing Sunday school teachers and other laity to the right resources. Every now and again, I sat in the office with the director and volleyed ideas about the future of Christian education in our denomination.

Bad days were paralyzing. I couldn't move past my front door. If I got out of bed and took a shower, the major accomplishment was moving to the couch. Eating breakfast was a feat. Shifting channels on the television was a solace. Sometimes I called in. Most times I did not.

"I'm not feeling well" sounded like a poor excuse for

skipping work. I wasn't even sad that I was fired. It was one more thing I didn't have to make myself do.

During a good afternoon, I sat in Professor Weems's office.

"So what are your plans for the summer?" she asked while shifting a pile of papers from one section of her desk to another.

"I don't know. I need a job."

"Go to Sunshine," she said, barely looking up from her work.

"What?"

"The grocery store on Belmont. The natural foods place. They are hiring. This is perfect for you. Go right now and come back."

I needed this kind of direction. All my brainpower went into my final papers. I was a child who needed to know what numbers to paint by. "Now?"

"Now. Just go. And then come back. I'll still be here."

Not ten minutes from campus, Sunshine Grocery was the only natural foods grocery store in Nashville. There was no Wild Oats or Whole Foods or Starbucks in Nashville; there was Sunshine. Sunshine Grocery was run by three long-haired white hippies who wore Birkenstocks and gave the impression that they were at Woodstock together. Sunshine had a small deli area, fresh produce, and meat substitutes. All vegetarians in Nashville eventually found their way to this little Mecca. I knew exactly where it was.

Everything was still done by hand. The stockers worked in the back with a tape gun. Working without scanners, cashiers memorized the fluctuating produce prices at the beginning of every day. When the owners were present, they served as the information booth, but they wanted cashiers who knew something about vegetarianism, vitamins, and herbal teas. Being a cashier was three jobs in one: mathematician, checker, veggie guru.

How long have you been vegetarian? Five years. Do you like to cook? Yes. You already shop here, right? Totally. You say you're a student? Yes, at Vanderbilt. Fill out these forms. You work four days a week, eleven-hour shifts, an hour off for lunch. Whatever you eat while you're working is free; 20 percent off groceries you buy. Will that work? Yes. Sign here.

Less than an hour after leaving, I bound back into Professor Weems's office like a first-grader showing a parent the gold star on her assignment. "I got the job!"

In her usual calm demeanor, Professor Weems smiled. "This is good. You'll be fine." This was how she mentored me. Not with hugs or meetings in restaurants. She didn't ask about my personal life. Rather, seeing a crack or deep puddle ahead, she picked me up by the scruff of my neck to keep me from falling in.

Summer job. Check.

Theresa came to live with me for the summer. When I invited her, I didn't know about her depression. I knew that the eternal frigid winters of Syracuse turned her into a recluse who couldn't leave her dorm room to go to class. I knew Aunt Maxine was worried. I knew they argued over what would best help her—if she needed help at all—or whether she just needed to be left alone. I assumed that the winters of upstate New York could do anyone in.

She didn't want to go home to Baltimore, so I said she could stay with me. Things changed between my family and me when I left home for college. Four years of schooling on the East Coast let me take the train down to Baltimore for Thanksgiving and Christmas, but we were no longer cousin-children sharing summer camps and holidays. We encountered each other as adults who had stronger intimacies with our chosen friends than with cousins, parents, or aunts. After our respective high school graduations, we missed major milestones and events in each other's lives. Conversations with parents were negotiations around visits, meeting significant others, and financial support for school. When we did see each other, we fell back into our childhood patterns. I don't recall any clear teaching from Grandma, Mama, or Aunt Maxine, but we knew that family doesn't need personal knowledge for bonding. You show up for family because they are family. This was the pattern of my childhood.

"Stay with me," I told Theresa. "What are big cousins for?"

Theresa is the artist in the family. Her ability to learn instruments and sing with a loud, strong voice always left talent show competition in the dust. Her quick spirit and tendency toward the dramatic often brought her accusations of melodrama at best, and "liar" or "just exaggerating" at worst. The family mistook her major depression for drama, and missed it. All of us did. From Grandma and her siblings, we learned to see deep grief, dull eyes, and despair as normal. We didn't know that it's the prelude to something death-dealing.

I knew it was depression when she arrived. She looked sad. And she didn't move. She was lying on the couch when I dashed off to work. I left bus routes on the counter and the Internet on the computer. When I returned, Theresa looked as if she hadn't moved.

"Have you eaten?" I inquired.

"No."

"Nothing?"

"No." It was the flattest "no" I ever heard. Without frustration or even resolution. Just honest resignation.

"I'll make something for us." And I shuffled around in the kitchen.

She didn't want to leave for the most basic things. Not the mall. Not the coffee shop. Not even the grocery store. She simply left a list of things she liked that I could bring home from work.

What happened to my cousin? When did her moodiness become mood swings? When did her solitariness become suicide attempts? When did she start going to psychiatrists rather than the pediatrician? Was this a just bad summer in what would be hundreds of seasons of her life? Or was this something she wouldn't get over? Something she would just have to manage?

I only knew that when it was bad, it was bad. It was bad that summer.

And still, when I thought of this bright-eyed, chocolate skinned, brilliant-smiled little girl running around with two braids . . . this girl who called me a "girly girl" because I was more interested in books and pianos than kickball and basketball . . . this girl who won the "Little Miss" pageant of her state and twirled around in light blue and lavender lacy dresses on Sundays . . . I could barely believe that the body on the couch that did not move for days, looking at TV but not really looking, was my cousin.

It frightened me. Knowing how close she came to self-destruction on a regular basis. She told me of the insidious ways she devised to undermine herself: the slow deaths through food and lack of self-care, and the faster deaths through overmedication or refusal to take the prescribed medication. It's not crazy at all. Any sane person would think this kind of life is worse than death. It's a need to feel something . . . anything. It's a desire to end the loop that dances between life and inhumanity. It's feeling trapped in something you cannot name but know is real. It's a taste for freedom.

When she was a professional, she was glowing. She moved and jumped and leaped and sang her way into everyone's heart. Her eyes became wide, her smile radiant. Her talent overshadowed her colleagues. I recognized her once again. But off the stage, on a bad day, she was another person. There was nothing I could say to make the bad times better.

The irony is that I was no different, no better, no

healthier. I just pulled off the daily life thing with more finesse, more deception.

That summer, we held each other up. I cooked. I gave her a home away from home. She rubbed my feet at the end of long days. We offered each other presence.

We didn't talk about our depressions. We fell into our own patterns. I went to work. I came home. I cooked. I watched TV with Theresa. I went to work. I came home. I cooked. We watched TV. I went to work. I came home. I cooked. We watched TV. We couldn't handle anything more complicated than that.

At the end of every day, I went to my room, closed the door, and pushed play:

Saying good-bye can be the hardest thing to do
when you really love someone.
You keep holding on,
Hoping another second will last
Last you forever, but it don't.

It was a simple piano melody of single notes and chords. No synthesizers, guitars, or drums. Just a melody—the kind that forms the backdrops of dreams. But I didn't even realize it—not when I woke up at least. Not until I heard it somewhere and thought, "This is the music in my dreams."

I put this song in the CD player of my boom box and hit "Repeat 1." I first heard it the dark night in Harvard's Memorial Chapel during the AIDS memorial service. Peter played the piano and sang the words over and over:

"Everything happens for a reason, everything happens for a reason, everything happens for a reason." He sang it in a desperate, pleading way. As if the reality of AIDS made us all doubt this pithy saying. "They say, they say, I don't know whether or not to believe them, they say, everything happens for a reason."

I later learned that this was a ballad buried on the album of R&B duo Zhané: two tall, thin women with closely cropped hair, one a dark sepia brown and the other a glowy high yellow. They are best known for the funky summer hit "Hey Mr. DJ!" Like most of my friends, I bounced to their hit at frat parties and turned up the dial when the song came on the car radio. But it was this little ballad sung so movingly by a man I loved that made me buy the CD.

I played the song over and over. I remembered Peter: the moment he caught my attention, the things that made me love him—his deep raspy voice, a willingness to give his musical skills to the ministry of touching something deep within people and suggesting that God may have an answer. I remembered Peter: the things he said to me that long night, the look on his face, the way he felt on top of me. I cried.

I felt over and over again the words of the song:

Saying good-bye can be the hardest thing to do
when you really love someone.
You keep holding on . . . hoping. . . .
Everything happens for a reason, they say. . . .
I don't know whether or not to believe them.

I don't know whether or not to believe them.
I don't know whether or not to believe them.

The song repeated as I drifted off to whatever sleep I got.

Theresa was just a wall and a bedroom door away. I emerged from my room to shower, go to work, and ask if she needed anything. I came home. I did it all over again. I needed the routine. There is healing in regular things, I told myself.

Theresa and I didn't talk about . . . anything. Not my doubts, my fears, my sleeplessness. It was nice to know she was there . . . around . . . family . . . someone who loved me. She must have known I was in turmoil. What else could she think of someone asking over and over how "everything happens for a reason"? How rape can happen for a reason.

I tried to recreate that night and morning in my journal. Sometimes I thought it was a bad dream. Sometimes I thought I exaggerated. Then I remembered the ache between my legs when I took a shower that morning.

I was not crazy.

11

GOOD DAY, BAD
DAY

Nashville, Tennessee: Two Months after the Rape

Nancy recommended a group. "I don't really know what you're experiencing. It could really help to talk to other people who do." Nancy didn't offer any suggestions. She knew that I had to take the next steps on my own.

I sat on my couch and said the word out loud several times. "Rape. Rape." And slowly I said it to myself, "I was raped." "Peter raped me."

It took two months to learn to say it. I wanted to say it earlier. I wanted someone to hear it. I wanted someone to hear it and say, "My God, what has happened to you?" Someone to hold my arms from their thrashing, rub my stomach from its convulsions. Someone to yell "I love you" over and over until I really believed it.

I opened the yellow pages to *R* and found the Rape and Sexual Assault Center of Middle Tennessee. When the quiet, kind voice answered the phone, I repeated the awkward sounding phrase, "I was raped, and I need help."

I played with my hair, pulled on the edges of my clothing, and crossed and recrossed my legs. I longed for my favorite teddy bear. The counselor looked toward me and said, "Would you like to introduce yourself?"

Char already knew my story. We spent an hour doing the intake one-on-one before the group met. Char's gray hair was cut into a soft bob, and her clothes seemed to both hang and drape off her thin body at the same time. She always looked comfortable, which helped me to feel more comfortable. I liked that she received her doctorate at Vanderbilt. It made me feel like she understood what it was like to be a graduate student.

We sat around the edges of the room, two or three sharing a couch or sitting in comfortable stuffed chairs. I turned toward the six other women in the room and said it out loud again, "My name is Monica, I'm twenty-one, and I was raped."

Even though it was the middle of July, the room was dark and felt cramped. The shades were drawn. The room was decorated in olive green, dark blues, chocolate browns, and that neutral tan color in offices and spec houses that is supposed to appeal to everyone. It was as if we couldn't tolerate the light. That was the world out there and we needed another place, a different world, a transformed space, to tell our stories.

Of the seven of us, three were former alcoholics, five had children, and one was married. I was the only woman whose rape occurred within the previous two years. Four years. Six years. Fifteen years ago. It was clear: you could deal with rape, or rape would deal with you. Rape found its way into every part of your life—your job, your parents, your friends, your lovers—if you managed to ever have sex or love again. Even if this was the first time you ever told anyone, it left its mark on your life. It changed you, and people noticed the change. Even when it had no name.

Week after week, each woman shared what happened to her. Who knew. Who never knew. What they did. How they didn't do anything. How everything fell apart. Every. Thing. Noses turned red, Kleenex was passed around the room, and we cried. We cried when we realized that even years after the rape, there were still times when we needed someone to take care of us. We cried when we complained of the fear and anxiety we felt at night, or even around our closest male friends and relatives. We cried when we tried to imagine what it might be like to trust again, love again, or feel safe again.

Char's firm but reassuring voice comforted us. "You can stop whenever you want."

"No, I can do this," the storyteller replied. Deep breath.

It was so hard that I never expected to see a full room when I returned the following week. I knew that one harsh word stood between rubbing our eyes with Kleenex and bolting out the door into the sunshine and the quietness of secrecy. Each week, I was amazed that any of us were still alive. That we could still talk. That we could still walk upright, out of the shaded safety of that room, into the muggy sun—and back again in seven days. We returned, I suspect, because we didn't want to cry alone anymore. Because we preferred tears to paralysis.

"I don't sleep," one woman said.

We all nodded. We needed each other. We needed other people who understood us—from the inside out. Without explanation.

The group gave me the courage to talk about what happened to me. I began slowly. First with friends. Many of them knew Peter. Would they believe me?

My male friends took the role of the big brothers I imagined. They became angry and asked if I needed them to "take care of it." I loved the idea of one of them walking around Harvard's campuses, tracking Peter down between classes or on the way to the dorm, dragging him into a dark alley, and pummeling him into the bricks.

"No, you can't do that," I said time and time again. I smiled wide so that they could hear me through the phone. We laughed aloud. And they looked after me. They called to chat. About their grad school programs. About the weather. About nothing. They made sure I wasn't alone.

I wanted to tell Professor Weems. I wanted to explain myself somehow. Why I needed so much reassurance and direction. Why I needed another job. I called her and asked if we could meet.

I almost stammered when I asked, "Will you look at something I wrote? It's not long. A page or two." I wanted her to say yes. I didn't want to impose.

We met at the bookstore. I was already three mouthfuls into the pasta with artichokes and olives when she sat down.

I handed her the short piece. It began: "Rape. The sound of the word hurts my ears."

I continued to eat. I focused on my food. I was afraid of her gaze, afraid that she would tell me it was crap.

"It's good."

"You think?" I looked up. I smiled.

"Yes. It's good. It's fiction, right?"

"No."

Perhaps she put all the pieces together. My breakdown on the phone. My stumbling exit from her classes. Needing a job. The weariness on my face. Within seconds, she stood up, letting her bag fall to the floor. She moved to the other side of the small round table where we sat. She didn't cry, or look shocked. She bent over where I sat, and hugged me.

Professor Weems's response was an intensely personal version of what I encountered at Vanderbilt over my second year. One by one, I told my professors, and they all received me warmly—in their own way. Some gave me extra time in advising meetings. Others made a concerted effort to stop and ask me how I was doing.

My class in crisis ministry was the real turning point. We had to pick a crisis to research. I knew a crisis. I was in crisis. Since rape was all I could think about, I decided to research it. I approached the professor. She had that comforting voice I desperately needed.

"Are you sure you want to pick this for your topic?" She

looked me up and down, as if to see if I would crumble in front of her.

"Mm hmm."

"It might make things worse," she said.

"I think I can do it."

I went to the library. Ann Burgess and Lynda Holmstrom's "Rape Trauma Syndrome" in the *American Jounral of Psychiatry*. Judith Lewis Herman's *Trauma and Recovery*. Marie Fortune's *Sexual Violence*. Mary Pellauer's *Sexual Assault and Abuse: A Handbook for Clergy and Religious Professionals*. I learned that what I experienced was normal for a rape victim. I had words for what the six other women in the group and I struggled with. I learned that I had rape trauma syndrome. I learned that I had post-traumatic stress disorder. I heard about what prisoners of war went through. I saw television shows about Vietnam vets. I didn't know that abusive childhoods, domestic violence, and rape could cause the same effects. The things that so often happened to women were wars on our souls. I understood: you're not supposed to be okay.

It helped to read about what rape survivors typically experience. It didn't get me to sleep any faster. It didn't make me any less afraid. But it kept me from being frustrated with myself. The things I experienced were part of the process. They were part of the recovery process. It wasn't my fault. I wasn't weak. I was raped. I wasn't supposed to be okay.

These books were sparkly flecks in the muddy river of my life. I dipped my pan deeper because this was where the gold was. I read as much as I could—decades of articles and books by feminists who started rape crisis centers, psychologists who studied women's lives, and activists who gathered women's stories.

Understanding rape better didn't keep me from hurting. I still cried. A lot. Every day. Sometimes before I went to bed. Other times, I cried as I drove up the hill to my apartment complex, the tears blurring my vision, my hands barely steering, knowing where the turns in the road came. I pulled into a parking spot, pressed my forehead into the top of the steering wheel, and wailed. Snot dripped from my nose to my open mouth. I didn't care. I turned up the radio to drown out the sound.

In many ways, the knowledge gave me strength to heal. Understanding rape reminded me that it was okay not to be okay. I sat in class twirling the earring in my left ear. It probably looked like a nervous habit to my classmates. I turned my new knowledge over and over in my mind. I thought about Lanh. Yes, healing from rape was like knitting. Simple stitch by simple stitch. I survived each day by doing one regular thing after another. Counselors taught me the basics. I read some books. Like Lanh, I would teach myself the rest. I could count the good days.

I expected the emotional trauma because I knew there would be emotional healing. In the center of my being, I believed that this would not kill me. Even when it seemed as far away as Columbus, Ohio, I knew there was life and love after rape.

Omar and I hit it off immediately. We met through a common friend, exchanged numbers, and couldn't stop talking with one another. At six feet and two inches with a solid muscular frame, he made me feel secure in his embraces. I still didn't feel safe in my apartment. I cluttered it—with Theresa, with music, with books. Omar's house enveloped me. His interest in Africa was draped all around him. Wooden sculptures from various countries in Africa. Printed African cloth hanging between rooms like the string of beads in the 1970s. Paintings of black families interspersed with pictures of his family. The eye of the Egyptian deity Heru bent into silver on a chain around his neck. The aroma of spicy incense beckoned to me in the way a baking pie beckons toward the kitchen. I sat on the couch and flipped through books of poetry, back issues of the newspaper he published, coffee-table volumes of Nigerian art. I never knew how much I was holding my breath until I leaned into the crook of his arm and exhaled.

He talked about his marriage, divorce, and young daughter. He told me how he started his newspaper. He shared his career dreams with me. I told him about the rape, the survivors' group, and what I was reading. It was an easy and comfortable friendship.

He was substituting for an English teacher at one of the city's high schools. I often met him at the end of the day, blending in with the high school students when I dashed up the stairs to his classroom. I leaned against the desk while teenagers straggled out of the doors.

"Hey you." Sugar dripped off my words of greeting.

"Hey you." He smiled broadly. The hug again. But not as long. "The kiddies, you know."

"Yeah." I winked back.

He gathered his books and papers, stuffed them in a backpack. "Whatcha doing today?" We never assumed we would take up all of each other's time.

"Don't know. Been thinking about reporting."

"For real?" He looked up from our walk down the stairs. He held my hand. I kept talking.

"Yeah. I want to be counted. Like there needs to be a record of what happened to me."

"Yeah. How does it work?" he asked.

"Don't know. I guess I just go to the police station and tell them." I shrugged.

"Just like that?"

"I don't know how it works. But sure, why not? Just like that," I said.

"You can do it. You're strong enough." We leaned against the brick wall of the school, the sun beaming down on our faces. He held my hand tighter. I felt like a teenager meeting up with a boyfriend after school, before our parents came to get us. But we weren't teenagers, and I wasn't his girlfriend. He put his fingers to my chin. turning my face toward his. "You can."

We hugged again. I briefly kissed him on the cheek as if I were greeting him, not like I was walking away.

He called back when we were a couple feet apart. "Coleman?"

"Yeah?"

"Call me when you're done."

I smiled. "Cool." How hard could this be?

Technically, it was easy. I drove up to the station and said I wanted to report a rape. Mine.

When did it happen? Six months ago.

Are you okay? Pretty much.

Two other officers came. One was a woman. They asked me what happened. I told them. They gave me a yellow pad of paper and asked me to write it down. Again? I wrote it down. They took the pad away. I waited. They brought back a typed version of what I wrote. That looked right. Sign here. And here. I left names, phone numbers, addresses. It was simple.

There was no evidence. I took a shower.

They asked why.

What did they mean why? Because the bathroom door had a lock on it. Because I wanted to get clean. Because it was the most natural thing to do. What did they mean why?

Did you go to the doctor?

No.

Did you tell anyone?

How could I tell someone what I didn't tell myself?

What were you fighting about again?

Really?!

Three times in ninety minutes I said what took me three months to voice. But with details and contact information. To people I didn't know.

I drove home and called Omar.

"How'd it go?"

I told him about the yellow pad of paper and the pen that leaked. I told him about the guns riding on the officers' hips. "Is that supposed to make me feel safe?"

"Never much liked police," Omar said.

"Me neither. Rodney King and all." I was on the bed. I rolled from my back to my side. I eased into a fetal position. "Wish you'da come with me."

"You didn't ask. I would've," he said plainly.

"Didn't think it was a big deal. But I shoulda had a friend with me." I rested the phone against my cheek and reached for my teddy bear. I knew that I would be in bed for the next two days.

"I'm your friend."

"Thanks. That makes me smile."

I pulled myself through two days in bed and a week of classes. I told Mama and Daddy that I reported the rape to the police. I had told them both about the rape a couple months earlier on my summer trip home. At the time, they looked broken and sad. They asked if I was okay. They asked if I needed anything.

But now they were angry with me.

Each syllable came out distinctly:

What

Were

You

Think-

ing?

Don't you know what will happen? It could go to court!

171

You will have to tell everyone what happened! Everyone will know!

"It's not a secret. I didn't do anything wrong!" I yelled back.

"It will only make things worse," they insisted.

"That's not possible. It can't happen. Nothing . . ." I paused in the middle of my tirade. My tone was equal parts scream, cry, and defeat. "Nothing . . ." I began again. The tears choked my voice through the phone. "Nothing can be worse than being raped. Nothing."

"But I don't understand," Mama continued. "What will people think?"

"What will people think? What will people think? Is that what you are worried about?!"

In a separate phone call, Daddy sounded no different. "What will people say?"

I had them pegged. My parents didn't care about me. They cared about themselves and about their middle-class friends. About how it would make them look if people knew that I was raped. As if they somehow failed as parents. As if they failed to protect me.

To Daddy, I said, "I don't care about them. What about me? What about what I think? What about how I feel?" I tried to be calm and respectful. I was almost screaming. I knew he would say something about how I was "raising my voice at him."

He did.

He replied, "I don't care what you think or how you feel."

As he said these words, something in me broke. Or rather, something in me fused. I was raped, but I was no longer the teenage girl cowering at the kitchen table. The broken pieces in me gathered themselves into a mosaic that knew I was worth more. I was worth talking to someone who cared about my thoughts and feelings. I exhaled, lowered my voice, and spoke calmly to my father.

"I can't do this. I'm not doing this with you. I love you and I'm hanging up now."

Click.

It was okay with me if I never talked with him again.

In my conversations with Mama, I pleaded. "Just support me on this."

"But I don't understand why you're doing this."

I took a deep breath. "I know. But why do you have to understand? Can't you support me just because? Because I'm asking you to. Because I'm the only daughter you have. Because this is what our family does. You taught me that!"

"My baby," Mama cooed. She asked if I needed her to come to Nashville. "No, I know you have work." She offered care packages. "I'll take some Michigan bread if you can mail it."

I had no idea why reporting my rape caused such chaos for others. I thought that disclosing would liberate me. I thought I would become lighter with each telling. I thought I was reclaiming some of my own power by insisting on recognition.

I couldn't make Mama or Daddy understand. I needed them to help me. I needed them to hold me up. I just needed them to be on my side. Their inability to be what I needed made me feel disappointed in them. I concluded that their love didn't understand me. My family missed Theresa's pain. They missed mine. They loved me, but they couldn't see inside of me. I quietly concluded that I would have to find others who could see me. I always had.

There I was, trying to jump from one good day to the next one—when there might be weeks in between. I couldn't find the language. I lacked the energy. Everything I had went into getting up, getting dressed, eating breakfast, going to school. I was so focused on the everyday tasks of my life that I could not see beyond it. I didn't understand that rape unravels everyone's life. It ripped holes in the fabric of my being, but it also frayed the material of which Mama and Daddy were made. Rape leaves many victims in its path. Rape hurt me, but it also hurt people who love me. People who picked me up from my crib, rocked me in their arms, and vowed to protect me from all bad things in the world. I could not see that they were in crisis as well.

If I had read Lee Madigan and Nancy Gamble's *The Second Rape*, I would have known better. Madigan and Gamble describe how reporting rape to law enforcement often feels like another violation. They detail the humiliation and frustration of working in the criminal justice system. They talk about how taking legal action negatively affects one's loved ones. Reporting was not nearly as horrific for me as it was for the women in the book. But had I known this, I would have had someone go with me to the police station. I would not have told my parents that I reported. I would have been prepared for a bad day, a bad week, a bad month.

12

SILENCE

Nashville, Tennessee: Five Months after the Rape

In all my research and steps to healing, I was not prepared for what happened to my faith. I was a minister who wasn't talking to God. I didn't have anything to say. Church made that experience bearable. If I couldn't get to God myself, I could at least surround myself with those who found faith for themselves. What else would I have done on a Sunday?

Leaving Payne Chapel was a technicality. My degree program at Vanderbilt required a structured internship in a church. Payne Chapel was not one of the qualifying congregations. Scanning the list, I chose a church with a black female pastor. Until that point, I was trying to be something I hadn't seen. I looked forward to working with a black female pastor.

I met with the pastor of Payne Chapel one last time. We had an appointment, so he was expecting me. He leaned back in the padded leather office chair on his side of the desk. I slid into the chair on the other side. There were diplomas, plaques, and awards on the walls behind him. Recognition of service to the community, college degrees. A small television sat atop the file cabinet behind my head. He was watching the baseball game when I went in.

"Just wanted you to know what's going on with me." I sat upright. I wore the black-and-white suit uniform of clergy-in-training. I spoke clearly. I must have looked like I had it all together.

"Do I know him?"

"You've met him." Peter had come to church with me on visits before we broke up.

"Well, I've heard of things like this happening to other members in the church." The pastor paused and looked at the baseball game playing above my head. He turned back to me. "But no one's ever told me themselves."

I don't know what he said after that. He might have asked me if I was okay. He might have asked me about counseling. He might have asked me about Peter. I couldn't hear another word. I tracked his eyes moving from me to the baseball game behind me, and I knew I had to get out of the room. I made up some excuse. "I have another appointment." "Yes, I'm fine." "It's been a good year worshipping here." "God bless you too."

When the church door clanked behind me, I knew I'd never open it again.

I tried again. Sitting in the office of another black male pastor, I just knew I'd made a better choice. I visited the church before. There were female ministers in the pulpit. His preaching indicated that he knew something about people in pain. In a more spacious office, we were separated by the oak tabletop of his desk. He leaned forward, deeply interested in what I had to say, in why I asked for his time.

I began again.

"A couple of months ago . . ."

As I finished my story, he leaned forward and, using a gentle tone, began to ask questions. I only remember the first one.

"Why was he in your apartment to begin with?"

It was a simple question. Maybe he just wanted more of the story. After all, he didn't know me that well. Maybe he just wanted more of the story.

I didn't hear it that way. "Why was a man in your apartment?" "You let him in your space." "Were you teasing him?" "Did you give signals that you planned to have sex with him?" "What did you do to lead him on?" "You put yourself in that position?" "What did you expect?"

I cried for hours after the meeting. I told myself over and over again: "You have the right to trust someone you've known for a year and a half." "You have the right to think an argument will not lead to rape." "You do. You do."

In my head, I knew this was true, but inside, I replayed every hour, every moment. What if I had said something else? What if I had told him he had to leave? If, if, if.

I told myself that the internship church would be different. The pastor there was well known in the area as one of the few female pastors of a black church. The small church was located just two short streets off a main road. The bright blue carpeting that lined the sanctuary contrasted with the white painted wood of the altars and pews. It was a church, but it felt like a comfortable home. The pastor and I gathered Vanderbilt's paperwork and began to set up our supervisory meetings. She busied around the office, shifting papers and moving books while chatting with me.

She wore her hair in a short, relaxed bob that complemented the round shape of her face, and her dark-rimmed glasses were stylish without being trendy. She had pictures of her family on the desk. She seemed as excited about working with me as I was about learning from her.

I gave a short version of the story. "Earlier this year, I was raped. I'm still post-traumatic."

She moved her chair to the other side of the desk and sat quietly. She waited for me to say more. Her eyes asked, how are you?

"It's hard," I continued. "But I've been in a group. I've got a good therapist. I don't sleep much. I cry a lot."

She began to share with me. She didn't tell a long story either, but she said that she knew what I was going through. She was also a survivor. Of childhood sexual abuse.

I felt my muscles relax; my shoulders shifted down. My comfort became audible. "Yeah?"

"Yes. Now let me tell you," she continued. "Depression is a tool of the enemy. Cast it out in the name of Jesus."

My shoulders tensed up again. I felt my eyes become slits. I heard the sentences I wanted to say in my head: "Are . . . you . . . serious?! I'm *not* possessed by some demon.

Casting out will not help. I . . . am . . . a . . . victim . . . of . . .
rape. I'm not supposed to be okay!"

Is this what ministers tell people? Is this what they tell
people like me who finally muster up the courage to share?
That it's our fault? That the devil is making us sad? That
taking blame onto ourselves or doing some kind of exorcism
will heal us?! Do they preach this to people?!

I disclosed the rape to ministers like trying on new
shoes. Pick out a style, estimate the size, and slide foot
inside. Walk around, look down, look up, walk, look down.
Only to find out that the pretty looking shoes pinch the toes
or leave gaps in the heels.

I was in Nashville with no God and no church.
Nashville! Nashville! No Starbucks, no subways, no rude
people. No taxis to hail, no busy streets to run across. No
old bookstores with the stale smell of wisdom. No brick
sidewalks. I was in Nashville to be something I didn't want
to be any more. I turned my life upside down for a calling
from a God that I wasn't talking to. I changed my career
plans to be committed to some place that made me feel
worse when I left than when I entered.

I returned to living life in two colors again. There was
a bright and yellow side where I was healing. I went to
individual therapy. I went to group. I had a language for
what was happening to me. I wrote academic papers about
it. I knew I was not alone. I had friends who cared about me,
and I didn't fear my tears. I knew that they were part of the
process. I could sit in a chair and tell a near-stranger that I
was raped without falling apart.

Inside, however, I was gray. Listless and groundless. The faith that spent mornings in quiet time with God was gone. The faith that believed that God would deliver dissipated overnight. I had gotten in the habit of turning to God. I pressed toward the wooden altar of the church to make things better. But all of a sudden, I couldn't. It's not that I didn't want to. I just couldn't. I didn't trust God to take care of me. I didn't trust God to hear me. And I didn't trust the church to understand.

I kept this pain to myself. I didn't talk to Nancy about it. I didn't share it in group. When Tanya asked how God and I were doing, I simply said, "Pass." She didn't push me. Who else could I tell? Lanh? She burrowed deeper into the faith of Christian Impact. I closed the door. Bible studies and praise songs felt a million miles away. The police didn't care about my spirituality. And pious devotion—or a lack thereof—didn't type the footnotes to a term paper.

So I swallowed it. I expressed my frustration, but I swallowed the pain like a daily vitamin. The silence with God created a pit in my stomach. And there was no altar, no choir, no preaching to tide me over. I wanted to give up. I wanted to surrender my faith, my church, and my commitment to ministry. The night had won.

But I had to go back to church. My degree program required an internship. I had fellowships. I couldn't just quit.

I pored over the list of qualifying congregations once again. Time was marching on. It was mid-October. I needed to find a placement.

Halfway down the list, I saw it. Metropolitan Interdenominational Church. The place where my classmate took me that Saturday evening. The church that stayed open while I, the strange girl, cried in front of the plants. This one had to work.

Reverend Ed's office was a mess. There were books and papers from one end of the room to the other. In stacks, on the floor, on the tables. I'm not even sure if there was a desk under the cassette tapes on the far side of the room. Like a black Santa Claus, Reverend Ed stood over six feet tall with a salt-and-pepper beard and warm eyes. Eschewing the traditional clergy sensibilities, he wore the same thing every day. "My uniform," he said about the khaki pants, blue blazer, white shirt, and red striped tie. For worship, he replaced the jacket with a simple black clerical robe. I liked that he kept it simple. He opened the door wide for me to enter first.

I sat in the only other empty chair in his office, two or three feet from what was clearly his chair. He held the requisite paperwork from Vanderbilt. He listed the church's ministries.

Tuesday night prayer group. Wednesday night Bible study. Thursday noon worship. Saturday evening service. Sunday morning worship. Ministry with the children. The HIV/AIDS ministry.

"Does any of this sound right to you?" he asked.

"Here's the deal." Talking about rape had become a burden. "Last spring, I was raped. I'm post-traumatic. I don't know until I wake up if it's going to be a good day or a bad day. I don't know how I can contribute to the church. In fact, I really need someone to minister to me. Can you work with that?" My voice contained the weariness and exasperation that I felt. And probably more defensiveness than was appropriate. I was desperate. I had to land somewhere. I also had to be honest about where I was. Nowhere.

"Okay." Reverend Ed didn't move. He didn't lean over to touch and reassure me. He didn't ask any questions. He didn't suggest a magic formula for getting better. He put the paperwork in his lap, and looked me right in the eyes. "Okay."

"Why don't you just show up when you can? The ministry will find you."

I bit my top lip and blinked my eyes to keep from crying. *Show up when I can. Show up when I can. I can do that. I can do that. I. Can. Do. That.*

I knew then that I would be okay there. This church—or at least this pastor—knew what to do with people who had been victimized: don't ask us for much.

I inhaled and exhaled through my nose. I looked down before I returned his gaze. I smiled. "Okay."

Perhaps I was asking for too much. That's the first thing I thought when I found out that the district attorney wasn't taking the case. I should not have been surprised. I asked friends who were lawyers. Shit, I watched *Law and Order*. Word against word. He lived in another state. No rape kit. No evidence. I waited to report.

I was in the kitchen, books on the counter, dinner on the stove, when the phone rang. It was the beginning of someone's third shift, and she asked for me.

"We just want you to know. . . ." She wasn't mean. Just matter of fact.

I don't know what I expected of the police. I knew rape was a criminal offense and I didn't really want Peter to go to jail. I just wanted someone to know. Officially. I didn't really expect justice from the police. I knew way too much African American history for that. The refusal to prosecute wasn't about me. It's about whether or not they could win. And how much it might cost them to lose. I knew all this in my head, but I heard the news one way: I didn't matter.

Yes, I was counted, but no, I did not matter.

I called Omar and asked if I could go over. I needed to feel the embrace of his home, the incense, and his arms. I needed to be seen.

Within an hour, we were lying on his bed, staring at the glow-in-the-dark stars he adhered to the ceiling. We listened to Brian McKnight's sophomore CD. The half moon shone through the window and reflected off of the nine glasses of water on Omar's ancestral altar in the corner. Nine, for the ancestors, he told me the first time I went in his room. "Gotta honor them, you know."

Although I had learned about Yoruba religion at Harvard, Omar was the first person I knew well who practiced it.

Omar explained about the ancestor to whom he felt closest. "Obatala rules my head."

"The orisha of the white cloth," I replied.

"Yeah. So all the white." I thought to how Omar dressed when we were at his home—white jeans, white cap, white T-shirts.

"Cool."

The longer we lay on his low futon, the brighter the room became from the greenish sticker-stars and the nine round glasses. It started to hurt my eyes, so I closed them. I turned toward Omar.

"You wanna talk about it?" He asked me quietly, as if he if he were afraid of offending me but not like he was afraid of what I would say.

"No. I don't." I didn't ever want to talk about it again. "Can we just hang?"

"Yeah." He brushed the twists of my hair away from my face, sliding an arm beneath me. He pulled me into his chest. I craned my neck up, remembering his height again. I started kissing his collarbone, then his neck. I moved to his left ear. He pulled me on top of him; his hands slid below my waist. As we kissed, I removed his T-shirt. His arms rose above his head before returning to my body. I removed my shirt.

Our breathing heavy, he pulled back. I admired his muscles, the curly hair below his navel. I moved my nose toward his belly button. Mmmm.

"Coleman?"

"Mari." I used my nickname for him. I tickled my tongue amid that hair below his navel.

"No, look, look at me," he said.

I looked up to his face. I pressed my fingers into his fade.

The curls on the top of his head made two complete loops. I pulled them out gently between the nails of my index finger and thumb, and watched them bounce back.

"C'mon. Sit up," he said.

"What . . . is . . . up?!" A little attitude dripped from each word. "You're killing the mood here," I said. I gave a half giggle.

"I need you to tell me," he said.

"What?"

On the third repeat of the album, I heard Brian McKnight sing: "Lucy and Linus and Charlie Brown, Oh how Snoopy never left the ground, Oh that is true, You remember me like I remember you." A song about being children. I felt very adult. For the first time in months.

"Tell me," he said. "Tell me what you want." He was kind, but insistent.

"I want you."

"You want me what?"

"I want you, Mari. I want this. I want to . . ." I couldn't find the words. I couldn't call it lovemaking. We didn't love each other. We liked each other. We respected each other. That was better than love.

"I want to have sex."

We sat straight up on the mattress. It seemed dark again. I could only see the contrast between his dark brown skin and my own fair skin in our interlaced fingers.

"Are you sure?" He looked directly in my eyes.

I smiled. "Yes."

"Are you sure?" he asked again. Not joking. Not flirting. Just asking.

"Yes, I'm sure," I repeated.

"Tell me again."

"Again?" I asked. This time, gently tickling his stomach, I pressed myself against him, both of us falling back on the bed.

"Again," he whispered loudly.

"Yes." I kissed his cheeks. "Yes." I nuzzled my nose into his chest. "Yes," as I reached for the button on his jeans. "Yes," as I moved his hands into my pants.

Yes, yes, yes.

On the first yes, I was a rape victim. A couple yeses later, I was a number in the state statistics. By the last yes, I was a woman again. A beautiful, attractive woman whose no was previously ignored, and whose yes was deeply honored now.

Good day.

13

DINAH PROJECT

Nashville, Tennessee: Eight Months after the Rape

I asked for a ceremony.

"Reverend Ed?"

"Yes, daughter?" I liked that he thought of me as a surrogate child. He was quickly becoming a father figure to me.

"Can I have a minute with you, after church? To ask you something? . . . I'm wondering if I can use the church space for a small ceremony. A ritual."

For the previous two months, I showed up at Metropolitan.

Tuesday night prayer circle.

Wednesday night Bible study.

Saturday evening service.

Sunday morning service.

I did minister things. I read litanies. I said prayers. I handed tissues to people who cried. I stood when everyone else stood. I sat when everyone sat. When people closed their eyes in prayer, I kept mine open: scanning the sanctuary to see who looked distressed or puzzled. To see whom I needed to stand next to with words of prayer. To see to whom I should bring tissues. I tried to pay attention and anticipate people's needs before they expressed them. I was as much a minister-fraud eight months after the rape as I was in the days that followed the rape. I was talking about God, but I was not talking to God. This church knew and didn't care.

The more time I spent in the church and in the Nashville community, the more I realized that Metropolitan was known for welcoming the people with whom no one else wanted to worship. This church was known for its members who were known or suspected to be HIV-positive, crack and alcohol-addicted, openly homosexual, and homeless. This church was known as "the gay church," "the AIDS church," and the "AA church." Reverend Ed explained our reputation simply: "For God so loved the world that He gave His only begotten Son so that *whosoever* believes in Him should not perish but have everlasting life." I had heard John 3:16 more times than I could count, but this church simply said one word in return to my empty stares: whosoever. We were known as a church of "whosoevers." Just two months at Metropolitan and I knew that this was an accurate portrayal. The open attitude attracted whosoever poor, whosoever disenchanted with other churches, whosoever gay, and whosoever straight. We had whosoever wealthy and whosoever homeless, whosoever sick, whosoever black, and a couple of whosoever whites. We were known for loving and accepting those no one else would, and, in that season of my life, I needed "whosoever" to be me.

This was probably no surprise to anyone in the church. When I wasn't being a minister-fraud, I was crying. After the sermon, when people were invited to come to the altar and pray. In the hour before service, when I used my key to let myself in, disable the alarm, and play the piano. In the hour after service, when all but the church leaders left and I sat before the potted plants. In the front of the church, while the choir sang a song that perfectly expressed how much I needed God. I cried because everything still hurt. I cried because I was tired of the energy it took to go to school, go to church, just leave the house. I cried because I missed God.

I trusted God enough to think that God heard me. But I could not find words for God. I could not feel God. And I could not feel peace.

Rituals were supposed to help. That's what all my reading told me. When we aren't paying attention, rituals get into our skin and teach us about our deepest values. They reassure us of community. Professor Weems writes, "Rituals are routines that force us to live faithfully even when we no longer feel like being faithful. Until our heart has the time to arouse itself and fits its way back to those we love, rituals make us show up for duty." You take the wafer and juice. Eventually you learn that you are forgiven and you can forgive. You pour water over children. Eventually you learn that community grows one person at a time. You go into buildings with people who share your faith, and eventually you learn that you are not alone in the world. And when the old rituals don't work, you create new rituals that embody the lessons and values you want to impart. That's what the books were telling me.

"I think I need a ritual. A ceremony."

Reverend Ed looked at me and waited for me to continue.

"A healing ritual. Like a laying on of hands."

Something that would make touch holy for me again. Something that would make embracing warm again. Something that would stop me from being afraid when a stranger accidentally brushed up against me in a crowded room.

"I think I can invite some friends. People close to me who know." I needed other people. Not because one needs people for ritual. I needed them for their faith. I needed people who were still on speaking terms with God. If people with great faith in God could surround me, and they stood in a circle around me, and put their hands on me . . . I might feel human again. I might be healed. I hoped their faith would transfer into me through their palms. I hoped their strength would seep into my spirit. It might not work that way, but it couldn't hurt. It had to be better than the oscillation between student, minister-fraud, and human geyser that I had become.

"So," I continued, "maybe one evening at the end of the month, while my friends are on Christmas break."

Reverend Ed leaned back in his chair. Without letting

much time pass, he replied. "Monica, that's fine. But I think it could be bigger. I want you to pray about this. I think it could be bigger."

In that moment, with my own desperation for the faith of my friends and my pastor's word "bigger," the Dinah Project was born.

The Dinah Project was named for Dinah, the daughter of the biblical figure Jacob, whose story of rape is told in Genesis 34. Actually, the Bible does not tell the story of her rape. It tells the story of what all the men around her—her father, her brothers, her rapist, and his father—do after she is raped. Genesis 34 is about how Jacob negotiates her bride price, how her brothers kill the men in the village of her rapist, how the Israelites end up in a war with the neighboring tribe. It's not about Dinah. A fellow minister suggested the name "Dinah" when Reverend Ed announced the initiative during a staff meeting. "Monica is working on a project for women who have experienced intimate violence."

"People who have been raped," I said with a less gentle touch.

I never noticed Dinah. I read the entire Bible at least twice between my own curiosity and divinity school assignments, but I never noticed Dinah. She never speaks. There were no sermons about her. She was practically invisible. Yes, that was the perfect name for a ministry about sexual violence. When there were no bleeding wounds or television reports about what a stranger did in a parking lot, the closet, or one's bedroom, survivors of sexual violence felt invisible. Like our pain could not be seen to those around us.

Reverend Ed kept encouraging me to think bigger. I was so focused on my own need for healing, faith, and community that it was a struggle to think that an entire ministry could come out of this pain. But I knew what Reverend Ed was trying to say: There are others. They need what you need.

The Dinah Project, or just "Dinah" as I came to call it in my mind, was an attempt to give other people like me what I needed. "Dee-nah," said my Hebrew Bible professor, reminding students that there is no long *i* sound in the ancient Hebrew language.

So I returned to all the books I read. The books affirmed that churches don't do much in the face of sexual violence. They say that churches should do something. Ministers should do something. They detail all the issues that arise in pastoral care. And the important theological issues. And the critical ethical issues. And the anguish that survivors of sexual violence feel when nothing is done.

I completely agreed. But they didn't tell me what to do. I had to figure that out.

If Dinah was invisible, if I felt invisible, I had to do something that said "bigger." I needed something that said, "There are others." I needed something that said, "You're not crazy. You're just in pain. But you are not alone." I needed something that said, "God has not abandoned you. God is right here. Loving you." "And until you feel that, we, the church, will stand in the gap."

These are the kind of things I needed to hear. I needed to hear them over and over and over again until I started to believe them. And if I, who read and researched and stood behind a pulpit every Sunday, needed them, then I could only guess how many more people needed to hear them.

Dinah was the only ministry I could do because rape was the only thing happening in my life. Therapy, research, classes on religion and sexuality. Every morning when I woke up, I was aware that I was raped. Eight months after the rape, most days I felt like I did when I first called the crisis center: "Hello, my name is Monica, and I was raped."

We started with worship. What is more public, more communal, or more visible than worship? Reverend Ed gave me a couple hundred dollars, a date, and freedom to plan. I forgot about my personal laying-on-of-hands ritual. I delved into this new ministry. It took months to make it happen. Church members volunteered to help. Professor Weems agreed to preach; I used litanies from the books I read; I sent out press releases. Dinah was born.

I took all my spiritual needs and wrapped them up in Dinah. In a way, it was hugely self-centered. I projected my wants and my hopes and my desperate need to have my faith restored onto an entire church and entire community. I imagine that's how it looked to some people too. But I also think that my personal experience informed the work of ministry. I think it's an asset to know firsthand about the people we want to engage.

The truth is that I needed Dinah. I needed Dinah to help me celebrate that no matter how empty I felt inside, I was actually still alive and pretty sane when the first service took place. I needed Dinah for the places that were still hollow. I needed Dinah so that my pain was not in vain. I needed Dinah to be the church I didn't find every time I sat in a pastor's office and relayed my story. I needed Dinah to assure me that I was still a minister, not just a fraud. I needed Dinah to find the other people out there like me—the people who might have had therapy or gone through the legal system or been to the hospital but still didn't know how to pray. I needed Dinah for community. Most of all, I needed Dinah to show me the way back to God.

As I opened my story to the world through Dinah, I also opened my heart to love. Omar and I were still friends, but we were not in love. After our night together, we returned to the friend zone. The day love reappeared, my morning scripture meditation took me to the thirtieth verse of Psalm 104: "And God shall renew the face of the earth." Nearly a year after the rape, I felt like God was renewing the face of my world. With the first Dinah Project event in the planning, I was actually enjoying ministry. Individual members of the church connected with me and sat next to me during Bible study, asking questions, sharing their lives, looking for a word of comfort. After months of feeling like I was falling apart, I realized that I didn't have to be whole to be present for others. Whatever sanity I had, came from God. I clung to the scripture in 2 Corinthians 4: "But we have this treasure in earthen vessels, that the excellency of the power may be of God, and not of us. We are troubled on every side, yet not distressed; we are perplexed, but not in despair; persecuted, but not forsaken; cast down, but not destroyed."

I met Darrell at a conference for black students in seminary. Instantly, I was attracted to his preppy style of striped dress shirts and tailored navy pants with the belt matching the shoes. I found myself looking for excuses to touch him casually during conversation. A hand to the shoulder when he said something funny. A brush against his pant leg when crossing my legs.

Our attraction for one another grew as we realized how much we had in common. We were both in divinity school. We both attended elite colleges. We both were active in evangelical Christian campus organizations—InterVarsity for him, Campus Crusade for me. Neither of us had met many black people who knew the songs that these largely white organizations sang during worship. We shared our favorites. We both knew what it meant to have quiet times, to be disciplers, and to teach Bible study in a college setting.

When I asked Darrell about his quiet time that morning, he pulled a Bible out of his briefcase. It was marked with pen, pencil, and highlighter and stuffed with sheets of paper.

I laughed a bit. "My Bible looks like that too."

He smiled and opened to the book of Psalms, "When you send your spirit, they are created."

I spoke along with him, knowing the rest of the verse from memory: "and God shall renew the face of the earth."

"That's an obscure verse to know, Miss Monica," he said, invoking a nickname I instantly liked.

"It was my meditation this morning," I said with both calm and surprise. This was the kind of resonance Lanh and other friends in Crusade talked about when they described how they met their spouses. They said God brought them together. They talked about scripture. I thought that that was what was supposed to happen in Christian dating. I was surprised that it was unfolding in my life.

"For real?" he asked.

"Yeah." I leaned in closer to him to read the rest of the psalm with him. We talked about what this meant in a world of environmental change. We talked about what it meant for the churches where we worked. We talked about what it meant in our lives. I told him about Dinah, and he listened. He didn't look at me like a rape victim. He looked at me like a fellow minister.

After minutes of silence, he leaned toward me.

I stroked the shaven shadow of his caramel-colored cheek with the back of my forefingers. I moved my hand to hold the back of his fade.

The kiss led to months of plane travel between the cities in which we lived, as we developed a relationship that we believed God was anointing. During the summer months, we spent weeks on end with each other. During our last year in seminary, we traveled to his preaching engagements together.

I spent most of the relationship in awe that I could actually love and trust again. It happened one idiosyncrasy at a time. We bought devotional books for couples so that we could read and focus on the same scriptures every day. We prayed together on our knees whenever we made important decisions. We shared about our previous relationships and vowed to wait until marriage for sex. I learned his habits: the way he made an old dot-matrix printer portable by wrapping it in towels and packing it in his suitcase, the fact that he wrote sermons between one and three o'clock in the morning, how many T-shirts he wore under his dress shirts and how he tucked them in layer by layer. We developed code numbers so we could page each other when one or both of us was in class: 001 for "I love you," 002 for "I miss you," 003 for "Call me soon."

I was surprised that I loved Darrell. I was surprised that Darrell loved me. I was surprised that love came so easily and in such small acts.

Loving Darrell reminded me that I once loved Peter, and remembering that helped me to forgive him. I remembered that I once chose to love Peter, just as I chose to love Darrell. I remembered that there was something lovable in Peter.

Reverend Ed said that forgiveness comes by finding kinship with the person you are trying to forgive. I didn't want kinship. I didn't want to have anything to do with Peter. I'm not even concerned with following a divine edict to forgive. I just remembered that Peter was lovable. By someone. At one time, that someone was me.

I practiced writing it in my journal. "The man who raped me." I wanted to see what he did as something he did, not as the totality of who he was. Someone loved him. He was also someone's son, someone's brother, and someone's friend. He was more than "a rapist." He was also a man who sang for me and cooked for me. Remembering this didn't make me love him again. He was still "the man who raped me." Remembering this made him human.

For 95 percent of the time, acknowledging Peter's humanity and his relationality to other people is my version of forgiveness. It is sufficient to free me from the vitriol I feel when I imagine his face or the sound of his voice. But there is still a 5 percent: after nightmares, around the anniversary, when I edit my own written thoughts because I fear someone will read the words of my journals. In those moments, I hate him. I hate him with all of my being. I feel it surge in me from an empty place in my stomach, up my chest, and out my eyebrows. I hate him. I hate what he's done to me. I hate what he's done to my life. I hate what he's done to the people who love me. I hate what he's done to my future: will I always have to explain to potential partners that I am a survivor of rape? So please go slowly.

I don't eschew this 5 percent place. I assume it will always be in me. I don't see it as a personal or spiritual failing. Rather, it makes me human.

The ability to love and to forgive after the rape was nothing short of miraculous for me. Speaking in tongues and walking on water were nothing. I knew that miracles were the impossibilities around me: feeling secure in ministry again, loving after violence, sleeping through the night.

Darrell and I imagined a future together from the

beginning of the relationship. We believed that God brought us together and that God would keep us together. We treated our dating like an engagement. "Breaking up is not an option," we repeated to one another. I knew I could be angry and fight with him, but it would not end the relationship. We met each other's families and priced engagement rings. We picked a city to live in after graduation. We went on outings with other couples. Darrell flew in for major events of the Dinah Project. I flew to the East Coast twice a month.

I felt like I was returning to the life I imagined for myself before the rape. I was a minister with a ministry that meant something to me. I was in love with someone who understood that. I had a man who prayed with me. I imagined dressing our children for church. I imagined a church volunteer watching them on the front row while we both took our places in the pulpit. We would be a ministry team!

The Dinah Project ministry grew into more than I expected. Within a year, there were preachers coming from around the country to preach and teach, Bible studies, trainings for clergy, trainings for social service workers, collaborations with the local crisis center, activities for children, and group therapy. We had an advisory board, with Carol, a church member who was also a psychiatrist, serving as my chief advisor. I spoke on local radio shows, local television programs, Take Back the Night events on college campuses, and national conferences.

It wasn't easy. I talked about rape all the time.

Classmates told me what their pastors said about me: "Well, you see those skirts she wears. . . ." "She's probably a flirt." I could only imagine what people said to folk who weren't my friends. I had a script for speaking out so I wouldn't have to actively recall the rape each time I spoke about it. But when it came time for questions and answers, there I was again, talking about that night, the weeks afterward, and what churches could do. Some days, it dealt blows to my self-esteem. I went out for ice cream before heading home.

The Dinah Project drove me back to the classroom. I constantly encountered people who had up-close intimate experiences of suffering. I wrote my master's thesis on Dinah, but I still had questions. I could not tell people that they were sexually violated for a reason, or that God had a plan, or that all things were working together for their good. But what could I say? I needed tools for writing sermons that could speak to them and their experiences. With just one semester left in my degree program, I decided to audit a class on how to preach on themes of suffering and evil. The instructor believed that preaching emerges from what one deeply believes, and so we spent a lot of time exploring our beliefs about suffering and evil.

The professor assigned a book on process theology. Process theology offers a way of talking about God and the world that affirms that everything is constantly changing. Process thought talks about a God who is radically present. It explains that God is present with everyone at all times in all things. God is not just present with us but knows us better than anyone else. God knows us from the inside out.

And as God knows us, God feels with us. God rejoices in our happiness and weeps in our sorrows. Process theology also says that God takes our freedom seriously. God gives us real freedom to operate in the world the way that we choose. God doesn't coerce. God calls. God calls all of us to relationships of beauty and peace. But people use their freedom in all kinds of ways—and sometimes we say no to what God hopes for us. This made sense to me.

I told the people I worked with that God hopes for justice and beauty and adventure in the world. God calls each of us to do our parts to help make this happen. Sometimes people say no to that call. That often creates evil and suffering in the world. The assault was not willed by God—let alone a devil. The person who assaulted did not heed God's call. But God is with us. In our broken, hurting, weeping ways, God is there. God weeps with us. That was what I began to tell the people I met in the Dinah Project.

I didn't take the class just to help me become a better minister; I also processed my own ideas about suffering. The suffering I experienced after the rape changed everything in my world. It changed my relationships, my affiliations, and my faith. The rape reminded me that I was not safe. I did not do anything wrong. And God did not protect me. God did not intervene to stop Peter like God parted the Red Sea or tumbled the walls of Jericho. My silence with God was my way of asking: where are you, God? Process theology suggested that God was crying every tear with me. God might, in fact, have wept more because God cried with me and for Peter—weeping for Peter's pain, weeping for what

Peter did to me. God wept tears I would probably never cry. Process theology also suggests that God called me. God did not make me become a minister or force me to start Dinah. God called.

I knew this was my calling. I wasn't called to pastor or visit the sick or preach every Sunday. I wasn't called to help the homeless or feed the hungry. Dinah was my calling. Unlike my call to ministry, I didn't ask God or wait for a response. (After all, God and I weren't on speaking terms.) I just knew. I knew that God wanted me to talk about Dinah, and since God wanted me to do it, I knew God would give me the courage I needed to do it.

Courage came in sporadic bursts right when I was ready to quit. When it seemed that my words fell on apathetic audiences or I heard yet another remark about what I must have done to provoke the rape, something happened. An e-mail. A letter. A whisper after church. A rape survivor told me what a difference a Dinah Project event made in her life. How the sermon touched a part of her heart. How he never heard anyone talk in church about what sometimes happens to little boys. How now he understood what happened to his daughter and had an idea of what to say. This was how I knew Dinah wasn't all me. This was how I knew that Dinah was about God.

I gave my life to Dinah. No matter what I did at school or what I did for a living, everything was Dinah. I woke up, I thought about Dinah. I went to bed thinking about Dinah. When I graduated from divinity school, I worked two or three jobs at once so I could afford to work at the

Dinah Project for nearly free. I reached that stage that the books talk about—owning my own power, telling my story, becoming an activist.

And then Darrell and I broke up. Between the two of us, it was peaceful. We prayed together and went bowling. We concluded that we tried but were wrong. We weren't meant to be. When I talked to others, I said it the only way I understood it: "I've got Dinah here in Nashville. He's got the church where he is. God is calling us to grow where we are. And," my voice lowered, "that's not in the same place."

Once alone, I cried. I wept as if he trampled my heart. These were the tears of someone who was cheated on or abused. I cried on the way to class, at the gym, in the shower, and at home at night.

I could not name what I slowly came to know. I wasn't just crying. I was mourning. My connection to Darrell was largely our love for the songs and spiritual practices of Crusade and InterVarsity. We spoke the same spiritual language. We had the same faith. We dreamed of being ministers in churches. In dating him, I was reaching back for the faith I knew. The faith that brought me to ministry. I desperately wanted to be who I was, and to believe like I did. I knew and understand that faith. I knew and understood what the future looked like with that faith. My dreams with Darrell were how I imagined ministry and love and career unfolding. Dating Darrell was my last taste of the life I had before the rape. It didn't work. Neither dating Darrell nor Dinah helped me feel God again. I did all the right things: I prayed. I ministered. I preached. I organized. I read. I wrote papers. I had quiet times. I even forgave. I wasn't static, but I lost the feeling. I could not find my way into intimacy with God.

14

THE DANCE

*Nashville, Tennessee: Two and a Half Years
after the Rape*

"I had come into the city carrying life in my eyes amid rumors of death."

Black Arts poet Sonia Sanchez says these words over Sweet Honey in the Rock's rendition of "Stay on the Battlefield" on their *Sacred Ground* album.

This line well summarized the way I felt. As though I were supposed to be the bearer of life among a world and people who were the living dead. After graduating from Vanderbilt, I worked with victims of sexual violence and victims of domestic violence. Every day, I worked with women—and sometimes men—who lived close to the threat of death. Some faced it in their homes; others wrestled with the aftermath of violence from years ago. Honestly, I was still in a spiritual haze from my own encounter with violence, so I knew something about the living dead. But I also knew something about life. I knew it was possible to have a life after rape. I knew that people could offer life to others. I extended hope, safety, or maybe just my presence. I heard Sonia Sanchez and Sweet Honey talking about community activism and social justice work. Ministry. Dinah.

"I had come into the city carrying life in my eyes amid rumors of death."

I made this line the signature on my e-mails.

Korey recognized the verse. My signature verse was automatically attached to an e-mail I sent to the black graduate student and alumni Listserv at Vanderbilt. Korey, a doctoral student in history, e-mailed me back: "Is that from a song by Sweet Honey in the Rock?"

I was impressed. The folk singing civil rights acapella group has their own following—primarily of women. Here was a man who knew Sweet Honey in the Rock well enough to recall a line from a song on an album that was over ten years old.

I typed back, "Yes. One of my favorites."

Several e-mails later and we agreed to meet at a local poetry club. We laughed when we met because we'd seen each other at previous events at the club. We embraced each other tentatively. I was drawn to this deep brown man with long dreadlocks, silver hoops in his eyebrows and ears, and eyes the color of Godiva-dark-chocolate-cherry-cordials-when-you-lick-them-before-you-bite-in. He liked books. He liked music. We began to talk. We began to date.

He was a drummer. He drummed through high school

and college, and in Nashville, at the Village. "You should come by the Village and dance some time."

The Village was Nashville's African-centered cultural arts center. They offered an after-school program and summer camp for children, but they were best known for the drum and dance classes. Housed in a bright yellow renovated warehouse, the dance floor occupied most of the space. The shop with jewelry, the waiting area, the women's locker room, and carpeted border altogether took up less than an eighth of the space. You could rarely enter the Village without hearing the sound of drums and seeing women, children, or men dancing. The Village Drum and Dance Ensemble danced around the community—at street fairs, art shows, schools, and cultural festivals.

The lead drummer at the Village also played the drums at Metropolitan Church. He told me to come by some time. Take classes.

I kept saying that I couldn't afford it. Graduate student budget and all. After graduating, I said, "Well, you know I work nonprofit, right? On a budget." Outside of the party and club scene, I never danced. Doing the running man, cabbage patch, Kid 'n Play, or even Bankhead Bounce to a DJ is different from ballet, jazz, or tap. That was real dancing. West African dance looked tremendously difficult.

"Don't worry about the money," he yelled back each week as I scooted out the door of the church.

At Korey's invitation, I drove to the Village one weekday evening for dance class.

The first few times I went to dance class, I was quiet and

shy. I didn't know the other class members, who seemed unified in friendship and dance. I stumbled across the floor and hobbled back in line, tired and exhausted. When I was close to the drummers, Korey said snidely, "Struggling?"

I was struggling. I thought of myself as being in good shape, but dancing was more intense than running or lifting weights. It was over an hour of intense cardiovascular activity. I started going to the gym just so I could be in shape for dance class. Still I struggled.

Da-dada-da-dada-da-da. This was becoming a familiar sound. It's the sound of a break. When the drummers play that sound, the drum beat changes, the movement of the dance changes.

"Listen to the drums," the instructor said. "Don't just count the beat, listen to the drums. Start after the break. Change on the break."

"I don't hear the break, I can't remember the movements," I told the instructor.

"You will," she reassured me. "Just stick with it.

Almost two months into dance class and Korey stopped teasing me. One evening before class, Korey leaned over to me while removing his drum from its bag: "Monica, you are trying too hard. Stop trying so hard. You know the steps. Just feel it."

I tripped down the floor once again.

"Just feel it," he mouthed from the end of the dance floor. "Just feel it."

I stopped thinking about putting my right foot first and arching my arm. I stopped thinking about a straight back

210

and the direction in which to rotate my hips. I let the motions take over my body. Arm curved up to the right, arm curved up moving across my body to the left, back and head then down, head and back up, do it again. Arm curved right leads me into a circle, left arm led me to turn the other way, dance forward with my shoulder leaning. My body did the motions. Da-dada-da-dada-da-da. I felt it! Before I knew it, I was on the other end of the dance floor.

The women in the class rushed me. They clapped and hugged me. "You got it, sister, you got it!" I smiled. I was part of the group.

Twice a week, I was at the Village to dance. I put all my stress and energy into the movements. Into my feet and legs and arms and back and head. And back into the world. Da-dada-da-dada-da-da. I danced toward Korey's drum.

Da-dada-da-dada-da-da. Dada-da dada-da dada-da dada-da.

Unlike dancing to a DJ, this dance meant something. These movements meant something to the people who originally danced them. It reminded me of the woman in Professor Matory's video. Professor Lorand Matory was the anthropologist who taught my West Afro-Atlantic Religions class during my junior year at Harvard. One class session, he wheeled a VCR and TV into the classroom. He pressed "play."

There was a woman turning and spinning. She threw her head back and walked tall and proud. She walked toward another person in the circle around her; she resumed the dance. The drums in the background gave the rhythm for her dance: da-dada-da-dada-da-da. The woman changed her movement. The camera shot in black and white, and the dark-colored dress moved right along with her. She never lifted the skirt to give her legs freedom. Professor Matory fast-forwarded the videotape a bit; she turned. "She has been dancing for hours," he quietly commented from the side of the monitor. Her dancing slowed, she stopped. She fell to ground and appeared to faint. Women rushed in around her, tending to her needs. Massaging her arms and legs? Giving her water? I couldn't tell. As they were tending to her, the camera moved to the drummers—still drumming. Da-dada-da-dada-da-da. Done.

"The woman is possessed by an orisha." Professor Matory told us of his fieldwork among the Oyo-Yoruba in southwestern Nigeria. A devotee of this traditional religion might be male or female, but this time a female was possessed. By an orisha, the ancestors who reside above one's familial ancestors; the ancestors with stories and adventures and faults and strengths and associations with nature. "She was mounted by Shango. Who is?" He turned to the class. We had just memorized the characteristics of major orisha for the last quiz.

"Thunder and fire," said one student.

"The color red. Lightning," chimed another.

"The husband of Oya, the whirlwind, the woman who walks among the graves," I added.

"Exactly," approved Professor Matory. There was pleasure and pride mixed into the toothy smile he gave when his students grasped the material. Professor Matory explained the video. The orisha came into—he mounted, he possessed—the human, well, "host." You could say the person was hosting the spirit of the orisha, but indeed she or he became the orisha. The woman could not be told that she was not Shango. She had Shango's characteristics, his mannerisms, his dance, his bad habits and his good ones. The drummers recognized Shango and played his rhythm. Shango came for a reason because it is not his festival. He was there to convey a message to the people. To tell them something they needed to hear. This is one way the Yoruba connect with their past and their gods. It is also how the past and the gods connect with them. The dance means something.

At the Village, the dance instructors told us the stories of the dance and taught us the songs that accompany each dance. We sang in a call and response.

Kuku, the dance of the harvest. The motions symbolize planting the seeds, picking the crops, giving thanks to the Creator for the harvest. Dundunba, the dance of the warrior, a strong heavy dance with stomping and raised arms. Ekonkon, another harvest dance. And Mandiani, a rite-of-passage dance for girls.

They taught us to recognize the dance by the beat of the drum.

"Listen," they admonished. "The drum will tell you everything. It will tell you what dance, when to start, when to change, when to finish. Listen to the drum."

I danced. I danced with other women for hours every week. We danced the harvest, the fast strong rhythm of the warrior, the praises to earth and ancestor. It wasn't just a workout. We learned the language of the drum and danced the cycles of life.

It was hard to allow my nonintellectual senses to guide me. I had to cultivate and rely on my ears, my feet, and my own spirit.

I danced ancient rhythms. I danced for the ancestors. I danced the harvest for Grandma and her siblings who picked cotton for low wages. I danced the harvest for Nana who taught me how to make biscuits and cakes. I danced the warrior for Granddaddy who tried to be strong for his family but didn't know how. I danced for my family ancestors. I danced with them.

I was surprised by how much it felt like worship. I adopted the stories of the dance as my own. I knew the labor of working hard. I felt the joy of reaping that reward. I wanted to transition from one phase of life into another. I danced and sang. I danced and prayed. I danced and thanked. I danced and celebrated. My body spoke in ways my voice could not: Thank you for the earth. Thank you for the harvest. Thank you for my sisters. Thank you for the ancestors. Thank You. Thank . . . God.

This was where I began to feel God again. After the crying. Outside of the Bible and church and even Dinah. With sweat running down my face, torso, and arms. With callused bare feet. In a renovated warehouse. With African cloth tied around my waist. The dance did for me what years of ministry, church, and Bible reading did not. It returned me to God. It returned me to God the same way I lost God—through my body.

My body became my words. The dance became prayer. The chanted songs became scriptures. The drum was the choir. Moving down the dance floor, toward the drum, I found faith again.

A random e-mail, Korey's response, and a couple months of our casual dating got me back to God.

Korey lived in my old apartment complex, the one I lived in during the rape. Dating Korey was my first return to the complex after I moved out. I moved to a small house on another side of Nashville when I graduated from Vanderbilt. I was surprised by how much a change of scenery helped. In the move, I threw out the sheets and bedspreads Mama and I bought with the new bed that marked my graduate school journey. I guess that's why I never thought to get rid of them earlier. Why hadn't I thought of that before? Why did I keep the sheets? Why didn't I move? Why hadn't a therapist suggested it? Why did it take me so long to realize that I was living in and amid everything about the rape?

Korey didn't know about the rape. He didn't know me as an activist or minister. He knew me as the woman who danced toward his drum at the Village. He knew me as someone who loved black poetry and history. For just a moment, in that relationship, I got to be the regular woman I was before ministry and before the rape.

I stood in the bathroom mirror behind Korey with a piece of Godiva chocolate.

"Look," I said, licking the cherry cordial. "Your eyes really *are* this color."

"You are so silly!" Korey turned around, put his hands on my waist, and pulled me toward him.

We sat on the couch to talk about graduate school, music, and families. He was nice. I relaxed. Before we knew it, hours passed. Korey said that I should not drive home. It was too late. "Just stay."

Then the clanging. I cursed his neighbor for hanging a metal wind chime on the balcony. It was rainy and windy outside, and the damn wind chime kept banging into the wooden pole on which it hung. But something else was wrong. I started itching from the inside out. I left the bedroom and turned the lights on. I paced the hallway. I wanted to go home, but it was too late and too dark to walk out to my car and drive home alone. I watched early morning TV in the living room while Korey slept. But I didn't like being alone. I wrapped myself in a blanket, sitting straight up in the bed next to Korey. Watching him sleep. Cursing his neighbor. Waiting for the sun to rise. Waiting for Korey to wake up. Waiting for the morning. Itching, itching, itching inside.

In the calm of the morning, the wind chime stopped its clatter. The sun was up. Korey looked at me compassionately.

"Didn't sleep well?" he asked while rubbing the night's rest from his eyes.

I blamed it on the wind chime.

He pulled me backward into his chest and whispered, "I know you're scared, but one day you will dance in the rain."

Dismissing his reassurance, and eager to leave the sleepless night behind, I nodded. "Yeah. You know, I'm gonna go."

He turned my head to face his. "You okay?"

"Yeah. I'm okay. I'll be okay. I'll rest when I get home. I'll call you."

I didn't know until I turned the key in the ignition, backed out of the parking spot, and turned toward the gate. Then I heard it. I heard the slick sound of the car's tires on the wet asphalt. It was the same sound. The same sound I heard when I left my apartment after the rape. The sound of rubber on wet tar.

I said it out loud. I screamed it as I drove the car down the hill toward the highway. Rain. It was raining.

I didn't remember the rain. In all the times I talked about, wrote about, and recounted the rape, I didn't remember the rain.

But I remembered that sound. The sound of my car's tires on the wet blacktop. In that apartment complex. The sleepless night. The apartment building. The slick sound. It was raining. It was raining. It was raining.

I didn't remember the rain. I only remembered the sound of my tires. That slick sound. Every cell in my body knew it clearly. That slick sound was the sound of death.

15

WHEN I DIE

*Nashville, Tennessee: Nearly Three Years
after the Rape*

DAY 1090

I died.

The night I was raped, I died. I was twenty-one years old.

The loss was total, but I dealt with it piecemeal. School assignments. Meeting with Tanya. Trying to sleep. Losing my job. Getting another job. Telling people. Going to group therapy. Sharing a house. Going to church after church after church. Going back to school. I was so busy trying to stay alive that I didn't know that I had died.

That's why it took me years.

But everything was gone.

My sense of safety. My sense of trust. My faith. The woman I was for twenty-one years ceased to exist. To whatever extent I get those things back, they will not be the same. Because I changed. I cannot go back in time. I cannot be who I was before the rape.

That long night and morning while it rained, I died. I could not grope or date or pray or hope my way back into being the woman I was.

It was an invisible death.

No one brought buckets of fried chicken. No one rocked back and forth on the mourner's bench while wearing a black suit. No one wailed over my lifeless body. It didn't look or sound the way I knew death should.

This realization sent me back to therapy asking Nancy what I was supposed to do now. Now that every rain shower made me an anxious insomniac.

She looked at me earnestly and said, "Monica, you're a minister. What's the expression? Marry and bury? You know. You know what to do when someone dies. You know what to do."

"No, I don't. I don't want to be dead. I want my life back." The tears streamed down my cheeks. "I want my life back!" I yelled this time. "I don't want to be dead. I was a good person." Liquid flowed from every opening on my face. I wiped my nose and mouth with my sleeve. I whispered this time. "I wasn't bad. I didn't . . . do . . . anything . . . wrong. And I want it back. I want my life back!"

"I know you do." She spoke calmly without patronizing me.

I swallowed hard.

Nancy waited for me. She asked the important question

in a soft voice. She knew the answer. She asked me so I could say it aloud: "How long has it been?"

"Three years." I looked down, reached for several tissues, and looked back up. "I'm not getting it back, am I?"

"No, Monica. You're not." She waited a couple minutes so it could really sink in. "But you do know what to do."

When someone you love dies, you mourn. I needed to mourn. I needed to mourn the part of me that was lost rather than to try to convince myself that not everything about me had changed. I began to separate myself into "me" and "her." "She" was the person who had died. "She" was the person I was. "She" was the person I knew best. At church and in my relationships, I kept trying to reach back and get her. Mourning meant that I had to stop trying to be her. Because I couldn't bring her back from the dead. I came to see that dying is a consequence of being raped, even when you live to tell about it.

I tried to treat her like I would treat any other loved one who died. I went through pictures of her. From Vanderbilt. From Harvard. It had to help. It helped with Grandma—to go back and tell stories and laugh. Theresa and I did that a lot.

As I tried to mourn her, I dreamed about her.

I saw her—as she looked, how she dressed—blue Levi's 501s, white turtleneck, wool jacket. She reached out her hand to hold mine and yet she was sucked into this black hole or this swirling pool of water and I was screaming and shouting and reaching out for her hand but there's a space

221

and our hands could not touch and her hand grew further from me. No matter how I tried to reach, my shoulder muscles hurt. I reached so hard. And I wanted to hold on to her, but the pull from the undercurrent was too strong and if I had been able to reach her hand, she would have pulled me under with her. Either way, I had to let go to live, and it hurt more to hold on than it did to let go. I heard the screams like echoes. My screams. Like a grieving mother over a child. Hysterical.

I awakened in a sweat. Screaming grief.

What made it bearable was feeling like God was holding me. Holding me as I cried. I conjured up the image I started using to go back to sleep: God rocking me, smoothing my hair back, and whispering, "I know, I know." Whispering, "I know, baby." And I burrowed my head in the breast or chest or stomach of God and I was rocked.

On the nights when that didn't work, I turned to music to calm myself. I hit play on the cassette player as Sweet Honey in the Rock sang:

> They are falling all around me—the strongest leaves of my
> tree
> Every paper brings the news that the teachers of my sounds
> are moving on
> Death it comes and rests so heavy—your face I'll never see no
> more
> But you're not really going to leave me
> It is your air that I breathe, it is your song I sing, it is your path
> I walk . . .

You're not really going to leave me
And I will try to sing your song right
Be sure to let me hear from you

I tried to reason with myself: So if I can mourn *her*, if I allow myself to cry for her, I can go on. I will try to think of her like an ancestor. She's not really going to leave me. She's still with me, somehow. I will try to sing her song right. Every time I do Dinah, I sing her song. Every time I speak out against sexual violence, I sing her song. I sing her song when I invoke her memories of Grandma and college. I sing her song when I find comfort in the music I learned in Crusade. When I play the piano, her voice will tell me where to place my fingers. She's not really going to leave me. And if I treat her voice like one of the ancestors, perhaps she will come to me. Maybe she can guide me to a place of peace.

I voiced what seemed frightening, but obvious. When she died, her faith died. All the efforts in the world did not retrieve that. Not Darrell and not church. Trips to see Lanh and contemporary Christian music no longer connected me to God. The words of my first sermon were a blatant lie: God could not keep me safe.

But Sweet Honey in the Rock and the drums and the dance became worship. They were how I found my way to God.

I kept on with the mourning process. I considered how she died. Once again, I replayed the rape in my mind. I replayed her death:

I was confused. I blamed myself. I believed all the shit

Peter told me. I see it now. I didn't go in my room for days. I slept on the couch when I slept. I didn't eat. I didn't clean anything and I never called it rape and I blamed myself the whole time. How did I do it? Make it through those days? I went to class. I wrote my papers—all the while in hell. Yes, it was a miracle. That was my life's miracle. Living through it. She preached through it. She got that GPA through it. And every night, she cried. So confused. She tried. She tried to keep praying—to simultaneously grieve it and understand it, to feel it and to conceal it. It killed her. Not in one day or one instance, but it killed her. She died with all those tears and screams and silences. And Tanya and Cynthia and Professor Weems—they didn't just keep me alive as I thought. They delivered, or rather midwifed, me slowly. Slow enough that I didn't know it was happening. Through their hands, I came forth. Through and into their hands came a sensuality, a sexuality, relaxing, admitting the fear, talking about it, trusting a little. The death and birth was slow and simultaneous.

I remembered how Cynthia came to my apartment. How she tried to cast away negative spirits with olive oil and prayer. I thought of Paul D in Toni Morrison's *Beloved* and how he tried to cast Beloved out of 124. But, unlike Jesus or Beloved, I was not resurrected.

I was reborn. A new person—me. On Easter. On the highest holy day. This was my hope. That when *she* died, *I* was born. This new three-year-old me. And I wasn't half bad. I kinda liked me.

I was still alive. *She* might be dead, but *I* was still alive.

If the Yoruba were right, if the dance was right, if I trusted my teenage faith that prayed to Grandma, then I knew that *she* was spirit.

Sweet Honey in the Rock helped me to see her as an ancestor. When they perform their popular song "Breaths," based on the poem by Birago Diop, they move their hands into the shape of a bird and form their voices into birdcalls. This helped me to have a new picture of *her*. *She* was a dove. A small to medium-sized bird. Her spirit went into a bird, and I saw her fly out of clasped hands opening. She was not in a cage. I could open my hands and set her free. This image brought me peace.

Peace was the goal. If I couldn't be safe, I could have peace. I could cultivate peace in my home and in my relationships and in my spirit. This was the new three-year-old me. I lived in Nashville. I had friends. I had friends from the Nashville chapter of the Black Women's Health Project and dance class and the poetry club and church. They only knew *me*. They never knew *her*. They didn't remember her straight hair, makeup, or wool blazers. They only knew me. And you know what? They liked me. I could play dress up like her, but I just couldn't ever be her again.

I was okay with that.

What to do about this?

I came home from dance class with a bag of groceries. I turned the water on and dumped in the contents of my last open bag of bath salts. I put soup on the stove and lit every candle I found. I placed a bottle of filtered water and some incense on the edge of the tub. I thought I would stay in there forever. Bathing forces an intimacy with the body that showering speeds over.

When I got out, I dabbed myrrh oil on my wrists and feet and knees and neck. I put on a white tank top and tied two yards of white cloth around my waist. I wrapped two yards of white cloth around my head in the Yoruba style I learned from the women in dance class. All of my hair was covered as the cloth cut across half of my forehead. I secured it with a crisscross of the long ends of the material at the nape of my neck. I tied and tucked the ends on the sides of my head.

White cloth. White pants, white Keds, white jeans. White tank top, white blouse, oversized white men's shirt confiscated from an ex-boyfriend. White cowrie shell earrings, a pearl in the third hole. White cloth around my head.

Wrapping myself in white cloth, I treated myself like a dead body from ancient times. I thought of Jesus, wrapped in swaddling clothes in the manger. I thought of the women who went to Jesus' grave with the intention of wrapping his body in cloths, and in spices, to prepare him for a proper burial. There was myrrh at Jesus' birth—one of the gifts from the magi. And, my Bible dictionaries tell me, myrrh at Jesus' death—a common embalming spice of the day. It was Lent. I died during Lent three years prior. I became the walking dead again—as I was for those days after the rape. This time, I walked around knowing I would be reborn.

I garnered attention. The students in the class I taught at

Tennessee State University asked why I was wearing white. Before I answered, they asked if I was being initiated into something—like a new religion or a priesthood. I knew that they were referring to an African spirituality. Some of my dance friends were being initiated into a traditional Yoruba religious community in Nashville. They shaved their heads and wore white during their seasons of initiation. They went to work and the grocery store and dance class this way. Life did not stop because Spirit was moving. I was not being initiated, but yes, something new was happening.

I smiled and said, "In a way."

"Cool," one student replied, justifiably proud of herself for noticing and connecting faith and practice.

Wrapping myself in white cloth marked the end of my mourning. It allowed me to stop missing her. I gave myself permission to stop trying to be her. It allowed me to let her go. I wore white and began to make plans.

I made plans with myself: Say good-bye to her. Could I bury her somewhere? Set a marker? Write an obituary? Scatter her ashes somewhere? She lived—she died at my old apartment. That's why I had to move. I was living in a grave. Like a restless spirit, I would not be driven from there until I was ready to leave. Maybe in the woods beneath my balcony, I could light a candle, sing a song, and let . . . her . . . go.

I called on the things I learned by being a ministerial intern at Metropolitan. I thought about Grandma's funeral, and Nana's too. I tried to visualize the various funeral programs of great-aunts and great-uncles that Grandma stuffed into her Bible. There's a format for remembering the dead.

I called the new managers at my old apartment complex and asked if I could hold a memorial service there. "A friend of mine died and used to live there, and I'm just wondering if I can use some space outside." Not a full explanation, but not altogether untrue.

I scheduled it for the Saturday after Good Friday, a day before Easter Sunday. A week prior, I walked the property. Parking in the same spot I used when I lived at the apartment complex, I grabbed a sweater as I closed the car door to stave off the unusually chilly winds. Through the breezeway, past the end of the concrete walkway, I made my way to the grassy lawn and the beginning of the woods. One could walk from the edge of the woods and down the bluff to the water, but it was too narrow and steep. I scanned the area trying to imagine how to turn a neglected piece of property into a sanctuary. I envisioned chairs at the edge of the forest in the natural cove with moss that juts into the forest. I remembered all the days I looked out of my apartment window into these woods, the stream sparkling in the sunlight below. Yes, I thought, this is the perfect place.

"I can do this. I know what to do. I'm a minister, I know what to do." I repeated these words to myself over and over. I kept planning.

How to adapt a eulogy and Bible readings and hymns about going home to glory to the death of *her*? There was no body to look at sideways. There was no name to wail out in tears. It would make no sense to talk about mansions prepared in the sky.

I thought of my days in Catholic elementary school where going to church was an entry into clouds of incense and dripping holy water. The space needed some kind of holy smell. I decided to find a handful of myrrh incense sticks and burn that. The sweet smell of death.

The hymns on which I was raised would not work. What sense would it make to sing "We're Marching to Zion"? But it's not worship without music. I circled the grassy expanse and remembered that I had a classmate who wrote a song about Tamar, a biblical character who was raped, for our class Sexuality in the Bible. I asked her to sing that song for me.

Most funeral programs have two readings from the Bible—something from the Hebrew community and something from the early church's witness. I couldn't give the usual verses about God leaving peace or telling me to remember my faith. I needed something that I could feel. Something that acknowledged my grief. I chose the words that helped me shortly after the rape: Jeremiah 14:17 and 8:18–9:1 and 2 Corinthians 4:16–5:8, 16-17.

Speak this word to them: Let my eyes overflow with tears night and day without ceasing; for my daughter—my people—has suffered a grievous wound, a crushing blow. Therefore we do not lose heart. Even though our outward woman is perishing, yet the inward woman is being renewed day by day.

229

I kept walking. I closed my eyes and sensed the apartment complex's back lawn transform into a holy Clearing space. I knew what to do. I would use songs from the Holy Bible according to Sweet Honey. Like any other church service, there would be a processional. We would march in to "They are Falling" so that I could remember that she was an ancestor and my job was to "sing her song right." It wouldn't be so painful. It would guide and comfort. The way ancestral voices should. Like Grandma's.

I needed a song for the faith I grew into—a faith that was danced. A song I could dance to. Instantly, I knew that I would ask my dance teacher to help me choreograph something. I chose Sweet Honey's "When I Die."

When I die, you can bury me up on the mountaintop
When I die let my spirit breathe
Let it soar like an eagle to the highest peak
When I die you can cast me out into the ocean wide
When I die, let my spirit cry
Let it add to the tears that make the ocean deep and wide
When I die you can bury me down deep in the ground
When I die let these bones take root
Like a seed that's been planted
Let 'em come up bearing fruit
When I die you can toss me out into the winds of time
Oh when I die let my ashes roam
Blow here, blow there

I know I'm going to find my true home
When I die, oh when I die

I returned to my car and sat in the parking lot for nearly an hour. I pounded on the steering wheel as I cried tears for every funeral I ever attended. Grandma, Granddaddy, Nana, Great-uncle Robert, Great-aunt Zelda, Mrs. Wingo. *She* was as dead as they were. The plans made it as real as shaking the hand of the funeral director of the community mortuary.

I spent the next week trying to make an appointment with my dance teacher. By the fifth phone call in our game of tag, she concluded that our inability to coordinate schedules was a sign that she wasn't meant to help me.

"You can do this on your own, Monica. It's your dance." She didn't say it like the words of encouragement I needed. She said it like the busy working mother that she was. Then she hung up.

I knew I had to dance. Pushing the couch back to the living-room wall of my new home, I tried to recall my favorite steps from class. I put the CD player on repeat until the movements flowed with how I felt during each part of the song. When Sweet Honey sang "let these bones take root like a seed that's been planted, let it come up bearing fruit," I did a part from Kuku that raised my right arm, then my left, then both together coming over my head, and I crouched down, head down, hands down and jumped up like a big X, my hands to the sky. The expanded crooked right and left arms of Lamban fit with the lines "ocean wide." I stopped thinking and moved. I rotated my hips and shifted my feet until I felt like I was dying. Until I felt like dying was okay. Until I knew that death was not the end.

Two days before the memorial service, the meteorology report predicted rain. Would I really be out there in all this white, soaked to the bone, dancing on rocky, dirty, muddy grass? I wanted to reschedule, but everything was in place. I couldn't tell the apartment management why the service needed to continue despite the rain. I convinced my friends—who barely understood—to attend. I began to realize that the coming rains were not ironic, but typical. It always rained when someone died. Grandma. Granddaddy. Nana. Even Mrs. Wingo. Even me.

I remembered Korey's words: "It's okay to be scared, but one day you will dance in the rain." How did Korey know? I didn't talk to him about death. Was it Spirit? Is this what the writer of the biblical book of Hebrews meant when it talks about entertaining angels unaware? That Korey and so many others were present for me to help me stay alive, find myself, or get to God? How did he know? *It's okay to be scared, but one day you will dance in the rain.*

I encouraged myself: I will be fine. I will not be scared. *She* died. It will rain. I will wear white and dance. I will not melt in the rain.

When someone dies a physical death, it's fairly obvious. You don't have to explain invitations to friends. In fact, as soon as they learn of the death, they ask you to tell them when and where and what food they can bring. Inviting loved ones is harder when there's no corpse. I started with my closest friends. Tanya and Cynthia automatically understood. Now living at opposite ends of the country, they were unable to come. Three years later, most of the people who walked the first thirty days with me were spread across the country in graduate school or working low-paying community justice jobs that made jumping on an airplane impossible. They promised to send something special for the event.

I trusted my new friends to understand and join me in memorializing someone they never knew.

I tried to explain it to Mama. She admitted that she didn't understand what I was doing, but she understood grief. We reminisced about Grandma and about all the times we played the cassette tape of the funeral in the days, weeks, months, and years after Grandma's death. We liked hearing Cousin Carolyn tell stories of Grandma. Cousin Grace's crisp diction reading Grandma's obituary calmed us. We heard ourselves crying through the reel on the tape. Mama said she understood grief and she understood memory, even though she didn't understand why or how the rape killed me. I appreciated her support, but I needed the people at the memorial service to understand what was happening. I didn't think I was strong enough to do all this and explain it again.

Carol attended in her role as woman of faith and church mother. She heard the tone in my voice that said: I really need you to get this. I really need you to be here. Another minister from Metropolitan came. I didn't know all of her stories, but I sensed that she knew how to live through and after things that kill some people.

Instead of a eulogy, I would explain myself. I would talk about how important it is to remember what we lose. I would talk about *her* best qualities. I would say what I would miss the most.

At quarter to nine Saturday morning, I returned to the grassy area beneath my old apartment. I set up folding chairs, a small boom box, the order of service printed on gray cardstock, and a large bottle of water. It was cool and gray, but it didn't rain. I thought I was ready for the rain. Then I felt myself exhale at the mere humidity. One fewer battle to fight this day.

Tanya planted a tree on an island off the coast of Seattle—as a symbol of my new life. I placed the picture she sent in a frame on the ground in front of the folding chairs. Cynthia e-mailed me a poem she wrote.

At nine in the morning, we made an odd picture. Four black women in shawls, sweaters, and raincoats huddled before cheap brown metal folding chairs. From our mid-twenties to fifty-something, we grasped papers and notebooks tracking what occurred. I hoped no one living nearby was awake or curious enough to interrupt us. I imagine that we looked like a coven of witches brewing up a secret something.

As the openness became altar, and trees witness, I said good-bye to myself.

I lit the sticks of myrrh that my minister friend held. I

poured water as a libation to thank the earth and ancestors for supporting us all. I paused. And I poured water for all the people who weren't there but who were there when *she* died: Lanh, who gave me a place to sleep and taught me to count good days; my classmate, who first took me to Metropolitan; Professor Weems, who helped me find a job and hugged me when touch had become frightening; Omar, who treated me like a whole person; Korey, who helped me remember the rain. They came into my daily life and then left. I wasn't "me" without their presence, and yet they all faded into the background of my life—accessible by phone or e-mail if we wanted to connect. They were my angels, real angels, who watched over me to get to another side. To get me to that Clearing.

Carol read the poem that Cynthia sent. The last two stanzas set the stage perfectly for the dance:

> *Why not dance with shadows?*
> *Grow acquainted with their theatrics*
> *Direct them with leading and twirling*
> *Insist that they entertain our dreams*
> *Why not dance with shadows?*

I did. Barefoot in the grass and dirt. Shedding the extra layers of white shirts I brought in case of rain. I danced with the shadow of death. I danced through the valley of the shadow of death.

At the end, I gave the eulogy. I described her death with the following words: "Rape. The sound of the word hurts my ears." I talked about her death. I used the same words I invoked whenever I spoke publicly about the loss of rape: "Rape steals. It stole my sanity. I learned to live on less sleep. It stole my pride. I no longer cared when and where I cried for hours. It stole my entire sense of control. I want my body back. He took it. I want my heart back. He stole it. I want to feel safe again. I want to be able to relax again. I want to trust again. I want to love. But he took it all. In one single night, and a couple of thrusts, I was robbed of what I thought was mine."

I concluded by talking directly to *her*: "I hate the way you died. So painful, so bloody, so wrong. I've given you my energy, my love, my passion, and all the tears I had within me. Because I missed you so much. But I can't be you again. I know this. I didn't know how to be anyone else but you. But now I do. Now I have. You have died and left behind a child who is growing, toddling, and becoming someone I think you would be proud of. You would be proud of me. You would like and admire me as I like and admire you for who you were. I want to say good-bye to you. And I want you to know that I love you and I'll miss you and I want you to become an ancestor. I'm still learning from you. And I still need you to speak to me."

By Monday, I was eating cake. Yes, I died, but I was also reborn. When people are born, we celebrate with a party. I wanted to be the three-year-old child that I felt like I was. I wanted balloons and games. I wanted things to be warm and orange. Mangoes and warm grains. I made a yam curry with golden raisins. And brown rice. I invited friends from dance class and from the poetry club that I frequented on weekends. I invited women from the Black Women's Health Project.

I said, "Three years ago, something inside me died, and I want you to celebrate with me that . . . that I am still here. And I'm someone new. Someone I like."

People understood that.

One friend brought balloons and the game Taboo. Another took pictures. Mama bought a plane ticket to visit and ordered a vegan cake from a local restaurant. I made shopping lists: cumin, coconut milk, sweet potatoes, more rice, and a piece of clothing that wasn't white. I found a bright turquoise blue African print with silver etching on it at Alkebu-Lan, the local black-owned bookstore, calling me as clearly as the white clothing had six weeks prior. I ordered four yards. Two yards to wrap around my waist and two yards for my head. I wrapped them around sandalwood incense sticks so I could smell like something other than myrrh. I wanted to feel alive.

My new life found expression in process theology again. Five months after my rebirthday party, a casual encounter at the coffee shop took me in a new direction. I ran into a current Vanderbilt student whom I recognized from an alumni event. He told me that a prominent process theologian was teaching a class at Vanderbilt in the fall semester.

"You should come today for the first class. Hear the lecture. At two o'clock."

I laughed. "You know I have a job, right? I can't just cut out of work to go to a lecture."

"Sure you can," the student boldly asserted.

I laughed again and paused. I thought of all the days I attended evening meetings in the low-income neighborhoods where I was a community organizer. Returning to the office at nine thirty at night to do paperwork, dragging myself home an hour later. It's not like I didn't work my forty hours plus.

"You're right. I probably can," I replied.

Marjorie Suchocki's austere brown bob framed a face full of smiles. She didn't seem to notice that I wasn't enrolled in the class when I slid into a chair next to my coffee shop friend. Suchocki wore clothing in understated greens and taupes, and her jewelry matched her cardigan, purse, and shoes. I took this as a sign that no matter how jovial she appeared, she was probably a stickler for details.

She passed out a two-page syllabus and began with an introductory lecture to process theology. She drew circles on the board with arrows. She talked about how God lives in us and how we live in God. The arrows penetrated her chalk-lined circles. Professor Suchocki talked about how everything in the world is connected and how we need God. And God needs us. She continued with notes on how the world feels God and how God lures us—usually without our awareness—quietly, biologically, spiritually toward the best paths that we should take.

We are constantly changing, Suchocki said. In each moment, we become something new. We are not the people we were yesterday or last year because we have new experiences and they shape who we are. Who we were, is gone. We are perpetually perishing, but we are constantly reborn. God interacts with us as we change and calls us forth to new opportunities, new ministries, new ways of being.

Enraptured, I leaned forward on the always-too-small desk attached to the right side of the chair and stared. As Professor Suchocki spoke, I gathered each word like a pearl from a broken necklace scattered across a bedroom floor. I gathered them up in my head and let them sink into me.

Professor Suchocki was talking about my life. I died, but I was reborn. And I did feel like God was in it. Like God was calling me. Through the drum and the dance, God called me. With the Dinah Project, God called me. I changed. I was still changing. And God's call changed with me. I was curious about this idea that God needs me. Is it possible that God needs me to be me and that that helps make the world a better place? I liked this theology that says that change is normal and that God is with me in it. This theology made sense for my life and the lives of the other survivors I knew. Metropolitan Church gave me a ministry; my new friends gave me community; the dance helped me talk to God. Perhaps process thought was giving me a way to talk about God. Instantly, I knew. I had to learn more.

I rushed to Professor Suchocki at the end of the lecture. Aware that I had to return to work, I hastily explained that I was an alumna and scheduled a meeting for the following week. When we met, I told her what I learned in my preaching class. I told her about Dinah and ministry. I told her that I thought I believed this.

Narrowing the distance between our chairs in her office, she pierced her eyes into mine and said, "You should write that. Come to Claremont."

"Just like that?" I asked.

"Yes. Pretty much."

There were few hours left empty after work, Dinah, church services, dance, and freelance writing. Over the next weeks and months, I squeezed in several drafts of my personal statement, GRE preps, the GRE tests, fellowship applications, and pleas to former faculty for reference letters. Once I had enough funding, I made plans to go to Claremont to learn the details of this theological system that gave academic parlance to my four-year-old life and faith.

I lay back in my bed and played every song about California I could find.

The Beach Boys crooned, "I wish we all could be California girlllllllllllllls. . . ."

LL Cool J hammered, "I'm going back to Cali, Cali, Cali. . . ."

I threw my feet in the air and wiggled my toes to the beat when Tupac rapped "California knows how to party. . . ." I sang loudly on the first lines: "Let me welcome everybody to the Wild Wild West, a state that's untouchable like Elliot Ness."

I left binders and budgets for the Dinah Project advisory board. I gave them a pep talk about continuing the work without me. I gave notice at my job. I asked my dance teachers for referrals to studios in L.A. I told my friends that I was living out my career dreams—ministry and the academy.

Shortly before I headed to California, Carol asked me if I felt like I had closure. Did the memorial service ritual and Dinah Project give me closure?

I thought about the previous four years. I thought about Dinah. I thought about my tears and the dance and the rain. I thought about the next week's appointment to talk about rape at the Women's Center.

"No," I told her. "It's not closed. It's still really here. It's still with me." No one had asked me so directly. "You know, Carol, I don't think I'll ever get closure." I paused. "But it's okay. I don't want it."

"So," she asked politely, "what was all of it for?"

The funeral and birthday party and Dinah were not meant to close the door on the rape. The rituals helped me integrate the trauma of rape in my life. They were there to tell me I didn't have to fight and wrestle and cry all the time. They helped me remember that rape is just one of my stories. It's part of who I am. But it's not all of who I am. I have other stories, and Lord willing and the creek don't rise, I will create new ones.

PART IV

NO MORE
AUCTION BLOCK

PHILOSOPHY: CALIFORNIA, 2000–2004

16

LIFE OF THE MIND

Claremont, California: First Year, Doctoral Program

I felt healthy, strong, and sane when I moved to California. I could barely wait to begin my doctoral program in religion at Claremont Graduate University. When I stepped out of the airport doors in Ontario, California, all I could see were the mountains. Holy things happen on mountains. Moses went to a mountain to commune with God. The ancient Israelites marched to and sang about Mount Zion. Jesus gave his sermon on the beatitudes from a mountain. In Cuba's Santeria, the orisha Eleggua is the bearer of the mountain and sits at the crossroads where important decisions are made.

These mountains were unlike the Appalachian Mountains through which Mama, Daddy, and I drove on holiday trips to D.C. Not the Smoky Mountains that Grandma pointed out on car trips down south. Those were large hills of trees and grass, like Midwestern forests, but on a large hill. These mountains were massive hunks of rocks, one next to the other, jutting into the clear blue sky, forming both a foreground and a backdrop to everything there was to see. The near-desert climate of Inland Valley in California mystified me. Sage grew in the unkempt lots between developed properties on the main boulevard. Roses bloomed in winter. Aloe sprinkled the edges of apartment and campus properties. Geckos scurried across the sidewalks. I felt the hot, dry heat baking my skin to a bronzy high yellow, but I didn't sweat. Like the corny plotline of a made-for-TV movie based on Gold Rushers or aspiring entertainers, I joined the millions of people who went to Southern California to find their futures. Mine was just the nerdy religious version. The mountain welcomed me to California and seemed to say, "Yes, you are embarking on a new journey. And it will be holy."

I planned to recreate the best of my Nashville life in Claremont. Before leaving Nashville, I looked up the phone number to the closest rape crisis center and found a West African dance studio in L.A. I planned to attend an AME church because I knew that any AME church would recognize my ordination. There were a couple AME churches within driving distance of campus. Activism around sexual violence, dance, and church. This would balance out the work of my doctoral program.

Within two weeks, everything fell apart. The rape crisis center required all volunteers to work the crisis hotline before they did any other kind of task. I was happy to return my pager to my employers in Nashville. I swore I would never again take a job that included the words "on call."

I also knew my own boundaries. I was able to talk and minister about rape, but I fell to pieces at rape scenes in movies. I would disintegrate if I had to coax someone through the hours or days after a rape. I didn't think I could bear the sound of a life falling apart without reliving my own. I just put myself back together. I didn't do crisis hotlines. Still don't. So no volunteer work at a rape crisis center.

I rode into L.A. for dance class with a new friend, the wife of a classmate. An hour and a half drive from our homes and fifty-five sweaty minutes of dancing in a small studio with no air conditioning, and I hit the floor. I collapsed into a sad heap in front of my new friend and strangers who gave me looks of pity as they offered bottles of water. I was thankful that my friend was driving so I could rest all the way home. The dance teacher told me it was heat exhaustion and I would feel better next week. Three days later, the doctor told me it was severe anemia and that he was surprised I even had the energy to dance at all. He placed me on a regimen of iron medication and fifteen hours of daily sleep.

"And try not to exert yourself too much," he cautioned.

The weakness sustained itself for months. In my evening class on Augustine and Origen, I curled up on the floor with a notepad. I explained my condition to the professor. My brain could engage the material, but my body was too weak to sit up. No dance classes for months.

My only outlet for worship was at church. I met Reverend Tyler on campus. I was surprised to see another

African American person walking the campus pathways. I was the only black person in my department, and I was one of two black people in the School of Religion involved in coursework. Sure, I saw other black students in the libraries. A couple students in religion who were studying for exams. Usually, the black students I met were working on degrees in education or political science. So both Reverend Tyler and I stopped and greeted one another when we ended up on the religious quad on the same day. Reverend Tyler taught a class in preaching for master's students. He also pastored an AME Church in Santa Ana, Orange County. A quick thirty-minute drive down Highway 57 on a Sunday morning took me back to the familiarity of African Methodist liturgy and practices. Each week, I slid into the pew, standing and clapping to hymns and gospel songs I had heard before. Reverend Tyler said I was welcome to sit in the pulpit whenever I wanted. I told him that I wanted to teach. We arranged for me to teach a six-week series on spiritual disciplines during Lent.

Otherwise, all my time went to my studies. My bookshelves with Zora Neale Hurston, Toni Morrison, Alice Walker, Octavia Butler, Paule Marshall, and Toni Cade Bambara collected dust. The books by Judith Lewis Herman, Mary Pellauer, and Marie Fortune that nourished Dinah Project work were untouched. I didn't even read the work by the mentors I garnered at Vanderbilt: Victor Anderson, Renita Weems, Sallie McFague, Peter Hodgson. They wrote lyrical theology and ethics that posed the questions that kept me up at night: Who is Jesus for us today? Do our beliefs destroy the environment? How do we understand violence in the Bible? How does African American culture affect theology and practice? Now, I hauled around tomes by dead men in my weathered backpack with the Harvard crest. Harnack, Schleiermacher, Kant, Plato, Augustine, Gadamer, Hegel, Dunne, Troelstch, Whitehead. I spent hours in the Claremont School of Theology library close to where my classrooms were. I then walked down Dartmouth Avenue to put in another couple of hours reading in Claremont Graduate University's Honnold Library. After dinner and an hour of watching TV, I propped up in bed with books around me. Hours and hours a day trying to understand the assigned material, and then more hours reading the referenced material that I'd never read before. If I understood half of what I read at the end of each day, I considered it a victory. If I made a comment in class that didn't sound completely unintelligent, I did jumping jacks inside.

I couldn't believe that was my life. I knew that philosophy was hard for me. The required philosophy class at Harvard kicked my ass. I had to barter an entire semester of my notes from another class to get one of my friends to spend the night before the final exam talking me through the take-home points of introductory Plato and Kant. I escaped the class with a B- and vowed never to read that crap again. Yet there I was. Two feet in. Just so I could learn more about process theology.

The belief system that answered my questions and made sense of my life was putting me through the paces. Process theology is a philosophical theology. It offers a way of thinking about the world. Theologians apply this view of the world to religion. To thoroughly understand the ideas, I had to read other philosophers of religion. I had to know how process thought stands in relationship to other ideas. I needed to know why it was so different from what I learned in church, and why it felt so familiar to what I experienced. Philosophy was the way there.

Three months into the program and two hundred pages into the reading by Harnack, I realized that I hated my California life. All I did was read. All I did was read and think and go to class and write papers and read some more. That's all I did. Who was I becoming? I knew that the degree was a necessary part of my plan to be a professor. I was excited about going to California to study religion in new ways. When I worked two, three, or four jobs at a time in Nashville, I barely had time to read academic books. I missed the way scholars engaged ideas and argued different points—sometimes just to see if the argument could be made. I wanted that. The "life of the mind." I left Nashville for the "life of the mind." I was groomed for the "life of the mind." This was my path.

To pursue the path, I left an entire life behind. No living-room meetings with my black female friends as we discussed health topics and our love lives. No lively conversations in the side room of the dance studio while we changed out of work clothes and into shorts and tank tops, wrapping yards of African cloth around our waists. No requests to pray with someone after something in the sermon rang a personal note. No calls from the rape crisis center to speak to an audience of college students about the process of healing. No e-mails from an editor, asking if I could turn around an article in three weeks. No lectures to students about the importance of the required reading in the classes I taught at Tennessee State. No peeking over the cubicle wall just when my coworker and I needed a break from filing reports. No trips to council meetings with neighborhood representatives. No excuses to buy shoes at the discount warehouse with my friends. No Bible studies. No poetry club. I traded in a full life of ministry and justice work and friendships for hours of reading philosophy. To be a process theologian.

I realized what happened to me in Nashville. I did not just teach and preach and organize. I had become a teacher, minister, and community advocate. That was who I was. But not anymore. In California, I was a student. A student who read all day.

It made me sick. Literally.

When I woke up, my limbs felt heavy, and walking from the bedroom to the bathroom made me light-headed. I assumed it was the anemic dip I had before every menstrual cycle. Not fun, but I was used to it. I thought I could push through it, even though I wanted to turn over in bed and try again tomorrow. Although it was only March, I had a two-day training for my summer job helping middle school students connect their faith to social justice. A bit of ministry for the summer months. A needed break from the incessant reading. Job training called, so I dragged myself out of bed and drove to campus. By the end of the day, I had a dry cough.

Within two days, the dry cough turned into a wet cough and my fever rose to 101 degrees. I took some Tylenol and canceled a speak-out at the Claremont Colleges annual Take Back the Night rally against sexual and domestic violence. I finally found a way to speak out against sexual violence, and I was too sick to go. After four days of coughing up yellow mucus, I decided to see a doctor.

The Claremont office of my HMO looked like the free clinic seen in impoverished neighborhoods on television shows where a ritzy doctor volunteers. The receptionist fussed at me for waiting so long to choose a primary care physician. She asked if I'd allow the doctor I saw that day to also give primary care.

"Yeah, sure, whatever," my sleepy, achy cough said.

Thirty minutes later, the doctor told me that I had the flu and gave me a cough syrup with codeine in it. The cough syrup helped me sleep, but I still coughed when awake. I was too tired to read for class. I went to class, but I only lasted an hour before my coughing interrupted the lectures so much that other students couldn't focus. My classmates gave me scornful side-glances. The professor suggested I go home and heal.

On day seven of my fevered cough, I woke up coughing. Within moments, I was gasping. I sat straight up, hung my legs off the side of the bed. I willed myself to cough harder. But I couldn't. My throat felt dry and tight. I saw tiny yellow firefly-like dots swirl in front of me. I recognized them from the anemic falls. I blinked to make them go away, but the fireflies were everywhere. I thought I was going to pass out. I stumbled to the bathroom door where I heard the water running. I knocked and quickly put my fingers around my throat in the universal choking sign.

My roommate immediately asked about calling 911.

I nodded.

The paramedics gave me smoky medicine in a plastic tube until I could talk on my own. In the ambulance, they told me that I had bronchitis and that I needed to throw away the codeine-based cough syrup and refuse to leave the hospital without antibiotics. After several hours, I received a lung X-ray, another bronchitis diagnosis, more of the smoky medicine in the tube, and a nonpenicillin antibiotic. Just knowing that someone diagnosed me correctly made me feel much better. I was on the mend. For two days.

On sick day ten not only was I coughing up mucus, but I vomited the medication and half of what I ate. I saw another doctor in the Claremont clinic office because I didn't trust the codeine-cough-syrup-administering doctor. The new doctor suggested clear liquids, popsicles, and over-the-counter cough medicine. I vomited popsicles, veggie broth, and apple juice. No more Claremont clinic for me.

The HMO hotline recommended urgent care, where another doctor prescribed something for nausea—although I wasn't actually nauseous. The pills helped me sleep, but I still woke up coughing and vomiting. On my second trip to urgent care, yet another doctor decided that I was having a bad response to the antibiotic. He gave me a different antibiotic, another cough syrup, and suggested regular painkillers for the fever. My fever broke and I slept for twelve hours.

The next day, I vomited everything, and a sharp pain in my lower back shot down my left leg. The HMO hotline again recommended urgent care. Doctor number six told me that I had sciatica—an inflamed sciatic nerve in my back. The violent coughing and vomiting probably caused it. She recommended the over-the-counter painkillers that I already owned. I alternated ice and heat on my back, per the doctor's recommendation. It worked for two days.

I was shivering with cold as I sat on my bed. At one in the morning, I was hungry and scared. I had vomited everything in the two days since I saw the last doctor. My back hurt so much that I couldn't sleep. I thought I needed to be in a hospital. I called a black graduate student I'd met once at a mixer. I begged this near-stranger to take me to the ER where I could get an IV. When the nurse arrived with a prescription and discharge papers, I started to cry.

"You can't send me home. I'm sick. I'm really sick! And I keep going from urgent care to the ER and back again." I begged. The nurse told me that I was not dire enough to merit admission to the ER.

I kept Mama abreast of every step of the illness by phone. I cried when I told her that they wouldn't admit me to the ER. Mama asked if I needed her to come out and help.

"Please, Mommy." I was a sick, helpless child.

Twelve hours, a flight, and taxi ride later, Mama got to my apartment and drove me to doctor number eight. This doctor concluded that I was being overmedicated. She told me to stop all medications except the one she prescribed. Like a fool, I took it. Popsicle. Applesauce. Peppermint tea. That weird tasting drink they give sick children to help them get electrolytes. Crackers. Water. I vomited everything. I didn't even try to sleep anymore. I hadn't been to class in three weeks. I called Reverend Tyler and canceled my Lenten teaching. I was too sick to get to Santa Ana, let alone teach.

When Mama called the HMO for a follow-up appointment, I refused.

Like a toddler throwing a tantrum, I propped myself up on pillows in the bed and said, "No. I'm not going. These doctors are killing me. If I die, I will die here in this bed." It was a little melodramatic, but I meant it with every inch of my achy body. "No more!"

I was resolute in my hatred of doctors, the HMO, and medicine. One of Mama's first cousins dabbled in naturopathy and suggested crushed papaya mixed with wheatgrass juice. Armed with my smoothie hand blender, little shots of wheatgrass from the juice bar down the street, and a grocery-store papaya, Mama made the concoction. She fed me green papaya mush in half-teaspoon doses. I kept it down. Mama repeated this every hour for two days until I could drink water without vomiting it.

For a week, I ate papaya, applesauce, water, papaya, cracker, water, papaya, pears, water. Mama refused to leave until I was able to eat food that required chewing and I could drive myself to class. Until then, she drove me to class, sitting next to me, taking notes. I negotiated with professors to make up the work I missed; Mama asked me about Wesleyan theology and feminist theory on the drives home.

I have a Mama who stopped her life for six weeks to save mine. I curled up next to her on the couch while we watched TV. She knew how to take care of me. I forgot that. Because she didn't understand my response to the rape, I forgot. But I knew then. My Mama still knew how to take care of me.

When Mama returned to Michigan, the pain still radiated from my lower back down my leg to my foot. I was so glad to eat that I decided to live with the sciatic pain. The sharp throb became a constant feature of my daily life. Because of the illness, my workload doubled. I didn't take Sundays for church. I read and read and read.

For philosophy, for process theology, for illnesses I could not have foreseen, I was bereft. No dance, no church, no Dinah. I saw then what kept me alive in Nashville. The net. I had made my own safety net. Each component of my life was a connected knot, binding me to other people and to practices that kept me alive. I stocked my quiver with a set of healthy warrior tools that I used to ward off severe depression. Miles away in California, my storage was empty.

17

RAZOR

Claremont, California: Three Months after the Illness

I don't know how illness became stress, and I don't know when stress became loneliness and loneliness became fear. I don't know when the pain shooting from my back down my leg and into my foot started to move into my soul. I can't name when the pressure of school and illness and being out of active ministry turned into listlessness. The doctor visits and vomiting used up all my internal resources. I stopped sleeping, and I started to cry.

I went to the gym at four thirty in the morning. I did over an hour of cardio. Tried to get enough endorphins to make it through the day. On a good day, I felt human until one thirty in the afternoon. I cried while I worked out. No one noticed because it looked like sweat. I ate breakfast. Cereal. Juice. Easy. I didn't want to eat after that. I wasn't hungry. I watched TV while flipping the pages of the books I was supposed to read. I had incompletes in two classes, but I couldn't focus on the words. I couldn't even remember the plots of the TV shows. It was noise and moving colors.

"What do you do about the depression?" Herb asked me one evening over the phone.

Herb wasn't usually so direct. We had been friends for years, but things between us were changing. I was always attracted to his sepia skin, shaved head, and athletic physique. We met in the small social world of black graduate students in religion. In the years that we both lived in Nashville, we interacted like shifting Venn diagrams. One day, we were in a group of six students grabbing lunch at the joint across the street from the divinity school. Months later, I was sitting in a common area looking pitiful, and he said, "C'mon, ride with me to the grocery store." He didn't blink an eye when I cried as we walked through the frozen food section. It was the second year anniversary of the rape. A year later, I called him and asked if he felt like going dancing. We met at a downtown club before they started charging a cover. We danced to P-Funk and R&B and hip-hop until our feet hurt, then we kicked off our shoes and danced for two more hours. For a week I hung out at his place, read books I pulled off his shelf, and took intermittent naps in his Papasan chair while he studied for exams. A year and a half passed without contact. We ran into each other on the street, went out for coffee, and talked for four hours.

As I moved into my role as a doctoral student, we found ourselves at the same conferences: in Washington, D.C.,

Denver, back in Nashville. Our interaction became more consistent.

Two thousand miles apart and three weeks into my doctor-to-doctor illness, he asked me directly: "What do you do about the depression?"

"What depression?" I replied as if he hadn't known me for three or four years.

He could have reminded me that I was up in the middle of the night, talking like I wasn't tired. He could've reminded me of the grocery-store meltdown. Instead, he started talking about St. John's wort and herbal teas. He talked about how isolating graduate school could be. He talked about depression like it was the common cold.

"So," he gently asked again, "what do you do about the depression?"

No one ever asked me. Herb spoke as if I were fully aware that I lived with depression and could have a rational conversation about it. He used the same tone that a person has in asking for directions.

I had no answer. I could have told him how I lived through my parents' marriage and divorce. Barely. I could have lamented about college nightmares. It was horrible. He already knew about the rape and Dinah. Therapy, church, dance, ritual. I never thought of them as depressions. They were concrete events. I had traumatic responses. That was all.

I wasn't lying when I said, "I don't know."

As I propped myself up on pillows in hopes of getting some sleep, I suddenly felt exposed. How did he know? How did he know about the river of sadness inside? How did he know that I always felt that if someone dug deep enough, they would find out how terrified and insecure I was? How did he know about the nightmares and sleeplessness? How did he know that there were times when I felt I would do anything, anything, anything just to feel a little bit happy?

I told Herb that I was sad and scared.

"About what?" he asked.

"I don't know. Just am." Pause. "Can't wait to see you." Translation: I'd rather you hold me while I cry than be here, alone, crying by myself.

"I'm your friend. I'm not going anywhere. I'm right here," he reassured.

"Yeah?"

"Yeah." He paused. "So what are you going to do?"

There he was, asking questions I didn't know the answer to. I should have said that I would go to the doctor. Or tell Mama. Or look for a therapist.

Instead, I started thinking about razors.

An activist-friend wrote to me about her experiences counseling women who were sexually violated. She wrote about the pain, the trauma, the nights without sleeping, the ceaseless crying. Yes, I remembered that. She wrote about teaching and counseling and encouraging women to tell their stories, to leave the shame behind. I did the same thing with Dinah Project. She wrote about the women who came into her office and removed their cardigans to reveal arms of scars from cutting.

This captured my attention in a different way. I tried to

imagine how I would feel, how I would react, if someone had come to Dinah Project with scarred arms. It reminded me of one of the last times I saw my high school boyfriend, Maurice.

When Mama and Daddy divorced, Mama and I moved to Ann Arbor—much closer to Detroit than I had been the three years prior. Top on my list of things to do: call Maurice. Although we were no longer dating and hadn't talked in months, I still thought about his hugs, long letters, and California accent. Finally, Maurice and I were geographically close enough to visit each other. Close enough, I hoped, to reignite our relationship. I called his home.

His mother answered the phone. "Maurice's not here, but he'll be back next week, Monica." She remembered me from our previous conversations.

"Where is he now?" I asked, thinking that perhaps he was with his father on the West Coast.

"He's in the hospital."

I didn't even pause before asking what happened. The images blurred together as Maurice's mother told me what she saw when she came home from work one day. Maurice's long lean body. His clothes in a pile on the floor. His lower leg dangling over the bathtub's edge. Blood filling the water that was still running. The razor on the floor. Pink-red water pouring over the tub's edge. I imagined his mother's scream and ambulance wail. Maurice was in a hospital on the other side of the state.

She continued talking about Maurice. I heard tones of

optimism in her voice. "But he is doing much better now. He's coming home next week. I know he'll want to see you."

I pushed my words through the silence that seemed to me a more natural response. "I'm glad he's okay. Really. I'll make sure I come down to see him. Like in a couple of weeks, if it's all right."

"When we talk tonight, I'll tell him you're coming." Maurice's mom sounded welcoming. "It will be good to finally meet you in person."

"I look forward to meeting you too, ma'am."

Two weeks later I was sitting on a couch next to Maurice. He looked the same except that his glasses were different. They made him look a little older.

I leaned into Maurice's torso, my back to him. He still wore those T-shirts made of soft cotton that feel good when you put your nose into them. He put his arms around me, and we talked about nothing important:

"You know I lost a year of school, so I'm a senior like you," he said.

"Come hang out down here with the class of 1991," I laughed.

I didn't know what to say. I was surprised by Maurice's suicide attempt. He had often been strong for me when I was sad. We had talked about parents, divorce, moving, and school, but that gave me no indication that he was depressed. But perhaps I should have known. I should have known from the way he told me that he understood me, from the way we both clung to our feelings for each other as an escape from the rest of our lives. Still, I didn't know it was . . . so bad.

Maurice allowed me to be quiet while I had these thoughts. We enjoyed doing nothing in the same space—something that phone conversations and letters didn't allow. I broke the silence when I said, "Can I see?"

"See what?"

"See what you did."

"The scars?"

"Yeah."

He turned his arms 180 degrees and I saw the horizontal marks across the inside of his wrists. They went up and down both his forearms. He was really trying to kill himself. I lifted his right hand to my mouth and began to kiss the darkened lines. One by one, wrist to wrist. I couldn't kiss away his pain and what it had caused him to do, but I tried. It was the only way I could think to tell him that I cared.

"It's a reminder," he said once I pulled his arms around me again. "Of how bad it can get and how bad I can never allow it to get again."

"I'm really glad it didn't work, Maurice."

"Me, too." He hugged me tighter. "Right now, I am too."

Attempting suicide seemed light years beyond my nightmares and journal ranting. What Maurice did, how he must have felt, was in a different category from my experience. I was sad sometimes, but I wasn't suicidal anymore. And even when I was, I didn't have a plan. That's what I told myself at the time.

I began to feel a kinship with Maurice, even though ten

years had passed since that fall afternoon when I last saw him, since I studied his scars. I understood better. I understood the perfectly reasonable logic behind cutting oneself to near death. I ran my fingers up and down the insides of my arms. I turned my arms over and over again, and I began to wonder if a razor might help me. The pain was so deep, diffuse, and inexpressible that I was like a sick child talking to a parent.

"Where does it hurt, sweetheart?" the parent might say while resting a hand on the forehead.

"All over, Mommy! All over."

It hurt all over. From the beginning of my days to the end and through the night. It hurt my soul. I was incapable of praying. Again, I was without words or a language to talk to God about it. It hurt my mind. I could not focus on anything besides the moving images on a television screen. And then, I wasn't watching, just staring. It hurt my body. My appetite, my energy levels, the nausea and stomachaches, the anxious trembling and rapid breath.

Where did it hurt?

All over.

But I didn't have a way to explain that to myself, let alone anyone else. And sometimes, no, every minute of every day I wanted to locate it. To say—*this* is what hurts and this is where. And a place . . . a stream of blood . . . a cut across otherwise smooth and soft arms could do it. It could give me a place to say, "It hurts right here."

The thought scared me. But the thought would not leave me. For days, and weeks, I contemplated cutting my arms.

How would it feel just to hold a razor in my hand? To feel it on my skin? So I started with an experiment.

I would shave my legs.

I hadn't shaved my legs for ten years. No reason really. It wasn't a political statement. It wasn't rebellion against mainline beauty standards either. Most men I met found my hairy legs sexy. I didn't care one way or the other, and not shaving my legs freed up several minutes of daily shower time. The convenience later turned to stubbornness and a refusal to shave my legs for any external standard. Unless, I decided in my early twenties, I just woke up one day and wanted to shave. Otherwise, I vowed that I would not.

I went to the drugstore two blocks from my house. I bought a three pack of pink plastic razors and shaving cream—designed for women and their legs with extra aloe, fragrances, and moisturizers. I was ready.

I held the razor up in the light while the water beat down on me in the shower. I turned it to the left and right, watching the water bead up on the blade. I put it on the shower shelf and picked it up again. Turning it, twisting it, getting a good look at the thing. No, I couldn't. I put it down and left the shower to get dressed.

Two hours later, I drew a bath and lathered up my right leg while leaning back in the tub. I picked up the razor again. I didn't even look at it. I wasn't going to hurt myself really. I just wanted to know what it felt like—metal on my skin. Cool, maybe?

It took me nearly forty-five minutes to remove years of leg hair. I looked at my legs, and they looked like someone else's legs. Like an alien body with my head and torso. I felt naked and exposed and foreign to myself. It was the perfect analogy. I was someone else. Someone different from the person I was used to being. I looked in the mirror and didn't recognize the person that I saw. Where was the Monica who is strong and confident? Where was the Monica who laughs and smiles through the day? What happened to the Monica who enjoys cooking and eating and going out with friends? Where was the Monica who can work hard and well and successfully at academics and community work? Who was this woman who hates herself and everything about her? Who was this woman whose memory betrays her, sifting out all the positive things, any joys and happiness and friendships in exchange for despair, loneliness, and sadness? Who was the woman who lies on the couch all day wishing she could just disappear into nowhere? Who was this woman I was living with now?

It was like being attacked by something from the inside. I looked the same, but I wasn't. And this new me, the one in the mirror, the foreigner, she was inept. I needed help remembering to eat. I had to ask friends to watch me to make sure I ate and talked to other people. I considered dropping out of school just because of the sheer difficulty of getting to class and focusing long enough to read hundreds of pages at a time. The intense privacy and secrecy I had with my inner life—which had been "sad" for over a decade—was there for everyone to see: my pale skin, the weight loss, the dry hair. Soon, it would be my failing academic performance, tardiness, and attendance issues. My secret was revealed. My privacy was gone. The Monica that always existed, quietly, carefully subdued, hidden. It was here for the whole world to see. Suddenly, I was exposed.

I told two friends about looking at the razor blade and shaving my legs. One drove from L.A. and took all my knives: paring knives, chef knives, razors, dinner knives, butter knives, every knife.

"How am I supposed to chop food?" I asked, as if I was really eating anything besides cereal. I sat on the couch as he rifled through my kitchen and bathroom.

"I don't really care, Monica. I'm worried about you." He wrapped them in newspaper and put them in a grocery bag.

I couldn't assure him that I would be fine. I just watched him like it was the most ordinary thing to do. As he headed out the door, he turned around: "I'll bring them back when you feel better."

Carol asked me if I was suicidal.

What began as a normal conversation to check in on the activities of the Dinah Project took a sharp turn as Carol heard the flat tone in my voice. Her psychiatry background trumped her role as church member. "Do you want to kill yourself?"

It was the wrong question. I wanted to live. I wanted to be happy. I wanted to feel something besides nothing. I didn't care how I made that happen.

I recalled the conversation Carol and I had years earlier when I lived in Nashville.

She asked me directly. "Would you consider taking

medication?" We were at her home one Sunday after church. Carol turned toward me on the couch. "If it ever gets so bad that you couldn't manage it with the techniques you have been using, will you consider taking medication?"

I told her about how, two years after the rape, I still felt scared and sad sometimes. I told her how much my therapist helped. She knew I was dancing and preaching. She knew that the Dinah Project brought me new life. She also saw what I was just learning. I wasn't so healthy and strong. I just had really good coping mechanisms.

I railed against the idea of taking medicine. I almost launched into my diatribe against the overprescription of the medical industry. I wanted to tell her about the economics of supporting multinational drug companies. She already knew how much energy it took me to take the iron pills for my anemia. She knew my answer before I said it.

"I just don't know. But if you are asking me today . . ." my voice trailed off. I couldn't even say it aloud. I turned my eyes from her face.

"Well, why do you talk to me?" she continued. "Why do you tell me, a psychiatrist, about your sadness? You know what I am going to say."

This answer I knew. I looked her in the face and said it clearly. "Because I need to tell someone. I need someone to know. And I thought that if I told you, you would listen. And you would watch. And you would notice me . . . in case . . . you know, in case."

"So what am I supposed to do?" she replied. Her voice held concern, but there were still traces of indignation.

"Just watch me, okay. Just watch out for me." I put my head on her shoulder and closed my eyes. She put her hand on my head. She didn't even have to say it. I knew she would.

That conversation was three years prior, and Carol was doing what I asked. She was trying to watch me across the miles and the phone conversations.

"Do . . . you . . . want . . . to . . . kill . . . yourself?" She enunciated every word to let me know that she was serious.

So many things wrong with that question.

Want? There's no want. There's no desire.

Kill? So active. So bloody. Killing would take energy.

She should have asked: "Do you think about dying? Do you think about hurting yourself? Do you think about being dead?"

18

DIAGNOSIS

Claremont, California: Four Months after the Illness

Depression mocked me. I was the kitten pawing, lunging, and chasing after the string that unraveled from a spool held by an entertained owner. Except there was no force outside of me playing catch-me-if-you-can with my life. The depression was inside of me, asking in every known language: "Will you take me seriously *now*?"

I cried at work. I was working with a local church leader and a Claremont religion professor to help a group of twelve preteens choose a social issue they cared about and connect their faith and activism around it. Some tears were acceptable. They were an appropriate response to being spiritually moved as the praise team sang about loving God and wanting Jesus. A slower song, hands raised, heads bowed in sincere prayer. That was acceptable. Twenty minutes after the band dispersed, I was still in my seat, head on my knees, crying. I couldn't explain it. One coworker tentatively approached me, quietly settled in the chair to my side, to ask if I was okay. I couldn't answer. I was supposed to lead these young people. Be an example. Help them understand their thoughts and feelings. Show them how faith and activism are avenues to justice. But I could barely talk. The workout at four thirty in the morning was supposed to get me to early afternoon, but by nine o'clock, I was toast.

Shifting from professor to minister to mother mode in two seconds, my coworker held my hand and asked if I had seen a doctor.

I knew I needed a doctor. Against my better judgment, I returned to the HMO that poisoned me. After all, I was paying the insurance premiums. There was a checklist:

Over the last two weeks, how often have you felt the following?

- *Little or no interest or pleasure in doing things*
- *Feeling sad or hopeless*
- *Trouble falling asleep, staying asleep or sleeping too much*
- *Poor appetite or overeating*
- *Feeling tired*
- *Feeling bad about yourself*
- *Trouble concentrating*
- *Wanting to hurt yourself*

Check, check, check, check, check, check, check, check.

This should have been cause for alarm, but it was my new normal. I wanted help. I wanted to sleep and eat again.

Unlike the ERs I was in a couple months earlier, this time a nurse led me to a small room without windows and asked me to sit in a chair that was half stool, half classroom desk. I climbed up and leaned my arm on the large padded armrest. I poised to give blood when I remembered that I was in the psychiatry wing. They didn't want my fluids; they wanted to know how I was feeling. The nurse held a clipboard of papers with my checklist on top. She asked me what brought me there.

I told the nurse that I was sad, tired, and uninterested in eating. She told me that I was depressed and needed medication. In fact, she added, I would probably have to be on medication for the rest of my life.

"Can't I just see a doctor? Isn't therapy included in my health plan?"

The nurse refused to schedule an appointment with a doctor until I agreed. Until I told her I would take medication for the rest of my life.

I was desperate, but there was no way I was letting these people give me another pill. Ever. I took my weak sad self home. Immediately.

That was my something. The thing I tried to do about the depression. The help I tried to get. I tried to answer Herb's question.

Then he came to visit. With him, I was a giddy teenager. I noticed his tiny habits. He licked his lips before he lifted a drink to his mouth. He was particular about ironing khaki pants even if he knew he would be sitting down long enough to wrinkle them again. He rubbed his hand on the back of his head and down his neck when he was tired.

We turned a weekend into a movie scene with background ballad music. He was in blue jeans and a black T-shirt. I wore a white tank top with a green-and-white batik skirt with dangling seashells and white sandals. I made an unpatterned jingle sound everywhere I walked. We drove up the narrow mountain roads to the nature trail where we asked strangers to take pictures of us. We snapped photos of cacti and mountaintops and scurrying lizards. We drove to the ocean and people-watched at Santa Monica's Coney Island–like pier.

We ended at the Third Street Promenade gallery of shops. I rattled on about a nearby vegan restaurant; he found a bar where we stopped for drinks.

It was bright outside, but the bar was dimly lit as we pulled our barstools up to the counter. We ordered and fell into a comfortable silence—happy to have a moment away from the din of tourists and shoppers that continued outside. I realized how much the noise bothered me. That didn't seem typical. I lowered my head to the counter and covered my ears.

"It's going to be okay, Monica."

Herb didn't have to explain. He knew that I was struggling.

I smiled in response.

He took my hand and looked me right in the eye. "What

you're going through doesn't obfuscate the beautiful person that you are."

Right there. That was the moment when I felt myself fall in love with my friend. We had been creating a long-distance romance story with the phone calls, e-mails, and trips. We snuggled, held hands, and talked about our work. We stole kisses in his kitchen and living room when I returned to Nashville for a church visit. In the nearly empty bar in Santa Monica, Herb cemented the feeling I thought I could live on for years. I was holding hands with a man who saw me, really saw me, and still loved me. I should have told him how much I needed that. I wanted to be strong enough to say, "I know," and mean it. I should have told him that that damn near made him my personal Prince Charming. Then we could have laughed, and seen our codependence. But I sat there, needy, satiated, romanced, and falling in love at the same. I said the wrong thing.

"Only a graduate student would use the word 'obfuscate' in regular conversation." I laughed.

The reasonable person in the room pulled me into his arms where I felt attractive and witty. We eased into a kiss.

Hours later, he drove my car down I-10 toward my apartment. I was tired, but the bucket seats prevented me from sliding over and nestling into his shoulder. I reclined the back of the passenger seat and slid further down. He turned and looked at me, and smiled. He reached his hand to the right side of my face and pulled me toward him. He played in the soft dreadlocks on the top of my head while keeping one hand on the steering wheel. We said "I love you" many times over the phone, but it always had the tone of friendship. I felt it differently with that little motion of his fingers in my hair. This felt like the word "baby," or like the Spanish phrases we used with each other: "Te quiero," "Te echo a menos." He did this thing in my hair at the end of a date, or after an argument, or as we sat on the bed watching TV. As he laced his fingers and tangled my hair, I could feel myself exhale.

When Herb returned to Nashville, I depended on that memory, that feeling, and the relationship to stay on the life side of the cliff. Feelings for Herb were the only positive feelings I had. Loving him was the only way I knew I was alive. It reminded me that I wanted to be alive—if only to love him. It gave me the energy to keep looking for a doctor.

I went to the office of the campus counseling center. I relayed my story and feelings again. I did the damn checklist. The therapist asked me about my schoolwork: Do you have any incompletes? Finished them out. What's your GPA? 4.0. How do you like your program? It's cool. I'm being challenged. Learning what I wanted to learn.

Her assessment: I wasn't depressed. I was lonely. I just needed better social connections. She recommended a local church I might like.

I had a church. I had God. I knew the difference between loneliness and illness.

I tried another psychiatrist—the mother of a good friend. She knew I was a minister. She even knew my Nashville church. I began to feel comfortable. As we talked on the phone, I told her about the terrible HMO people. I told her about the woman at the counseling center. I told her that I was looking for a referral for a psychiatrist in my part of town. She told me that I didn't need a doctor; I needed Jesus. I didn't hear a word she said after this. I made up an excuse to get off the phone. I tried to be polite because she was my friend's mother. But no, this was not about religion.

The conversation added an hour to my daily crying session. I wasn't feeling crazy. I felt sick. Why is it so hard for people to understand that? Aren't I telling people I am sad? Aren't I being clear? Aren't I asking for help? Can't they see how hard this is? How hard it is just to ask? Do I have to have blood dripping from my wrists for someone to hear me?

Maybe it was my fault. Maybe I suffered alone because I suffered in silence. I didn't tell anyone I was depressed. I didn't ask for help. I refused help when it came to me. Depression was my fault because I hadn't said anything. I cried alone. I journaled about my pain. But I never told anyone how bad it was. I never asked for help.

I flung my body diagonally across my bed and buried my head in the pillow while tears ran into my mouth. The same position I had in my teenage depressions. The same endless crying alone.

Wait! That's not true. Thrust back into the decade-old feelings, I remembered. I remembered asking for help. I didn't have the language, but I asked. It came rushing back. My Shakespeare English teacher. Mrs. Myers. I told them. My poetry told them. I used my words. My actions also told them. I was sullen. I was withdrawn. I locked myself in my room. And those people then, like the doctors now, didn't believe me.

But I believed them. I believed what they told me: that I was ungrateful or spoiled or picky. I . . . believed . . . them. And so I stopped talking. I stopped talking about all the things I felt inside. After Mama and Daddy went to bed, I stayed awake and played the popular Cherrelle song over and over on those nights:

Tears keep falling . . . from my eyes
And I can't keep it inside (keep it inside)

I tried to keep it inside. But it was spilling out all over. It continued to. In my friendships. In my schoolwork. In my job.

I was in my late twenties, but I felt like I was fifteen again. It was if I were still in Michigan. Moving into the fetal position on my bed, I was a scared, dangerously depressed girl who was trying to tell someone that I wasn't okay. Again. Was I really back there again? I thought I buried her in that clearing in Nashville. But there "she" was. "She" was here in full force. Haunting me. Taking over me. Telling me things I forgot. The things that only "*she*" knew.

Like a ghost. Or . . . like the ancestor I asked her to be at the memorial service.

"Do I sound crazy?" I asked Carol when I told her that "she," my former self, possessed me and told me things. I hoped Carol understood. She was at the memorial service.

"Actually, it kind of makes sense." She talked to me about how we all have an inner child. She told me that some memories can be very disruptive when they are recalled. "And," Carol added. "If you really think of everything that happened before the rape as belonging to 'her,' you may as well get on speaking terms. You're gonna need your memory."

Carol was right. I needed my memory to help me tell a doctor about my life. But I would also need some faith.

When I shared my doctor frustration with a minister friend, he started sharing his own experience of depression. I was humbled by his willingness to share something I found so hard to discuss.

He assured me. "It will get better."

"You think?" I asked, cognizant of how depressed I was, but unable to find a way out. All the things I used before, however unknowingly, were not working. No church. No ministry. Few friends. No family. Going to the gym without eating much no longer offered an adrenaline high. It only made me thin and pale.

"You have to have faith," he insisted.

"I do." I immediately replied. "I don't think God hates me or anything. I believe in God."

"No. Listen. You have to have faith in the medication. You have to believe it will help you. Or it won't. You're going to have to trust this too."

My resistance to medication was breaking down under my fear of the illness. There were no razors or knives in my house. I was awake for hours before sunrise and hours after sunset. I barely ate more than cereal and juice. I cried at work in front of children and colleagues. I couldn't remember what it was like to have pride. I had nothing to lose by considering medication.

"Hey, if it can get me to sleep, I'll worship it," I joked, hiding my insecurity and desperation.

He played along with me. "It's not idolatry. If you really believe God is in everything, if you really believe that, then you have to know that God is in the medicine too."

Three days later, I sat in the office of the twelfth doctor I had seen in four months. Lisa had short, dirty-blond hair and a thin athletic body common to Southern California. She wasn't like the women in the gym who are bony, or too thin for their large breasts to be natural. Lisa's tan looked like it came from days of hiking in the nearby mountains. I handed her the clipboard with all my information. I refused to fill out the checklist. Instead, I handed her a six-page letter I typed up the previous night. She might be nice, but I still didn't trust the person sitting in front of me to actually listen to me.

Lisa calmly asked, "Is this for me to read?"

I nodded. I remained standing.

"Now?" She swiveled the chair to face me as I moved to the center of her office.

"Mm hmm." I plopped down on the cushy chair that was clearly meant for clients. I held an identical copy of the packet in my hands. I read along with her so I could gauge the time I thought it would take her to finish.

The letter told her all my symptoms. The ones on the checklist, and the ones the checklist omits. The letter told her about the flu turned bronchitis turned vomiting turned sciatica. The letter told her about the doctor who told me that I needed Jesus.

The letter told her the truth about my hope and hopelessness:

> *I worry that I might get so sad that I might hurt myself even if I don't want to. I have life plans and things I want to do like be a professor and continue in activism and ministry, and those things mean more to me than almost anything else right now. They make me me, and they fill me and make me feel like I am all that I am supposed to be. But I find myself thinking—if I weren't here, how long would it take for someone to notice? I think: Who would get what of my things? I wonder who would know why.*

In the letter, I confessed that I was numb and tired. I either felt sad or I felt nothing at all. I couldn't feel happy or look forward to things I wanted to feel happy about. I couldn't even remember what made me happy anymore. Feeling nothing was better than feeling sad, but eventually I felt sad. I was losing my ability to function. I had to detach myself emotionally from everything just to keep from crying all the time, and still sometimes that didn't work. It took all my energy to get up and get dressed and be there and not cry through the day. I hadn't had a decent night's sleep in months and months. At first, it was because I was sick and then the sciatica was so painful I couldn't sleep. Most recently, it was nightmares or just anxiety.

My letter concluded with the only words of self-advocacy I had left in me:

> *I would like to be treated as someone who is very wary of all medications, but also desirous of assistance. I would like to be treated as someone who has a hand in my own care, but can also trust the expertise of clinicians around me. I would like to be treated as a whole person with an illness, not as a collection of symptoms. I am very anxious because I don't know you; I am sick of telling strangers how I feel; and the whole idea of medication terrifies me.*

Lisa read my missive politely and deliberately. She recognized my wounds without treating me like a sparrow with a broken wing. By the time she finished reading my narrative packet of symptoms, I curled up in an upright ball on the couch, gently rocking myself, running my fingers up and down my hairless shins.

Lisa didn't say anything about medication or symptoms. She began to ask questions about my past. She said that she wanted to understand what I was dealing with. With just a couple prompting questions, a pattern emerged: Grandma's death, Mama and Daddy's divorce, college nightmare, rape, the illness. Every two and a half years. I had not seen these as depressions. I thought of them as natural responses to difficult life events.

"What some people experience as disturbing or painful

or grievous," Lisa began, "you seem to experience with greater depth."

Depth. That was the word that Herb used when he held me and said, "Monica, you just feel things deeply."

I heard his words like a consoling coo from Grandma as she rocked child-Monica on her lap. Grandma's voice contained traces of her southern upbringing, "Baby, there ain't nothing wrong with you. You hear me now? You just feel things more deeply than others." That's how I imagined it. At night when the anxiety kept me from sleep, I wrapped myself in the blanket of these words and cuddled myself to calmer.

"But can you see the pattern?" Lisa asked me. "Can you see how this is different?"

I saw it clear as day. I remembered how old I was: Thirteen. Fifteen. Nearly eighteen. Twenty-one to twenty-three. Twenty-six. Like clockwork.

I nodded. Biting my lip, holding back tears.

Severe. Recurrent. Major. Depression. With. Anxiety.

The diagnosis should have made me feel better. I was studying philosophy because I like explanations—or at least good ideas—about how things work. I like language and systems and frameworks by which I can understand God and the world and myself. That was why I left behind church and friends and ministry for the holy mountains of Claremont. So I could learn a system with a good answer. Lisa sat before me revealing the layers of my questions, showing me forms, offering me language. This was supposed to satisfy me and take away the mystery of what was happening. But my needs were far more banal:

"So, do you think you can help me sleep?"

Lisa leaned forward in her chair toward me. "I can see you've had a bad experience with doctors and medicine. I'd be just as wary as you are. Let's just talk about this directly."

I was ready for a conversation about medicine. The previous night, I took to the Internet. I researched drug companies, mental health advocacy organizations, and chat rooms. If I was going to take any medicine, I needed to know exactly what it would do to me. With the last illness, I was in desperate pain, so I did whatever the doctors told me to. Now I was sick, but I was not so far gone that I couldn't be skeptical, smart, and protective of whatever part of my self was left in my body.

I read about SSRIs, tricyclic antidepressants, and MAO inhibitors. I was nervous about side effects—especially weight gain and loss of sexual appetite. I thought that being fat would only make me more depressed. And it was one thing not to have sex, but it was another not to *want* to have sex. I was nervous about medication making me sick. If medication was the best route to sleep and feeling better, then it was easier for me to promise to take it one month at a time. I thought I could handle thinking about it one month at a time.

Lisa pulled out a large three-ring binder and showed me the information on several medications. Ruling out the ones that cause weight gain and loss of sexual appetite, Lisa narrowed the list to three that she thought might be appropriate for me. She slowly moved to sit next to me on the couch. She shared statistics, possible side effects, and possible benefits with me.

For the first time in four months, I was being treated like a smart person who was sick. My brain slowly turned against me, convincing me of feelings and doubts that I knew weren't true. Lisa's trust in me and my ability to reason was the gift I needed. It made it easy for me to respect her expertise.

Lisa told me that being vegan made it hard for me to get tryptophan—that stuff in turkey that makes people sleepy, but also happy—but she didn't try to convince me to eat meat. She told me that the therapeutic dosage for the medication she wanted to prescribe was three hundred milligrams per day, but the trials were run on the bodies of white men and my black female body was clearly sensitive to Western medication. The medication samples came in a folded cardboard package with a foil back. The smallest dosage was fifty milligrams.

"Buy a pill cutter. Start with twenty-five milligrams. Do you think you can do that? For one month." She spoke in a slower cadence with the last words. "Just start with a month."

I held the green-and-white rectangle of pills in my hands. It was a simple question that required a tectonic shift in my own understanding of myself. Holding the pills in my hands, I knew that I was way past the point of "feeling things deeply." Rereading my six-pager in Lisa's office, I realized how powerless I was over my ability to stay alive. I could not will myself well or happy. I couldn't eke it out of a morning workout or conversations with Herb. No matter how many good things in my life that I could list, there was something in me that imagined a razor's blade as a route to release. I was no longer in the realm of the sad river Styx flowing between my true self and my outer world. The layers were peeled back, and my illness was here for everyone to see. I was in the place where there were only two choices: life or death.

"Yeah." I tried to give half a smile. "I can do that." Life.

I went home, took my twenty-five milligrams before bed, like Lisa recommended, and slept through the night.

19

REVELATIONS

Claremont, California: Five Months after the Illness

With a name for my lifelong companion and a week of sleep under my belt, I wanted to go backward. I wanted my privacy restored. I wanted to run back into the shell from whence I crawled several months earlier. I wanted to go back to being a regular student with hours of reading assignments and a couple friends who knew about my personal life. I wanted my secret back. But the razor's edge, my breakdowns at work, and finding Lisa changed everything.

The medication helped the worst of my symptoms. I was sleeping. Within two weeks, I stopped crying in public. After a month, I convinced my friend to bring my knives back. He unpacked them in the appropriate kitchen drawers saying, "You know, Monica, if I didn't see it with my own eyes, I'd just never believe it. I wouldn't be able to tell how sick you can get." Good, I thought to myself. Just the way I want it. I don't want people to know. Not unless I tell them.

Admitting my deeply depressed state began with Mama. Although depression courses through my veins, I didn't want my family to know about my pain. We had our family roles, and I was the one who was okay. I was the one who had it together. I was the one who went to Harvard and declared complete financial independence as soon as college ended. I was the one people were proud of. The one no one had to worry about. That was my role. Admitting that I was fallen-apart seemed to disrupt the unspoken but established code.

Mama should understand that. She and Aunt Maxine had their roles as "the twins." Grandma had her role as the one her siblings sent to school. Even Daddy had his role as provider in his family. Although the family's ability to eat, go to school, marry well, or relocate no longer hinged on the material success of one person, the weight of the role felt that heavy. No one told me that I couldn't fail. No one said that I had to succeed. It was an unspoken expectation as rudimentary and learned as brushing my teeth and saying my ABCs. The role was not rigid. I carved out and defended my own standards of beauty and class by eschewing chemically straightened hair and sorority affiliation. Still, the message was clear.

I was content to keep my depressive lows from my family—until I could talk about the lows in the past tense. Until I got on the other side. Then I could talk about them as something that happened.

Carol stopped my plans with five words: "You need to tell her."

I didn't say anything.

Since our conversation about suicide, Carol called weekly, checking in on me. She asked about symptoms, doctors, and side effects.

"If I had a child in this much pain, I would want to know."

Again, I was silent.

"If you don't tell her, Monica, I will."

"Okay. Okay." I knew she would. She would find Mama's phone number online, remind Mama who she was and how they met at Metropolitan a couple years prior, and tell Mama every gory detail of my emotional demise.

When I spoke to Mama, I chose my words carefully. I gave the barest sketch of how sick I'd been since she returned to Michigan. A different kind of sick. Not the vomiting kind. Then I insisted: "No, you don't need to come. . . . No, there's nothing you can really do. . . . I don't really need anything. . . . Well, maybe if you could help pay for the doctor."

I ran out of health insurance just as Lisa gave me a name for my personal hell. The fellowship money I negotiated for health insurance the previous year had long been spent on other essentials like rent, food, and books. And there was no way I was going to back to the HMO that nearly killed me. I still had pain shooting from my back to my foot. Lisa gave me medications from her pharmaceutical rep samples and agreed to a rate half of what she normally charged. Even with that, I needed a couple hundred more dollars than I had left over at the end of each month.

And Carol was right. Mama was concerned. Although I knew she wanted get on the next plane, Mama stayed in Michigan and sent a monthly check. When I went home for church business in late August, Mama looked at me. She looked at me when I was looking at her, and she looked at me even more intently when she didn't think I was paying attention. Like the summer after my first year in college, Mama looked at my pasty skin and low weight. I appreciated that she didn't try to soothe when there was nothing that could console. She just looked at me like she wanted to rock me like an arm-baby. For a week, she made my favorite foods.

Returning to Claremont for my second year of school, I didn't even see the mountains that drew me there. East of San Gabriel Valley but before the sprawl of the Inland Empire, Claremont is nestled in the Inland Valley where it is surrounded by mountain ranges. The smog can't blow out over the ocean or into the desert fields. It hides the mountains. The brown air hangs low and thick. The mountain behind the school is completely invisible. Veiled by the dense odorous haze of smog season, there were no signs of holy anything emerging from my side of the mountain.

If there was anything miraculous to my Claremont experience, it was buried far beneath the volumes of books, five prequalifying exams, program requirements, and my desperate attempt to feel anything good. I didn't know how to stay alive and keep my just-beginning career as a religious scholar. I was not in lively debate with my classmates over coffee and thick tomes. I was not losing hours in the library stacks, hypnotized by the smell of old paper and seduced by the books to the left and right of the call number that took me there. Every day was a hapless juggle of intense cardio workouts, dry mouth from the medication, eating when I wasn't hungry, reading, thinking, writing, language study, conference presentations, exam scramble, and gratitude—not that I was happy, but that I could feel anything. Usually sadness, but still a feeling. Inevitably, each day I dropped at least three things I needed to do.

An intense doctoral program was probably the last thing that I needed. It was unreasonable to ask so much of my brain just when my brain, my mind, my soul, and my body were so thoroughly exhausted and broken down. I forgot that depression is a brain condition. I forgot that depression literally taxes the brain; depression wears it out. My brain was already overworked.

But I needed to succeed. I placed a lot of pressure on myself. I convinced some of the country's largest and most prestigious foundations that I was smart and interesting. They invested thousands and thousands of dollars in my education. I imagined them writing a check and saying: "Don't. Screw. Up." I wanted to be smart. I wanted to get good grades. I wanted to write a dissertation that made a positive contribution to my field. I wanted to make them proud. They could not know, they could never know, that something was wrong with my mind.

I could not hide my depression from my roommate, Kirsten. Kirsten and I met briefly in the library at

Vanderbilt, and we both rearranged our lives to study process theology at Claremont. Kirsten had a husband and teenage children in the Midwest. She needed housing for her final semester of classes. I had a second bedroom. And . . . as much as I hated to admit it, it was better that I wasn't left alone.

Appalled that I didn't own a coffeemaker, Kirsten brewed coffee every morning in a portable French press. By the time she ambled down the stairs, I had been to the gym and was back watching TV in the living room.

"Uff-da," she mumbled under her breath, a Norwegian combination of "Oy vey" and "What am I doing awake so early?!" She pushed her brown-turning-gray bangs off her forehead with her left hand. She wore a long flannel nightgown that betrayed both her Minnesota roots and her middle-aged modesty.

I waited until she was deep into the first cup before talking. We talked about the news programming, the story on NPR, or the research paper ideas we were trying to work out. It was good to have someone else around who understood the insider philosophical language of my field.

My depression was so obvious to Kirsten that I never explained it. Kirsten noticed when I was awake, when I went to the gym, how much I ate, and how often I cried.

Too much. A lot. Not enough. Most nights.

Her "mommy gene" activated, she always asked me what I had to eat. If the answer was "breakfast," she suggested a peanut butter and jelly sandwich. "You don't have to be hungry to eat something."

Kirsten also insisted I tell my advisor, Professor Suchocki, about my condition. I preferred to muddle through in silence. I told myself that it was about stigma and my career. I had to put my best foot forward. Today's professors were tomorrow's references. I wanted them to think the best of me. I needed them to think I was smart and capable and worthy of the degree, and a job, when the time came. I didn't need them to know about a chink in my armor.

"You have to tell her," Kirsten prompted, talking about my academic advisor. "She's on your side."

I just looked at Kirsten from my side of the couch.

"And . . . you're going to need her help," she continued.

Professor Suchocki had been my advisor since I started at Claremont. I knew she put time and energy into me—and her other doctoral students. She combined her love of film with group mentoring and invited us all to her home to watch movies, pick apart the religious themes, and indulge on homemade soup and fresh bread. As we left, she distributed extra lemons and avocadoes from her backyard trees. I had not seen her since May—when she took me to lunch at a Mexican restaurant and helped me to cross topics off a too-long list of things I might write about in my dissertation.

My teeth chattered audibly when I knocked on her office door. I had an appointment; she was expecting me. Professor Suchocki opened the door, told me that I was looking pale, and acted like I wasn't performing my version of an awkward emotional striptease.

"So," she pulled out my file, "What do we need to do?"

I needed my advisor more than I imagined. By mid-spring the anxiety hit new highs, and Lisa added another medication. The new medication put me to sleep. When I awakened, I was less anxious, but my brain felt like rotten squash. I was too dizzy to drive and unable to sit through a three-hour class. I missed two weeks of classes. I took a class that met in the evenings. I was still getting up at four thirty in the morning to go to the gym. I was usually in bed at the time that I was supposed to be saying something intelligent about Hegel or Kant. Most weeks, I got my body to the class, but my mind was never there in full force.

I needed Professor Suchocki to talk with my professors. Make it easier for me to work out a way to get my work done. Tell them that I'm sick, so they know I wasn't just making excuses. Say I have a chronic illness that's flaring up. "Say that, please. 'A chronic illness.' Don't say what, okay?" I wasn't letting every professor in.

I also needed Professor Suchocki's help to leave.

I needed to leave.

Lisa told me that medication was not a cure-all. It treated symptoms. That's important. Symptoms can take a person out. But it didn't replace a support system. I needed more friends. I needed a church closer than thirty minutes away. I needed activism. I didn't find that in Claremont. If I wanted to be alive, and stay alive, I needed to move.

Deciding to leave residency in my doctoral program changed my already ambitious four-year plan into a near-Herculean feat. I crammed the work of three or four semesters into one year. I had to attend class—or at least do the work of the classes I wasn't attending often enough—and learn another language, pass the exam, take another prequalifying exam, draft my dissertation proposal, and arrange faculty, readings lists, and questions for five other exams before leaving town. Although all of this was technically allowed within the program, there was a reason why most people didn't do it. I couldn't do any of this without Professor Suchocki opening doors and making explanations every couple of weeks.

Telling Mama and Professor Suchocki opened a floodgate within me. Their responses were filled with concern and advocacy. Not the judgment that I feared. They offered me a feeling of acceptance around my secrets that quickly became addictive. Belief, care, and resonance were the only safety nets I had then. I craved them like a dope fiend.

I reached out to every friend—new or old—who had experience with depression. Most days I just wanted to hear the timbre of a familiar voice and talk about anything besides school or how I felt: stupid television shows, fashion trends, weather. I just liked knowing that the person on the other end of the phone understood all the things I couldn't say or explain. Sometimes I needed someone to tell me to hold on, that it would get better. "I know. Firsthand." This need was so desperate and so connected to the middle of the night that I became fairly indiscriminate about who met it. I talked with other grad students, other ministers, people I just met. I never knew if a friend, acquaintance, damn near anybody might have some compassionate response that I desperately needed. Their presence, words, and phone calls were lifelines.

Put together, all of this made me a pretty rotten girlfriend. Herb's new job had him in Atlanta—making our long-distance love affair a twenty-four-hundred-mile jaunt. Loving on opposite ends of the country was a constant negotiation of time zones, sleep schedules, cash outlays, frequent flyer miles, and questions about "the next time I'll see you." I lacked the energy to do the little things I relished during the chick-flick romance days of our relationship. No more greetings cards in Spanish from the local grocery that declared *mi amor*. No more long weekends spent holding hands and window-shopping. No more long talks with Herb listening to me, compassionately reminding me twenty times an hour that I was going to be okay. Yes, that's what I needed.

Focused on managing my internal and academic chaos, I was incapable of the reciprocity a relationship requires. I couldn't even remember the last time I asked Herb how he was doing. I needed to love and feel love. I needed to be reminded that my humanity was more than misery and philosophy. I needed something to be steady. I needed Herb like that.

I experienced every conversation as one that would make or break our relationship. We had one particularly bad fight where Herb accused me of holding too much inside, holding too much back, and providing false intimacy.

I screamed my retort: "I'm being more real with you than anyone else."

Equally angry, he barked, "Well, not real enough."

Click.

I hung up the phone.

I sobbed as I scribbled in my journal: It's over. I can't keep dating him. He doesn't know me at all. I am telling him everything. He is the one who asked me about the depression in the first place. He hears the tears. He holds me when I cry. If there is anyone who knows me without the masks I have worn to the world, it is him. How can he say that?!

I knew he was right. I was a shadow of myself. I admitted the depression enough to address it. But I was still bending over backward trying to pretend I was smart and capable and eloquent when my brain had quit on me months earlier. I wanted emotional support, but I didn't give it. I didn't want anyone related to my career to know that I was sick. Well, as few people as possible. I didn't want them to think I was crazy. I was fearful and ashamed. I acted like people do when they are afraid. I ran. I wanted to run to him where he would kiss my wounds, apply an invisible bandage, and make it "all better." I asked far more of him than was reasonable or possible. I blamed the distance. If we were in the same city, I thought, he would understand. I would be okay. We would be good together.

I decided to move to Atlanta. When I lived in Nashville, Atlanta was my weekend escape for urban black culture, salons that could twist and braid my head of thick natural hair, annual Sweet Honey in the Rock concerts and hole-in-the-wall Caribbean restaurants. In the four-hour drive between Nashville and Atlanta, I found a city that satisfied my thirst for the East Coast vibe I had from summers in D.C. and four years in Cambridge—but without the harsh winters. My fellowship money didn't require me to live in Claremont. It was my last chance to live in any city in the country without factoring in employment or family needs. I secured a summer job at Emory University working with youth and theology.

Herb kept telling me, "Don't move here for me." I wanted him to welcome me with promises of a normal relationship. One where he picked me up and we went out to a movie. Or he came over for a dinner I cooked for us. But his words were a sign. The relationship was on its last legs.

I told him that I couldn't pretend he didn't live in Atlanta. I couldn't factor out something that was there. He was in Atlanta. But so were Theresa and two other cousins, warm weather, and a city full of black people, churches, my gym, and African dance classes.

"It's not all about you," my bravado replied.

Professor Suchocki supported my move. That was clearest the day I emerged from my anxiety medicine haze and was ready to attend classes regularly again. I e-mailed her to work out a strategy. I planned to stop by her afternoon office hours. I ended the e-mail, "See you on Tuesday."

On Tuesday morning, the doorbell rang. I was wearing the faded green hospital scrubs I got from a med school friend that doubled as pajamas. I rubbed the sleepy crust from my eyes to open the door and saw Professor Suchocki standing there with a box of granola as a gift.

Noting my unpreparedness, she said, "Tuesday, right?"

"Uh . . . yeah. I meant your office hours. I was going to come to you."

"Whatever." She tossed the word out of her mouth with the same lightness that someone uses when skipping rocks. She walked in and plunked down on the sofa.

"So," she began, "are you ready?"

My moving date was three weeks away. I had a job and a new apartment. I gave notice to my landlord. I passed two required exams, arranged qualifying exams, and was halfway through most of my term papers. I only worried about the one evening philosophy class.

I lamented to Professor Suchocki. "The paper just isn't going well. I don't think it's very good, and meeting with the professor just doesn't seem to help. I'm thinking of taking an incomplete."

"No!" Professor Suchocki spoke in an unusually harsh tone. "Just get it done."

"But I don't think I can write an A paper for this one." I continued to protest. "I want to keep my 4.0 GPA."

Turning her body to squarely face me, my advisor said, "You don't want this hanging over your head. Take the B. Just take the B and go. Look Monica, I know you'll do well, but you can't if you're sick. Just go to Atlanta, get better, and be the scholar I know you can be."

I cannot imagine more perfect counsel. While I stressed

about my daily health, a crumbling relationship, and my career, my advisor talked me off the proverbial overachiever ledge with a solid dose of human compassion. She believed in me and facilitated my health. Most importantly, she proved to me that revelation of my condition would not turn everyone against me. I needed that more than I could say.

That year also helped me to accept the fact that I couldn't go back to living with depression the way I used to. The depression was more than a response to life events. It was more than a breakup or rape trauma. The depression was something that was with me. It had been with me for a long time. It was something that was *in* me. If I continued to ignore it, silence it, deny its name . . . it would take me out. No classes or papers or conferences trumped the fact that depression was a big part of my life. All those things—they were like the smog in the Inland Valley. But the mountain was still there. Even if I couldn't see it all the time, it was still there.

20

WILDERNESS

Atlanta, Georgia: One Year and Three Months after the Illness

I was trapped somewhere between sick and well. I thought that Interstates 10 and 20 were the roads to the Promised Land. It took three days to drive from Claremont to Atlanta. Mama came out the day after the movers took the boxes away, helped me load the car, and took responsibility for the AAA TripTik directions we ordered. Atlanta, here we come! I dreamed of doing research in the stacks at Emory's library, strolling down Abernathy Avenue to the sounds of djembe drums and the smell of spicy vegan food, finding a dance class and making new friends. I did not realize that the move from numb to sad was just a first step. I did not know what it would take to feel happy. In my need for health, education, and community, I forgot an important biblical lesson: between the holy mountain and the land of milk and honey, there is a lot of wandering in the wilderness.

My sojourn in Atlanta started at Emory. I taught in the Youth Theological initiative of Emory University's Candler School of Theology, a program to expose high school students to theological studies and the link between religion and justice. When teaching feminist theology, I looked for a worship experience with gender-inclusive language for God and humanity, women in leadership, and female images for God. I went to the Atlanta Quaker Meeting House where Circle of Grace Community Church met on Sunday evenings. Chairs were arranged in a semicircle facing a stark wooden lectern. Sitting in the congregation, one could see the green flora of a humid Atlanta summer through the windows on the west wall. Watching the sunset behind the trees during the service reminded me of my Saturday evenings at Metropolitan Church in Nashville.

Worship was led by a short middle-aged white woman wearing jeans. Her pixie haircut had a white streak dyed on one side. Reverend Connie Tuttle preached the Genesis story about Lot's wife. Like many others, I heard sermons about how God punishes Lot's wife for disobeying the commandment not to look back on Sodom and Gomorrah while fire rains down on the city. God spares Lot's family, but Lot's wife ignores that so God turns her into a pillar of salt. The lesson was always the same: when God blesses you to go somewhere new, don't look back or God will punish you too.

Pastor Connie suggested something different. She read the biblical text and reminded us of all the words and blaming and punishment that the tradition ascribes to Lot's wife, but that isn't even in scripture. She asked what kind of God punishes us for looking back—either with fondness or in grief—on a place where we have significant life events. She talked about people who move—military brats like her, students, job seekers, and nomads. She taught that salt was valuable and sacred in the world of the ancient Israelites. The lesson could be that God erects sacred memorials when we lose things, when we make transitions, and when we have to move on. She said perhaps the fact that there is no name mentioned for Lot's wife means that we could see her as any woman or every person.

I filtered the pastor's words through my recent cross-country sojourns, piles of unmet expectations, and all the reflection I did on the rape. I heard her sermon as permission to be sad. In the recovery of the rape, I learned that I didn't have to be the perfect, smart, pious preacher girl. I learned to accept my grief, my trauma, and new faith expressions. But I still had not learned to share my sadness with many people. I shared in the same desperate groping way I did about the depression: only because it spilled out, only because I thought I would die if I didn't. I still thought that I had to keep moving forward all the time, letting the world see that I acknowledged my blessings. That sermon was made for me right there, right then. I stopped being a minister, religious scholar, and teacher. I was the faltering believer who needed the message that it's okay to look back and remember where you have been. It's okay to mourn what is lost.

Generally, religion was intellectual for me then. I studied philosophers and theologians, and repeated their ideas on my exams. I mentioned their perspectives in church. I made an outline for my dissertation and followed it, as if by rote. I chased footnotes to call numbers to stacks in the libraries at Emory and read books and took notes. I didn't pray. I didn't worship. I didn't feel God. I went to church because I believed there was value in just showing up.

All I did was show up. I just showed up in every aspect of my life. After a year of medication, the disruptive symptoms that sent me to Lisa faded. I slept an easy seven hours most nights. If food appeared without expending much energy (frozen meals and eating out), I was content to eat it. I was no longer suicidal. I was alive, but I was not happy.

Moving to Atlanta didn't make me happy. I counted the happy moments of the previous fifteen months on one hand. Herb and I broke up a week after I arrived. I maintained an intense workout schedule, arriving at the gym at the slightly saner hour of six o'clock in the morning. The adrenaline and endorphin high kept me human and sensate until one in the afternoon. After one o'clock, my decision-making process turned frenetic.

I wanted to be happy. I wanted to *feel* happy. I made a mental list of the various things that could get me ten or twenty minutes of bliss. Maybe an hour.

- Sugary food
- Roller coasters

- Sex
- Alcohol

That was all I could think of. Everything on my list was self-destructive or expensive in some way, and the crash could be worse than the high. (The only reason that drugs weren't on my list is because I had no idea where to get them.) Most days, I just took my sad, listless body back to the gym. Some days, I reasoned which of the things on the list was the least self-destructive and could be arranged within fifteen minutes. I indulged, got my dopamine, adrenaline, endorphin, or oxytocin high, felt happy, and within an hour forgot why I thought junk food, an amusement park, sex with a friend, or the Black Russian cocktail was such a good idea. I was lucky if all I had was a bad headache.

Like a squirrel hiding acorns in the hole of a tree, I stashed these machinations away from view. No one knew the range of my furtive attempts to feel good. I lied. How are you doing? Fine. How are you feeling? Good. Things better in Atlanta? Definitely. Are you eating enough? Yeah. I lied and lied and lied. The habit bred under my childhood mask developed into a refusal to let anyone in. When my lips betrayed the truth, it seeped out through the pores of my skin. Those with eyes to see, noticed.

Pastor Connie was a noticer. I started attending Circle of Grace, and Pastor Connie and I met regularly to talk about religion, relatives, and things going on in Atlanta. When the conversation fell to a natural pause, Pastor Connie asked, "But how are *you*, baby?" Pastor Connie used the affectionate term "baby" for Circle of Grace children, her partner, and pretty much anyone she cared about. Such affection made me feel kindred.

I exhaled, looked down and then up to her face.

"Your eyes look sad," she said.

With her pastoral attention, professional skills as a therapist, and a good sense of intuition, Pastor Connie always disarmed my force fields of chatter and intellectual conversation. She signaled that every meal, every conversation, every church service was a safe place where I could take off the mask.

I replied honestly, "Well, I am sad . . . and thanks for noticing."

Being sad was a lot of work. I had to go over the river and through the woods just to get medication in Atlanta. Since I left campus residency, I no longer qualified for the basic health services that gave physicals and flu shots. I had generous fellowship support, but it wasn't enough for an adult with health issues. When I subtracted tuition, a cross-country move, and books from my fellowship monies, I was left with enough to cover rent, food, gas, and one car emergency—the flat-tire kind, not the rear-ended or side-swiped kind.

I knew that every state had services for people with low incomes. I was caught in the financial paradox of many graduate students—a pedigreed education and middle-class affiliation, but not much money. As an advocate and community organizer in Nashville, I spent weeks of my life in courts, in council meetings, at zoning hearings, and with social service workers. If I could navigate Tennessee's social service and legal systems for frightened women and their children, surely I could do that for myself.

It took me three weeks, a ream of paperwork, and at least seven nurses, social workers, and doctors to sign the forms that got me my medication—which didn't come in generic form—for $4.33 a month. I could only imagine how impossible that system was to anyone who needed to clock into a job or pick up a child from daycare. I drove to the county medical center for two days every month to meet with the doctor who approved my medication and then retrieved it from a back room. I delayed dental and vision checkups—at least until I could get a job—and prayed that I wouldn't get sick or have a car accident.

Depression brought me into the same orbit with people who seemed radically different from me. Unlike my former clients and many of the people around me at the state medical center, my bottom didn't truly fall out. If I was absolutely desperate, I had parents and family members who could help me. But they couldn't. Hard-working parents, an elite education, access to doctors, and a background in social services did not save me from the sharp edge of razors. Class and access mean nothing to depression. Depression doesn't discriminate.

And I still needed to find a therapist.

I got Jesse's name from another doctor. The journey to her office led through a rehabbed Victorian house to a dollhouse-style attic. I plopped down on the comfortable couch. It was the kind of space I imagined in the books I read as a child. The kind of room siblings shared, and when they opened the closet, they stepped into another world, or when they looked out the window, their teddy bears came to life. This was a space that I intuitively felt could incubate my deepest needs. With pale skin, freckles, and strawberry blonde curly hair, Jesse was a nearly typical hippie feminist wearing loose pants and tunics made of cotton or hemp. Her lean arms appeared bony, but felt strong and warm when she hugged me good-bye at the end of each session.

At the beginning of each meeting, I sank into the couch across from Jesse, simultaneously slouching and holding the teddy bear with the green gingham bow tie. I felt I could truly fall apart. When Jesse asked how I was doing, she waited for me to finish rambling about school, exams, the county medical center, or the trainer at the gym.

She then asked again, "How are you feeling?"

She didn't solve my problems, although I often asked her to. She was, to use her words, "a compassionate witness." She listened past the defenses I used with most of the world, and waited for me to let her in. She stood party to my daily wrestling with depression, leaning over to look at books I brought, asking how I felt about my desperate attempts at happiness, inquiring about my relationships with my parents or my church. She neither named my condition nor took copious notes while we talked. I felt like she wanted me to be well, and she knew that the road there could not be walked in silence or alone.

I didn't want to be sad alone. I wanted to find other

people like me. I didn't know where they were. I started in the bookstore. I discovered memoirs written by other people who lived with depression: Kay Redfield Jamison's *Unquiet Mind*, Meri Nana-Ama Danquah's *Willow Weep for Me*, William Styron's *Darkness Visible*, Martha Manning's *Undercurrents*, Tracy Thompson's *The Beast*, and my personal favorite, Nell Casey's edited volume *Unholy Ghost*. Some of the books scared me to the core. I read one section and went into a short panic attack: I'll never be able to have kids. Postpartum depression will kick my butt! What if it gets so bad that I need electroconvulsive therapy? I'll lose my memory. I need my memory. How can I ever work? What if I forget Grandma?

I was scared, but I kept reading because I needed their stories. I needed their experiences. I needed their words. I looked for the right words, the right metaphors to describe this thing that defies explanations. It was the high tide of an ocean overwhelming everything on the shore. It was a strong current pulling me under. It was darkness. I couldn't see and I felt alone. It was an unholy spirit that took over who I normally was. It was smog. It kept me from seeing what was right in front of me. It was a blues song.

I wanted to find the right words. I wanted to be able to explain it to people. I wanted to be able to explain it to myself. I wanted a language for what was happening to my life, for the thing I constantly fought, for the ways I still seemed to lose hours and days to nothingness. I needed to know that I wasn't alone. I wanted to know that there were other people—however far removed they might be—who also tangled with the same creature. I didn't need them to be wise or even heroic. I just needed to know that there were cojourneyers on this path.

I found my depression colleagues in strange ways. I met Dwayne years earlier at Vanderbilt. We met in the Office of Black Student Affairs. He was ten years older than me and tall, dark, and handsome in all the classic ways. Like many other black graduate students, we made our way to the office for snacks during exam season or the occasional meeting of the black graduate student association. He smiled and stopped for a minute to ask how I was doing. I didn't know him well, but he left an impression. We met again at an academic conference nearly a year before I moved to Atlanta. We recognized each other across a sparsely populated room.

"Dwayne?" I questioned, double-checking his nametag.

He remembered the Office of Black Student Affairs and those exam snacks before he remembered my name.

We grabbed dinner that night and fell into an easy collegiality that became friendship through e-mails and phone calls. He talked about his divorce and how he adored his daughter. I talked about how I ended up studying religion. We laughed about how we both fell asleep with books in our bed.

His call awakened me hours after I had gone to sleep. The medication made my early sleeping hours hard and dreamless. Waking up during that phase felt like hammering in the head, dizziness and nausea combined. I groped toward the phone and saw that it was Dwayne. It had to be important. It wasn't like him to call that late.

I tried to ignore my growing headache and answered the phone.

"Hey. You okay?" I whispered.

"Yeah. Just wanted to talk."

Dwayne's speech was slow. I thought he was drunk-dialing.

"Okay. What's up?" I asked.

Within five minutes, I knew that his daughter was upstairs sleeping, and Dwayne had just taken more medication than he was supposed to. He chased it with some kind of hard liquor.

The headache and mild vertigo disappeared when I realized that he was in the middle of a suicide attempt. I sat straight up.

Damn. We were eight hundred miles apart. What was I going to do?

I tried to use all the tools I learned answering crisis lines in Nashville.

I started asking him questions about what he took, how much, where he lives.

"I'm not telling you. I don't want you to call the police." Dwayne was suicidal, not stupid.

I ran to my computer, trying to boot it as quietly as possible. I kept talking with him. Forty-five minutes and still talking.

I looked up suicide hotlines and websites. I couldn't get off the phone with Dwayne to call them. I tried to e-mail them questions. I searched for every resource in his city. Reverse phone directories. An address. Anything. I tried to keep him from hearing my nervous breathing.

Tell me about your day at work. What did your daughter do today? What did you make for dinner? So you're seeing a psychiatrist?

"Me too," I volunteered.

"Yeah?" he asked. We were ninety minutes into the conversation when I heard this new tone in Dwayne's voice.

"Yeah." I said.

"You never said anything about it before."

"We weren't that close." I replied. We both chuckled. Laughter—good.

I told him about my summer breakdown. I told him about the undoing of my relationship with Herb. I told him the name and dosage of my medication and its side effects. Without thinking, he told me his.

Yes! At the computer, I searched, e-mailed, and instant messaged pharmacies and suicide hotlines to find out what happens if someone overdoses on that.

Two and half hours later and we were still talking. The sun would soon rise.

He said the one sentence that let me know we made it past the break: "I don't want my daughter to wake up and find me. . . ."

I heard him cry. I heard him flush the rest of the medication down the toilet.

"I know you love her," I reassured.

"I do." I heard him smile through the phone.

Three hours later, I had a couple instant messages from suicide hotlines telling me that I did the right thing and that I was a good friend. A pharmacist assured me if we had talked this long, Dwayne might feel like shit, but he would live. I exhaled.

I lay back in the bed and tried to talk with Dwayne like we normally do. "What are you teaching tomorrow? How's the book coming?"

We both needed to pretend the last three and a half hours were a bad dream. We needed to feel a little normal.

"Damn, it's almost morning. I got to get my girl to school." He sounded tired.

"You okay?"

"Yeah." He was probably lying, but I didn't mind.

"Okay. Hang in there. I'll call later. Like tomorrow."

"That would be nice," he said in a soft voice.

I lay in bed wide awake for hours. Trying to figure out what to do, what to say, how to find Dwayne, and where to send police if I needed to had created enough adrenaline to keep me alert for most of the day. But that wasn't what kept me awake. Rather, my sunrise insomnia came from the questions I kept asking myself:

How did he know? How did he know about my depression? How did he know to call me? Why did he call me? How did he know? God that was scary!

As soon as it was a decent time on the West Coast, I called the friend who removed the knives and razors from my apartment just over a year earlier.

"I'm so sorry. I'm so sorry I put you through that. I'm

so sorry." I was almost crying. "I must have scared you to death!"

"Yes, Monica, you did."

"I'm so sorry. I didn't know . . . I'm sorry."

He said that I didn't have to apologize for something I couldn't control. He ended the conversation saying, "I'm glad you told me. I'm glad you're okay."

Yes, that was how I felt about Dwayne. And that was what I said to him in the afternoon when I called back. "I'm glad you told me. I'm glad you're okay."

I continued to wonder how Dwayne knew to call me. Was it something I said or did or let slip that let him know that I knew enough about depression to talk him through the night? Were we part of an invisible tribe walking stealthily among normal people? Did he have radar that could hone in on me? After I stopped fearing that I was doing something that sent a blip onto his screen, I wondered if perhaps I could develop the same sense. Maybe, I could find my clanspeople.

I looked for my people, frog by frog, until I met a prince—finding them more by accident than intention. I tried the weekly meetings of a local chapter of a national mental health advocacy group. I drove down a windy asphalt road to the outpatient center of a large hospital. Three doorways, an elevator, and another hallway later, I sat in a room of white people twenty years my senior, sharing medication nightmare stories. They treated our diagnoses like addictions, "Hi, my name is Mary, and I have severe bipolar depression with rapid cycling and some dissociative identity disorder." Everyone else in the room chorused together, "Hi, Mary." By the time we moved around the table to where I sat, I wanted to lie about my name and keep my diagnosis to my damn self. Frog kiss.

I met my tribe—two women who didn't know each other—in ordinary ways. Through a friend who said that we study similar kinds of philosophy; through another colleague who thought we should work on a book project together. We sat at coffee or lunch, talking about our work until someone slipped and mentioned a therapist, or reached for medication, or talked about reading in the middle of the night when sleep was elusive.

"Me too," one of us whispered.

The conversation erupted into comparisons about meds, therapists, symptoms, how no one understood, what we liked about our doctors. We ignored the business that brought us together and laughed. Other days, we met without the need to cheer someone up. Some afternoons, we walked briskly, begging an hour of endorphins out of a tough day. We drove to each other's apartments with bagels or salad if one of us said, "I'm just not getting out of bed today." We hugged good-bye tightly.

There is no radar or secret handshake or knowing look that depressives give one another. I'm not even sure most of us are self-aware enough to know our own symptoms embodied in someone else. I can barely see sadness in my own eyes. I don't see it in others. The secret is courage. One random day, someone pushes past a fear of judgment and risks vulnerability. We recognize a kinship. We know each other because we live with the same behemoth. We need each other so that we won't have to battle the dragon alone. We huddle together around a campfire lit by the breath of the beast that keeps us from leaving the cave on the fairy-tale island.

21

FATED

Atlanta, Georgia: Two Years and Two Months after the Illness

Sharecropping occupies a space between fate and freedom. It's better than slavery. No overseers, whips, or gang labor. No forced rapes or breeding for children. But it's not freedom either. Picking cotton from can't see to can't see for a wage you never get. Being tied to land you know, land you work, a land that knows the prints of your feet and the crevices in your knuckles. Owned by someone else, the land owns you. Sharecropping means owing a debt you can only repay by the next year's labor, and the year after forever. Sharecroppers often lived in conditions only slightly better than when they were slaves. Getting out requires working more than is sane. Finding enough cotton or some loophole or a way out in the middle of the night. It is a life that is not your own. No longer slaves, but not yet free. It could drive anyone into madness. I should not have been surprised that my sharecropping great-grandfather killed himself. It's a wonder that more sharecroppers did not.

"You need to know about the noose." Theresa called me with urgency in her voice. "You need to know what I found out about Great-granddaddy."

Theresa had been visiting one of our older cousins when the story of our great-grandfather's suicide was revealed.

"He planned it," she said. "He was teaching Uncle Robert how to tie knots for some period of time. Weeks, probably."

"As if they were going camping?" I asked, projecting my contemporary sensibilities into the 1920s South.

"I don't know what he told Uncle Robert. But there is more. He had Uncle Maydee lift him up. Uncle Maydee was twelve then! He had to understand what was going on. Great-granddaddy told him to come back the next day to make sure he was dead."

I was stuck between silence and screaming. Who does that? Who gets their children to help them? Who puts their kids in that position? Who teaches their kids to help them kill themselves?

Theresa continued. "Everyone seems to know. I mean, all the cousins from down South. When I ask, they tell me. It's not like it's a secret."

There was a long pause on the phone. I moved from bustling around in the kitchen to a slump on my futon. I had more questions than I shared with Theresa. Why didn't anyone say anything about this? Didn't they think that this was an important part of our family history? Why were they so nonchalant about it? Maybe they were ashamed. Maybe they thought suicide was a sin. A lot of Christianity teaches that. Maybe they thought it was better if no one talked about it. As if giving it voice would give it power. Would make it more real. Would make them hate an ancestor they didn't even know.

Theresa broke the silence. "This," she sighed, "is our family."

Our cousins knew this. Did these cousins, an easy ten to fifteen years older than Mama and Aunt Maxine, know what to do with this story? Did they know that they should pass this on along with the stories of "Uncle Sam," the former slave who raised their parents? Did they know that they shouldn't hide the bad memories? Did they know that we—Theresa and I and our cousins in this generation—needed them, that we needed to know who we were and where we came from? Did they have an idea that this was part of our medical history? It was as pertinent as knowing that our people tended to die of diabetes and heart disease. This story was just as complex as any other disease—some savvy combination of genetics and diet. Passed down the generations like hair texture and the recipe for sweet potato pie. It was shared quietly and with intention. It was in our family stresses, seemingly harmless lies, the silences in the face of pained circumstances. It was in our poverties and strivings. They needed to tell the children. And not like a fact but like a harsh warning. Don't get too close to the fire; you will be burned. Don't start drinking; you might not be able to stop. Watch out for the things that go bump in the night.

Or did they believe what I was told? That Great-granddaddy was overwhelmed. That he didn't know what to do without his wife. That the idea of raising eight children alone was frightening. That was how they told the story of him "dying of grief." They, Grandma and her siblings . . . I heard it as if for the first time . . . when they told it this way, they blamed themselves. They blamed their father's suicide on their existence.

I wanted to run back in time and hug Grandma, Uncle Robert, Aunt Ozie, Uncle Maydee, and the rest of them. I saw them as children and I wanted to gather them in my arms and tell them that it wasn't their fault. That there was more going on there. That their father was despondent and desperate. He had decided that death was his best option. That made sense to him. Enough sense to ask his sons to help him. It was better, he must have felt, than living the way he was living. I understood that. I understood how death could seem like the best option available. Perhaps I understood because of Great-granddaddy. Maybe this depression was genetic, like so many books said.

I found my new diagnosis in a book. I did all my studying in the Borders Bookstore Café in Midtown Atlanta. It was noisier than a library, but better than sitting alone in my apartment where I missed human contact for days on end. At least I saw other people. They saw me. I was deep into rereading books for my dissertation. After three or four consecutive hours, the words blurred on the page. I took a break by roaming through the bookstore.

I had exhausted the section on African American literature the previous week. I didn't really have time to read anything unrelated to my dissertation, so I only scanned bindings, the endorsements on the back covers, and the tables of contents. I wandered into the psychology section. A book on bipolar depression caught my attention.

I can't explain why I went to this book or flipped to the section on Bipolar II. No longer referred to as "manic depression" . . . the manias are lower . . . hypomanias . . . rapid speech . . . quickly jumps from one idea to another . . . increased energy . . . severe deep depressions . . . often develops in teens and early twenties . . . does not usually interfere with functioning . . . personable . . . the life of the party . . . bright . . . professionally successful . . . rarely seek help for it . . . underdiagnosed and misdiagnosed . . . usually only seek help for the depression . . . may be the more common form of bipolar, with Bipolar I as the extreme . . . careful with treatment . . . some antidepressants can push an individual into a mania. . . .

It sounded like me.

It sounded like me! Was I . . . Bipolar II?!

I dashed out the door, almost alerting the security system because I had the book in my hand. I threw it on the table near the door and pulled my cell phone out of my purse.

Let her answer, let her answer, let her answer. "Lisa?"

I told her what I read. I asked if it sounded right to her.

I had only been able to see my sadness, but there were signs of something else. I thought of all the times teachers said that I had a lot of energy. I thought of how people complained that I spoke too quickly—like Vanessa's friend on *The Cosby Show*. I was a natural multitasker holding several things together in my head at once and keeping track of them.

Mama laughed when she told people that I had always been that way. "When she was a child, she would hold a pencil or ribbon between her fingers in one hand and do something else with her other hand." When I was in high school, Mama barely believed that I could talk on the phone, watch TV, and do calculus at the same time and do them all well. She tried to stop me, but I told her that I couldn't do just one thing at a time. She allowed me as long as my grades didn't slip. They didn't.

Even in high school, my mind moved quickly and sometimes onto random topics. I once wrote pages in my notebook wondering what happened to dandelion fuzz after you blew on it. But I didn't tell anyone about that. My ability to excel at school, church activities, community service and still run track, play the piano, and maintain a circle of friends was rewarded by my parents and everyone else around me. Was this how I was able to do it? To pull off all the things on my résumé even though I'd been dangerously sad? It wasn't like my life was spinning out of control. It wasn't. Nothing was easy, but it wasn't difficult either. I put time into studying, practicing, and playing piano. When I wasn't sad, I wasn't "high"—I went back to normal Monica, back to me. That was the "me" I missed when I was depressed. The "me" the book called "hypomanic."

I recalled the note that Carol sent for Lisa when I first started seeing Lisa. I asked Carol to make some notes for whatever doctor I found. "Can you translate all this stuff for me?" I asked Carol. "You know, psychiatrist to psychiatrist."

Carol was reticent. "I'm not your doctor. I'm your friend. I care about you."

"I know," I sighed. "But I trust you. And maybe you can explain the things that I can't. In a language the doctor will understand."

The note said this:

My presence in [Monica's] life is that of a surrogate mother, confidant, and social support. The majority of the time I have known Monica, she has been what I would classify as extremely high-energy, bordering on hypomania. Her speech is generally very rapid, though usually not pressured. She is effervescent and expansive, and her thoughts are expressed in rapid fire, always logical and sequential in progression but at times challenging to follow. She is able to manage a large number of very demanding tasks simultaneously, is very goal-oriented and productive; doesn't spend a lot of time spinning wheels unfruitfully if at all. Without any regularity that I have discerned, there have been periods of time when Monica would complain of a low mood, often associated with some stressor, but not always. Monica could mask these dysphoric periods quite well, and they often seemed mixed with hypomanic high energy.

I missed it when I gave Carol's note to Lisa. I didn't know what "dysphoric" and "hypomanic" meant. Sad *and* happy. Depressed, but not always. Buoyant, but not out of control. I liked that Carol could see me, even when I could not see myself. She heard that I was sad, but she sifted between sad me and happy me, the stress and despair, the mask and my natural energy. They all felt jumbled together to me, but Carol explained it.

Did this mean something to Lisa? Did she know all along? Was this note a factor in the way she chose my medication?

"Do you think," I asked Lisa, "that I have Bipolar II?"

Like a good psychiatrist, Lisa told me that she hadn't seen me over enough time to know; she wasn't going to diagnose me over the phone, and I really needed to find a psychiatrist in my local area. I had a psychiatrist. The man at the county medical center who got me my cheap meds. I didn't know him or trust him. I told him enough for renewals on the prescriptions.

"But," I pressed Lisa again, "does it sound right to you?"

In a voice just above a whisper, she said, "I treated you as if this was the case."

Bipolar II, Bipolar II, Bipolar II.

Was this the right term? The right words to describe me? To name my condition?

It explained why the memoirs on depression lacked

discussion of the reward that I experienced when I lived through a bad episode. Those writers didn't echo my feeling of being able to work, and minister, and enjoy life as grandly as I did between depressions. It also explained why books on bipolar were also foreign to me. I never thought I was superhuman. I never sailed around the world on a whim, had wild spending sprees, or experimented with drugs or alcohol. When I read about bipolar, I always knew that wasn't me.

But "Bipolar II." It had a name. My condition felt like an episode of the television series *House* where patients with unknown illnesses come to be diagnosed by a team of specialists. They spend fifty-five minutes of the show running tests, trying to figure out what is wrong. Once they know, they can save the patient's life. That part takes less than five television minutes. There's something to be said for knowing and naming the condition.

It could mean something to my doctors. It would tell them not to give me certain medicines. It could guide them toward the medicines that would help. It was a code word for my condition. It's Bipolar II; not epilepsy or autism or brain cancer.

The naming helped me feel sane. Hearing myself described on paper, so well, down to little details, suggested that the happy, studious, successful part of me was not just a lie, a facade or mask that I wore to hide my depressions. Rather, happiness was part of who I was as well. I wanted to say it aloud: "Happiness is part of who I am as well." The name "Bipolar II" officially said that I was more than depression. There is—there has always been—another side of me. And it was no less real than the sad side.

Was all of this my fate? Was I destined for sadness and suicidal ideations? Was the bipolarity just the personal twist on the legacy I inherited from Great-granddaddy? Was this in Grandma, my mother and aunt, our cousins? Or did the household climate of fear on my young developing brain alter unknown chemical synapses? I couldn't sort it out. It helped to have a label, but I was the same person with the word as I was before. Only now I wondered if that was all there was. I wondered if I would always be fighting depression. Would I always be in this place trying to sort my way to happiness and then clinging to whatever peace I found with the grip of a rock climber? Holding tightly to that life before I made the next move where I might find a hold or might slip again? Was this dance with depression the main story of my life?

I meant to take these questions to Jesse, but they overwhelmed me. I could not bear to say them aloud. Instead, I told her about my monthly dinners with Herb—the arrangement Herb and I made in an effort to rebuild our friendship after the romantic relationship ended.

"We said we would always be friends," I told her. "We both know that we need to put that back together. Like a house of cards that fell over."

One dinner at a time, we tried to remember the years of friendship we shared before we argued over the phone lines. Some months, Herb picked me up at the door full of the aromatic musky scent in which I once nestled my whole body. I wanted to smother him in kisses and fall in love with him all over again. Other months, I was furious with him before we got out of the car at the restaurant. Some small comment, insidious joke, something bothered me. I repeated to myself: This here! This shit here is exactly why we'll never date again. God, I hate him!

Other months, I felt completely lost.

Between the soup and the entrée, I dashed to the ladies' room, pulled the crumpled note card out of my purse, and told myself to inhale, two, three, four, exhale, two, three, four, again. I read the card aloud in a whisper:

I am a teacher. I am a writer. I am a poet. I am a minister. I am church. I am dance. I am the breath of the ancestors. I am the joy of God. I am my grandmother's prayers. I am my grandfather's dreaming. I am incense burning. I am a woman. I am the natural dread. I am a woman who loves the company of other women. I am a woman who honors the ancestors. I am sister. I am daughter. I am a daughter of Oshun. I am a person who feels deeply. I am alive. I am whole. I am a woman who believes in freedom. I am a woman who fights for freedom. I am a co-journeyer. I am a friend. I am loved by many.

"Why do you do this?" Jesse asked when I told her about this particular dinner outing.

"Why spend time with someone who can make me feel this way? Because I want us to be friends again. He does too.

And . . . ," I paused. "We have to rebuild it. I don't think it will always be difficult. Time will help. We just want to be faithful to the process."

She asked again. "Why do you do *this?*" Jesse pointed to the note card that I read from.

"Oh," realizing I answered the wrong question. The answer spilled out of me before I had a chance to think about what I was saying. "Because I forget. I can't remember who I am."

"I feel lost. I feel like I'm just this sad person all the time. I feel alone. I can't get to any of this stuff even when I know it's true. So I wrote it down. To . . ."

I paused. " . . . to help me remember who I am. To help me remember that I am . . ."

I bit my bottom lip and blinked my eyes rapidly.

"To remember . . ." The tears rolled down my cheeks, "that I am more than this. That I am more than . . . this."

I needed to know that there was more to my life, more to who I was, than the pain. I had to be more than depression. More than bipolar.

22

FREE

Atlanta, Georgia: Three Years after the Illness

I needed to create. I needed to start something, work on it, finish it within a reasonable period of time, and call it beautiful. Most things in my life had no end in sight. The academic life did not offer immediate rewards. I followed the outline for my dissertation; I strove to make deadlines for a May graduation. But I knew that the work never ended. I could read more books and articles; I could edit and reedit the chapters; I could explore yet another direction I found from the last footnote I read. Physical fitness was the same. If I looked in the mirror or stepped on the scale after every workout, I would feel futile. It took weeks or month to get to my bench-pressing goal or to gain the strength to do pull-ups. When I made one milestone, there was another one ahead. Do fifty more crunches per day; lift half my body weight; add ten more minutes to my daily cardio. I needed something simple and artful. I wanted to see the fruits of my labor. I cooked new recipes. I took a ten-dollar jewelry-making class at a local bead store. I went to church where I learned to knit.

The Circle of Grace knitting circle met in a coffee shop in downtown Decatur. We pushed past the tables of freelancers with their laptops and artists dressed in black clothing, rubbing sleep out of their eyes at one in the afternoon. We crowded our cups of coffee and tea to the middle of the table while straddling the bags of yarn skeins between our knees. Circle of Grace numbered no greater than fifty—and that was if you included children and animals. The outreach efforts were scaled to capacity. One Saturday, we filled shoeboxes with coloring books, toothbrushes, and socks to give to foster children, who make hasty transitions from home to shelter. What would you need if you were seven years old and had no time to pack? We knitted hats and scarves for homeless men at a local shelter. Two members knew how to knit; the rest of us brought needles, yarn, and a willingness to learn. We began in August. It might take months to be ready in time for the turn of weather.

I chose a yarn of mixed browns and greens. I purchased needles that felt comfortable in my hands. While at the craft store, I bought a book on knitting 101 that was absolutely useless. I couldn't figure out how the drawings of loops were supposed to look on my needles. I needed a person in front of me to show me how to begin, how to cast the beginning stitches onto one needle. Before long, I was able to chat with others while knitting and purling from one needle to another. The scarf looked more like a day-camp potholder project. That, the group leader assured me, was how it was supposed to look when you are just beginning.

Knitting was slow and unsteady work. Sometimes I felt like I had the hang of it. I engaged in conversation without looking at the movement of the needles. I felt the bumps of the yarn and knew all was well. I knit and purled with ease. Other times, I looked down and realized that the last two rows looked funny. I unraveled them from the heap in my lap and began again. Countless rows later, I asked for help again. How do I bind off the scarf? How do I put this together into a hat? Can I borrow your circular needles for my first go at it? I dropped a stitch and noticed a tiny hole. Too late to pull out four inches of knitting. The lapses and tiny gaps, my elder knitting colleague said, is how you know something is made by hand, not machine.

Once a week, every week, for months, we gathered to knit. Pastor Connie, Linda, Margaret, Felicity, Jane, Trudy, Kate, and me. We ordered drinks, took over a corner of the coffee shop, pulled out bags of yarn, chatted about ordinary things I can't remember, and called it sacrament. With open hearts and basic skills, we were helping the homeless. We were wrapping them in concern and care. Laugh by laugh, stitch after stitch, we were doing something holy. Sure, we could buy hats and scarves from the Burlington Coat Factory located between my apartment and the coffee shop. But knitting them said that we took time to make something by hand. We put forth the effort. Knitting was my new spiritual practice.

I was waiting for another cataclysmic spiritual

experience. One stark moment of realization. A speaking in tongues. A holy dance. The sky breaking open with a booming voice from God. A vision. A burning bush. I needed it. I needed to know I was on the right track, doing the right thing, sacrificing for a purpose. I wanted God to tell me that I was still a good minister, a good activist, and a good theologian even though it didn't feel that way. I wanted to know that being sad wouldn't destroy me. I wanted to know that living with bipolar was not the only story of my life. I wanted God to tell me that I was going to be okay.

Revelation did not come to me in thunderbolts. God was just there. In the hot cup of tea. In the women who gathered. In our laughter. In the knitting. God was in my uniform rows of stitches. God was also in the dropped stitch that created an imperfection. This was what Lanh discovered in the hospital and in her fuzzy ski sweaters for Malcolm. There is something holy in the movement of yarn through fingers and needles. It grounds you. It keeps you from falling through the chasms around you. This is the radical incarnation of process theology. I was taking exams and writing and rewriting and digging through stacks of books, all to forget what knitting reminded me. That God is in every cell, every person, and every activity. Whether I know it or not. Whether it feels like it or not. God is creating. With yarn and needles, hiccups, unraveling, do-overs, a rhythm, and individual stitches, God is making something new. Something beautiful. I thought that my prayers and good intentions in knitting for homeless men were divine activity. I was knitting God into the hat and scarf. No. God was knitting me. With therapists, medication, meaningful studies, a small church community, a pastor who cared, friends who understood, and a name for my condition, God was knitting me. God was knitting me back together. It was a new way of thinking about God. Knitting gave me a new way of being faithful.

I haven't gotten used to losing my faith and finding it again. I always want the faith of my childhood. I crave the old deacons singing spirituals. I yearn for a return to Grandma's theology of wafers and juice. But I know that it changes. I know that as I grow and change, my faith will also morph. My spiritual practices will change; my beliefs will shift; what feeds me will evolve. What once worked will no longer satisfy. I will find new ways of knowing God. This is the lesson of my healing from the rape, right? This is what drew me to process theology and those tomes on philosophy. Still, I fight it. Even when I know that there is something new and positive around the corner of my spiritual journey, I want what I have lost. I want to go backward.

I reached back for the dance. Dance once saved me. I wanted it to save me again. I wanted to do something I knew how to do. I wasn't up for the work of finding an African dance class and fitting it into my schedule. I wanted to hit the clubs. And I wanted to dance with someone I knew.

I called Herb. "Nadir is coming to town." After a year and a half in Atlanta, we were on the happy side of our rebuilt friendship.

In the years between graduating from Vanderbilt and moving to Claremont, I grounded my social life in Nashville's black arts community. In the evenings between long days of work, the young twenty-somethings of Nashville came together in local clubs, with open mics and aspiring musicians who cut their own CDs in bedrooms-turned-studios, on sale that night for five dollars. One woman organized the monthly sets, sharing the venues by word of mouth, e-mail, and handbills.

Obafemi did a poem about a Jehovah's Witness visitor over the background of DeBarge's "A Dream." Shellie belted out spoken words about women who defined themselves outside of sex with men. Rahz freestyled hip-hop rhymes about hard work and freedom. Utopia State took over the stage as a hip-hop group with trombones and drums instead of turntables and vinyl. The GRITS breakdanced on the stage to the best Christian hip-hop I'd ever heard, while I stood in the front row, hair picked out into a large Afro-puff, wearing retro bell-bottoms and platforms heels, raising my arm up and down, chanting "All Fall Down."

Nadir was a funk performer, whom I remembered best for his rendition of Bill Withers's "Ain't No Sunshine." His wife stood in front of the stage, quietly blushing, while he looked at her, mic in hand, and intoned, "I know, I know, I know, I know, I know, I know, I know, I know. . . ."

When the movie *Love Jones* came out, we knew they were talking about our life at the Spot, late-night dinners at TGI Fridays, love affairs and all.

334

Nadir had a new album and was coming to Atlanta.

"Nadir's my friend," I told Herb. Which is true in the way that everyone who went to the Spot considered themselves friends, even if three or four years had passed since our last contact.

I replied to the e-mail announcing the Atlanta tour, "See you there! Can't wait."

I zipped on my chocolate brown suede boots with the two-and-a-half-inch heels. They were a perfect match to my brown-and-white V-neck top with alternating sheer and opaque panels. I pulled on my favorite dark blue boot-cut jeans. I applied a layer of magenta lipstick before Herb came to the door of my apartment. Herb told me that I looked nice.

When we got to the club, Herb and I positioned ourselves on two stools on the edge of the bar close to the stage. It was a small venue. Nadir had an entire band of background singers and musicians I'd never seen before. No longer one of many newbies trying out their sounds on old standards in small Nashville clubs, Nadir sang original songs from his album, some cowritten by members of our old crew. He grabbed the mic on an angle and threw his head back and forth so that there were moments when the audience could see only his longer-than-shoulder-length dreadlocks flying through the air. Rock star.

Herb ordered his favorite drink and pulled my stool close to his so that my back rested on his chest, my body between his splayed legs. We moved back and forth to the beat of "Daddy's Cane" and "Fortune and Fantasy." It reminded me of the early days of our wordless years of informal courting—reading books in his Nashville apartment, dancing until our feet hurt. Before we expected more from each other than several hours of companionship and a good time. Before I needed him to remind me that I was alive and human. Before he needed me to give whatever it was that I never offered. Before we forced ourselves to sit in the small booth of a local restaurant with a menu that one of us didn't really like, making ourselves become friends again because neither of us was willing to throw away the love we made.

Nadir sang a funky soul song about a woman with a great body. I moved toward the stage, dancing alone with a couple other people from the club. I quickly learned the words and dance, mouthing along with Nadir, "If the funk ain't good enough . . . you just gotta leave it alone . . . if the funk ain't good enough." Raising my hand in both solidarity with Nadir and sexy movement, I grooved like I was the hottest thing on the floor.

When the song ended, I returned to my chair still in the mood to dance. Herb smiled at the return of a Monica he hadn't seen in years. Nadir transitioned to a sultry song, and I danced with Herb while he sat on the stool. Gyrating my hips from side to side, nestling my nose in his neck and then backing up to look him in the eyes. "My love is so good, so good, sanctified," I sang with the band.

"Sanctified?" Herb mouthed.

Yeah, I nodded with a confidence I hadn't felt about myself in a long time.

Running my hands over his torso, I continued to dance in the suede heels, closing my eyes and lifting my head up, moving side to side. We heard a ten-second riff in the song that reminded us of Prince in the 1980s. We cheered—"Aww watch it now"—and I continued my seduction, adapting the words: "It feels so sanctified. My love is so good it's sanctified. I'm so good that it's sanctified." I closed my eyes and tilted my head back, teasing Herb with the memories of our better times together.

"You ready to go?" Herb smiled at me. We had the same thoughts of "sanctifying" one another.

Just as I nodded and Herb went to get our coats, Nadir began to sing a new anthem:

I don't wanna feel the pain anymore.
I don't wanna feel the whip across my spine.
Don't wanna be tied up.
Captive.
Chained to the hurt inside.
Don't you know I wanna live again, like a man is supposed
*   to?*
I don't wanna be a slave anymore.
I don't wanna be a slave for you.

I forgot about Herb for a moment and moved right up to the stage. With a beat too slow for the sway I was doing, I stood as if the song was putting me under a spell. Nadir continued to sing the words of my life:

And I can still recall the day you turned the key.
And locked me in this cold and lonely wretched misery.
I don't wanna feel the pain anymore. . . .

In the meeting of the low lights and strobe light rhythms on stage, it became clear. In my silence, attempted secrecies, and solitary crying, I let depression own me. I bowed to it daily as I chose one of a list of self-destructive approaches for getting twenty minutes of pleasure. I organized my life around it—fitting in my dissertation and teaching around the harried schedules of sleeplessness or sleepiness it creates. With a name, it was the fated cause for everything bad in my life—whatever relationships I couldn't sustain, whatever work I could not get done. But like a whip across my back, it was kicking my ass and had been doing so for years, decades, generations. I had been so focused on surviving day to day that I had not thought about how I would live.

I began small revolts after moving to Atlanta—with my little note card, in my sessions with Jesse, in meetings with Pastor Connie, with my new friends over coffee, while knitting scarves. Without any intention, I slowly, painstakingly carved out a life where I wasn't dominated by denial of or torture by depression.

African American historians tell the story of Harriet Tubman, the Moses of our people, who led hundreds to slaves from bondage into the Northern states where they could be free. The journey north was difficult, full of unknowns, dangers, and the constant threat of being caught—which meant sure death. Sometimes slaves begged Tubman to let them return back to what they knew. The same is said of the Israelites that Moses helped to free from Egypt. But Harriet Tubman cocked a rifle on her shoulder and turned to those slaves with a new threat—we're moving forward no matter what. Like a running slave, I know that with freedom there is no going back. I must keep moving.

I cannot get back what I lost. The relationships, how I understood the world, how I related to God—things that seemed clear when I went to college and into the ministry. I understood this when I processed the rape; now it has new meaning. The most I can do is mourn, remember, and turn the corner to new life.

Bipolar is no more my fault or responsibility than the rape. I do not have to wonder what I'm doing wrong or what I can do differently. I do not have to pretend nothing is happening to me. I cannot crawl back into the sheath of shame and secrecy. I can no longer pretend there is no name, no pattern, no real threat from within me. It is not my imagination. It is real.

And like the rape, something dies. I lose some of me in every depressive bout. It may be something I need to lose—like pride. It may be something I don't want to lose—like pride. But everything in my faith and experience tells me that if I can hold on through the night, there will be an empty tomb; there will be new life. I will see the mountain again.

My rebirths are not as dramatic as in human biology. No labor pains, placenta, or celebratory cigars. I feel it internally, like snapping a twig underfoot on a nature hike or the sunrise turning from orange to pink. I know when there is upward movement. Sometimes it is small—like the memory that I really did tell responsible adults when I was a teenager—that relieves me of the idea that I suffered alone by choice because I never told anyone. Sometimes it is large—like the realization that I don't have to define myself by my condition. Rebirth is the surety that I am more than this. I am more than this. I am more than this.

Nadir continued singing:

Don't want to be tied up.
Captive.
Chained to the hurt inside.

I don't want to be reduced to my symptoms and diagnosis. Tied down. I am learning the difference between captivity and rest, between an illness and a condition. There's nothing wrong with me. After all, this is the only me I've ever known. But sometimes I need to slow down, check to see if I'm okay; look at the emotional heap of yarn in my lap, undo a few rows, and try again. I need to know that the things I drop, the things I can't do the way I want, the hard parts of my life are not failure. They are evidence that I'm human. Not made by machine.

The Christian liturgical calendar denotes months of the year as "ordinary time." When there is no celebration of birth, death, resurrection, or powerful movement of Spirit, there is just "ordinary time." Biblical lessons during those months are about Jesus teaching, healing, telling stories, hanging out with his friends. Ordinary relation-ships.

I learned, monthly dinner after monthly dinner, how to rebuild a relationship that was ground into dust. I came to see that my relationship with God was being rebuilt as well. Sometimes, it feels nostalgic; other times, it feels obligatory. Staying in any intimate relationship has a component of loyalty—to what I know to be there, even when I don't feel it. I rebuild with God in the same way: meal by meal, prayer by prayer, stich by stitch, dance by dance, song by song.

The leaders of the civil rights movement always talked about how helpful it is to sing when you are scared. Singing also helps unite people, pass long hours, encourage yourself. Sing, they said, when you are in line to vote. Sing, they said, when the power structure tells you that things will never get better.

I sang along with Nadir: "Don't you know I wanna live again?!"

My life and my faith are intertwined. My faith demands that I fight for justice. It calls me to give myself over to God and to church and to fighting inequities. Depression tells me to cling to whatever part of myself that I can find. I can no longer rely on faith to motivate me to act in the world. I cannot always maintain a faith that is about making my corner of the world a better place. That is still important, and it may still be what ultimately saves the world, what will save me. But that has to be an extension of faith—not its definition. Rather, my act of faith is much smaller.

If I can believe—in the midst of my most wordless,

painful, razor-shiny moments—that God isn't doing this to me, then that is an act of faith. If I can believe that God hears me, knows me, loves me, and rocks me, then that is a leap of faith. I don't need more than that. I don't need the degrees, the title, the philosophy, the long robes, the approval of my denomination, or special prayers for sharing the bread and wine. The leap to believe that God does not abandon me is all I need.

I think about Grandma and her father. They had no name but grief to describe something far worse than losing life and love. They had no access to medicine or therapists. They passed on what they had—a faith in family, generosity, and ritual. It's strong and fragile at the same time. It got Grandma through. It wasn't enough for her father. I danced for West African ancestors and for the orisha. Now I dance for my own ancestors. I dance for Grandma and Great-granddaddy. I dance for my great-aunts and great-uncles who lived with the noose. I will dance warrior, growth, and the changes of life. I will dance their tears and their ability to live through them. I will dance sultry and sexy. I will dance the legacy they left me, and the freedom I eke out. They are with me in the dance, drum, and bass line.

Nadir was giving me a spiritual, and I continued to sing it as Herb offered me my jacket. I noticed that it was raining as we left the club. Herb asked if I wanted him to pull the car around.

"No. I'm fine." Shaking my dreadlocked hair, I quipped, "I don't melt in the rain."

He dashed down the street toward the block where he parked.

I lingered, grooving to the beat I still heard as Nadir's band continued to play.

I don't wanna be a slave anymore.

I walked at a natural pace, ignoring the water soaking into my suede boots. The rain dripped onto my hair, my eyelashes, my nose and chin. The rain fell on my shoulders and legs. I didn't have to rush. I didn't have to run. This rain was not death.

LYRIC CREDITS

344

ACKNOWLEDGMENTS

In the late 90s, I thought about writing this book and I wasn't even done living it. I talked to Kevin Powell about it, and he gave me the best advice: "Start from the beginning, and tell the truth." This is what I have tried to do.

My journey does not belong to me alone.

I could not have survived the Greenhills years without the caring guidance of Melvin Rhoden, Dick Tobin and Joyce Potts. My high school friends listened, studied and shimmied with me. Thank you Kafi Laramore-Josey, Kelli Wingo, Andre Myers, Aaron Thompson, Sonya Snedecor, Francine Weiss Ashe, Marc Coleman, Tracy Hudson Trauscht, Robin Meriweather, Thembelani Banda, and Wesley Muhammad. To my other-mothers, I love you all so much: the late Rose Wingo, the late Sandy Snedecor, Bev Jenai, S. Yvette Jenkins and Diane Meriweather. My Bethel AME Church family nurtured my faith and community. Thank you Robert Blake, Ruth Jordan, Helen B. Oliver, and Ronald and Lily Brown.

So many people who sat with me in difficult seasons could not be named here, but you are woven throughout these pages: Keith Levy, Doug Webb, Kevin Gillespie, Ray Howard, Mai Tran Duff, C. Regan Almonor, Ed Gray, Richard Harris, Eric W. Lee, David Danner, David Shawn Smith. To you who let me call your names: Darrell Armstrong, Tanya Marcovna Barnett and Herbert Robinson Marbury. You saved me. Each one of you.

I have had some of the most amazing professors and mentors in the academy. Your influence pervades this text: Henry Louis Gates, Jr., Werner Sollors, J. Lorand Matory, Evelyn Brooks Higginbotham, Renita J. Weems, Victor Anderson, Amy-Jill Levine, Evon Flesberg, Viki Matson, L. Susan Bond, Marjorie Suchocki, Sharon Watson Fluker, Karen Baker-Fletcher, David F. White, Elizabeth Conde-Frazier. You saw me, pushed me and held me.

I would not have found my way into ministry without the models I saw in Cambridge and Boston. To Gwendolyn Long-Cudjoe, Kanice Attles, Adetokunbo Adelekan, Jason Curry, Joseph Robinson, Stephan P. McKinney, Echol Nix, Trevon Gross, Ray Alston and Frances Cudjoe Waters. Cynthia Johnson-Oliver, my sister in the calling, your courage spreads to me.

I hope it is clear from this work that I'm a strong believer in the positive effects of therapy. This is true because of the amazing therapists I've had: Nancy Anderson, the late Karen Silien, Char Creson, Lisa Schmid Phillips, Jesse Harris Bathrick and Orly Bouskila.

I feel like I left rivers of tears in Nashville. There was also laughter and support there because of you all: Edwin C. Sanders II, Joanne Robertson, Neely Ann Williams, David

Cassidy, Cynthia Turner Graham, Barney Graham, Kenneth Hill, my Metropolitan Interdenominational Church family, the volunteers of The Dinah Project, Edwin C. Sanders III/Edwin Simunye, Sumayya Coleman, Korey Bowers Brown, Nomalange Eniafe, Olaomi Osunyemi Akalatunde, Baba Musa and The Village, Amiri YaSin Al-Hadid, Charles Bowie, my National Black Women's Health Project/ Initiative sisters – Tonya Burton, Tonya Horton, Lee Mayberry, Matajmia Hayes, Cassandra Finch, Jennifer Grady, Randi Greene Chapman, Lisa Swett and Joy Hennings; Kim Steger and the crew from The Spot – Rahz, Utopia State, Shellie Warren, Jeff Carr, The GRITS, Nadir Omowale.

In the midst of the Inland smog there were clearing breezes. Thank you Damon Young and Kirsten Mebust – for more than I can say. Timothy Tyler, Sandra Richards Mayo, Garland Pierce, your actions made such a difference.

My Youth Theological Initiative crew befriended me during a difficult move: BaSean Jackson, F. Douglas Powe, B. Chris Dorsey. YTI also brought me to Connie Tuttle and Circle of Grace Community Church. You all are my ATL family. Keri Dianich, Melissa Johnston and Kai Jackson Issa, you took the pain away.

These organizations invested in me without knowing how they would change my life: Mellon Mays Undergraduate Fellowship Program, Ford Foundation Diversity Fellowship Program, the Forum for Theological Exploration (Fund for Theological Education), Harvard/ Radcliffe Christian Impact, Sexual Assault Center of

Middle Tennessee, Penuel Ridge Retreat Center, Youth Discipleship Project at Claremont School of Theology, Youth Theology Initiative at Candler School of Theology, Emory University, and Youth School of Theology at Perkins School of Theology, Southern Methodist University. To my faculty colleagues at Claremont School of Theology, you gift me with the privilege to be my full self in my professional life. It's been that way from day one.

For encouraging me to write publicly about depression, I thank Johnnetta Cole, Ann Pederson, Deanna Thompson, Miguel de la Torre, Philippe Matthews and Amy Caldwell. For being amazing writers, role models and friends: Renita Weems, Gloria Wade-Gayles, Tananarive Due, Dolen Perkins-Valdez, Therese Borchard, Sarah Sentilles, Eric Jerome Dickey.

To the most fabulous editor in the world: Faith Adiele, you made my jumbled manuscript into a book. Michael Datcher helped me frame the pitch. Carolyn Roncolato and C. Yvonne Augustine did some of the detailed research. Tony Jones and "Theology for the People," thank you for believing in this book and working to make it happen. To the amazing staff at Fortress Press: my gracious editor Lisa Gruenisen; and Olga Lobasenko, Alicia Ehlers, and Michael Moore. To the world's best cover designer, Brad Norr – it's so easy to trust you with my stories. Thanks to Anne Simone who took the cover photo – she makes me feel fly and tells a narrative with each photo. Thank you Casey Brodley for my L.A. photos. Helena Brantley at Red Pencil

PR – thank you for your resonance, and work to get this book to the world.

To my RoD sisters, Beatrice Wallins Lawrence and Aisha Dixon-Peters, I can't imagine getting through the last year of this without your camaraderie and acceptance.

To my family: the ancestors, my cousins, my aunt, my great aunts and uncles – I can tell this story because of your sacrifices and love. Grandma, I still miss you. Thank you for your faith. Daddy, I wrote about you as I knew you – in your pain, efforts, prides and love. Mama, the strength of your love outweighs any pain you wish you could have thwarted. Harlem, you inspire me.

Ashe.